The Complete Guide to

Italian Greyhounds

Candace Darnforth
and
Rene Leighty

Publication Data
Candace Darnforth & Rene Leighty
The Complete Guide to Italian Greyhounds – First edition.
Summary: "Successfully raising an Italian Greyhound dog from puppy to old age"
Provided by publisher.
ISBN: 978-1-954288-06-5
[1. The Complete Guide to Italian Greyhounds – Non-Fiction] I. Title.

This book has been written with the published intent to provide accurate and authoritative information in regard to the subject matter included. While every reasonable precaution has been taken in preparation of this book the author and publisher expressly disclaim responsibility for any errors, omissions, or adverse effects arising from the use or application of the information contained inside. The techniques and suggestions are to be used at the reader's discretion and are not to be considered a substitute for professional veterinary care. If you suspect a medical problem with your dog, consult your veterinarian.

Design by Sorin Rădulescu
First paperback edition, 2023

Table of Contents

Chapter 3

Chapter 4

Chapter 5

Chapter 6

Basic Training for Your Italian Greyhound

Chapter 7

Socializing and Mental Stimulation

Chapter 8

Chapter 9

Chapter 10

Chapter 11

Chapter 12

Introduction

Did you just bring home your new Italian Greyhound? Welcome! You have joined the legion of those whose lives will be forever enriched by the unconditional love and unselfish devotion you will receive from these dogs.

From the first minute you lay eyes on your Italian Greyhound, his bold, striking coat, soft eyes, and floppy ears will steal your heart. But the Italian Greyhound is not just another pretty face, as he is packed with personality.

Italian Greyhounds are teeny versions of their larger Greyhound cousins. Italian Greyhounds have been beloved as pets as far back as 2,000 years ago, and for good reason. This breed is friendly, loyal, patient, and playful with its family. It is hard to find another breed that tries harder to please its owner.

This shy, gentle breed loves to snuggle, partly due to their need for attention and partly due to their need to stay warm! Once they have

bonded with their family, they will be inseparable and often are uninterested in other animals and people. They are considered "Velcro dogs" who love to be with their families.

Italian Greyhounds make excellent therapy dogs and lifelong companions. They quickly adapt to new situations and can be trained to do just about anything. They require early socialization to help them accept new people, animals, and situations more readily. The only thing your Italian Greyhound cannot learn is something you did not teach him. *The Complete Guide to the Italian Greyhound* not only covers basic obedience training but fundamental field-training lessons.

Italian Greyhounds are hunting dogs at heart and have an incredible prey drive. Rule of thumb: if something its size or smaller moves, then your dog will chase it. However, Italian Greyhounds do not make good hunting companions due to their size.

Whether you are a veteran Italian Greyhound owner or are new to the breed, this book will provide you with everything you need to help you care for, train, and bond with your new lovable friend. You will learn what your Italian Greyhound needs to be a healthy and happy dog long into his senior years.

So, without further ado, continue reading to embark on your exciting journey with your new best friend!

CHAPTER 1

Meet the Italian Greyhound

Italian Greyhounds are gentle and extremely devoted to their family or person, not to mention cute, from their short, glossy coats right down to their ever-wagging tails. Not only are these pups considered to be one of the most playful in the world, but they are also some of the friendliest, happiest, and most loyal of all dog breeds.

Italian Greyhounds' rambunctious personalities and love are contagious, spreading laughter and smiles to everyone they meet. They are often described as decorative couch dogs who love to cuddle with their families, but at heart, they are sprinting hounds with an instinct for pursuit. Your Italian Greyhound's happiness depends on the simple things in life, such as a short walk, a game of catch, a belly rub, or a snuggle on the sofa.

Coming home to an Italian Greyhound is never lonely. Your dog will run excitedly toward you simply because you finally made it back home.

What Is an Italian Greyhound?

Italian Greyhounds are miniature-sized Greyhounds with the same distinguishing sleek and graceful features. Greyhounds are also referred to as sighthounds. Sighthounds are a group of super-fast and agile dog breeds that use their sight as their main sense. As their name suggests, their sight is second to none. These canine breeds hunt primarily by sight and speed rather than scent and endurance, as most other dog breeds do.

Often, this toy-sized breed is referred to as Italian Sighthounds, Iggies, or IGs. The expression Iggy is derived from the initials of the Italian Greyhound—IG.

Italian Greyhounds make great family pets and have massive hearts with plenty of love to give. Maybe it is due to the fact that their hearts make up a larger percentage of their total body weight than other canine breeds. This breed quickly bonds with its human family and any other four-legged members of the family too.

Italian Greyhounds need to be socialized at an early age, as they tend to become nervous or aggressive in unfamiliar situations or while meeting an unfamiliar dog or person. When properly socialized, they make excellent companions for large families with children or for single households. They do not thrive in homes where they will be left alone for long periods of

time. Iggies easily adapt to different living spaces, such as apartment buildings or a house with a backyard. All they need is a human family nearby.

Italian Greyhounds thrive on the company of human companions and are always up for a game, an excuse to show their love and affection, or simply to be the center of attention—often, all at the same time! It is almost impossible to look down at your smiling pooch and not smile back.

This breed is considered to be low shedding and hypoallergenic. However, all dogs still have dander—a common allergen. No dog is completely hypoallergenic.

The liquid eyes of the Italian Greyhound can melt the hardest of hearts. These toy-sized pups are masters in getting their way. As a result, Italian Greyhounds tend to be spoiled and are considered to be the rulers of the house. If you are looking for a breed that is easy to train and will obey your every command, perhaps this is not the dog for you.

Italian Greyhounds are catlike in the sense that they thrive on sunbathing. However, care should be taken so they do not get sunburned or overheated. They also love to climb up to high places, such as the back of your sofa or even the dining room table, to observe their surroundings from a safe distance. Just like cats, Italian Greyhounds have a dislike for getting wet; often, they will refuse to do any bathroom business when it is raining outside.

Actually, cats make wonderful companions for Iggies as they love lounging and playing together. Many Italian Greyhound owners report their pup happily chasing the cat, but in the blink of an eye, the cat is then playfully chasing the dog. It is not uncommon to find an Iggy snuggled up with a cat for an afternoon nap in the warmth of the sun.

Italian Greyhounds love the company of fellow canines; however, care should be taken when introducing an Iggy to larger dogs. A bigger dog could accidentally hurt an Italian Greyhound. The expression "their bark is bigger than their bite" applies to this breed because they easily forget that they are smaller than they really are.

Their short coat requires minimal grooming and maintenance. They shed their hair seasonally. Once every six weeks, you will need to give your Italian Greyhound a bath and trim his toenails.

Italian Greyhounds require moderate exercise. Of course, they love going for walks and playing fetch in the park just as much as most dogs.

They have lots of energy to burn off and require about 30 minutes of exercise daily, preferably outside. Even though Iggies are sociable, playful, and cuddly dogs, they can be very stubborn. This can be a challenge while training them.

History of the Italian Greyhound

The exact origins of the Italian Greyhound are a mystery, but the current theory is that the breed was discovered in Southern Europe and is approximately 2000 years old. Two types of writing appear in Mesopotamia and Egypt depicting Italian Greyhounds, which look similar to small jackals. Ancient Greek vases have also been found with illustrations of small hound dogs believed to be Italian Greyhounds, and archeologists uncovered various Italian Greyhound relics in Pompeii.

It's thought that Italian Greyhounds were first used as sighthounds for hunting small prey, but thanks to their affectionate and extremely

*Photo Courtesy of
Sarah Evans
Divine Kennels*

loyal nature, they soon became a popular choice for household pets. During the Middle Ages, the demand for Italian Greyhounds rose, especially among the nobles in Europe. However, the "Italian" part of the breed's name came from its extreme popularity in Italy.

Toward the 17th century, the breed's popularity spread to England, and during the rule of Queen Victoria, Italian Greyhounds were considered one of the most fashionable dog breeds. They were often carted around by aristocratic ladies. In the 19th century, breeders tried to make the dogs even smaller, but this led to complications in the gene pool. The Italian Greyhound Club was founded in 1900 with the goal of bringing the breed back to its original form.

Sadly, during WWI and WWII, the dogs' numbers started to decline in Europe, though breeders in the United States and Canada made sure Italian Greyhounds weren't wiped out of existence.

Many people associate Italian Greyhounds with racing Greyhound dogs, and with good reason. The appearance and characteristics of the breeds are strikingly similar, except for the size. IGs are much smaller, which is why they're considered a miniature version of the Greyhound and a toy breed.

An Italian Greyhound's personality is one of the breed's best traits. They can be sweet-natured one minute and silly the next. In between snuggling and sunbathing, they can have random bursts of energy that send them zigzagging and zooming around the house or yard. Their unpredictability can be quite entertaining, but one thing's for sure—Italian Greyhounds will love you with all they have. They are considered one of the most loyal dog breeds and are truly a person's best friend.

FUN FACT

Italian Greyhound Club of America (IGCA)

The Italian Greyhound Club of America (IGCA) is the American Kennel Club (AKC)-recognized parent club for Italian Greyhounds. The IGCA strives to educate the public about the breed, and its members participate in many obedience, performance, and conformation events throughout the year. The club is funded through merchandise and affiliated vendors. For more information about the club, visit www.italiangreyhound.org.

General Description

Size – Italian Greyhounds are considered a toy dog breed, measuring an average height of nine to 15 inches at the shoulder, which makes them perfect lapdogs. Typically, an Italian Greyhound is considered full-grown between 12 to 18 months of age.

Weight – This breed usually weighs around eight to 11 pounds. Italian Greyhounds are prone to weight gain, especially as they age. It is important to give them a healthy, wholesome diet and plenty of exercise, as obesity can shorten the dog's life span and cause serious health problems.

Eyes – The most common eye color for an Italian Greyhound is dark brown or black. Just a warning: don't be manipulated by your pup's big, warm, dark eyes. Behind them is an intelligent pup who knows how to get what he wants from you.

Nose – The Italian Greyhound's button nose is one of the breed's most endearing features. Often, they will have either a black, charcoal-colored, or brown nose, which will get into plenty of trouble if you don't keep your garbage in a tightly closed bin.

Torso – Like larger Greyhounds, Iggies are sighthounds that are physically built to be fast runners. They have slender torsos, deep chests, narrow heads, small hips, and skinny legs and tails. Their muzzle and ears are tapered and pointy. They may not seem very muscular, but don't let that fool you. Their muscles are tightly compacted in all the right places to give them amazing speed.

Coat – The Italian Greyhound's coat is typically short and glossy, which means they are light shedders and hypoallergenic. This breed has a short, silky coat that is easy to maintain. The smooth coat lacks an undercoat, which is why they don't shed much at all. Their hair can come in several colors. The most common colors are:

- Sable – Reddish hue with lighter tones.
- Fawn (blue and red) – Red fawns are a burnt orange color, and sometimes they can lean toward a dark, reddish-brown. Blue fawns

are a cream color with a hint of a blue hue. Sometimes it can lean toward a light brown.

- Seal – Similar to dark chocolate, slightly lighter than black, with hints of gray or brown hues.
- Black – All black with zero hints of any other color. Also known as "jet black."
- Cream – Solid light cream or tan color.

Some breeders may have more color choices, such as yellow, slate, gray, blue, white, etc. IGs don't have patterned fur with different colors, like brindle, but they may develop a stripe of darker hair down their back. Their fur markings are divided into four categories:

- Solid – The entire body consists of one color. Almost no white fur.

- Irish – White fur can be seen around a portion of the underside, the neck's collar area, and the feet (not much elsewhere).

- Wild Irish – White fur can be seen past the neck, even on the sides of the body. The legs may be covered in white fur.

- Pied – Spots of one color in small areas of the body. White fur can be seen in many places, like the head, feet, legs, torso, and tail. It may seem like there is more white fur than colored fur.

If you want an Italian Greyhound with specific colors or markings, you can use the terms above to communicate your preferences. For example, "Do you have any solid black Italian Greyhounds or a red fawn Iggy with wild Irish markings?"

If the breeder insists that they can provide an IG with brindle fur, then it is NOT a purebred IG. They probably crossbred it with another breed, like the whippet.

Behavioral Characteristics

Italian Greyhounds are rambunctious, affectionate, and highly intelligent canines who are always looking for ways to please the family. They are considered fiercely loyal to their immediate families, which can be a very endearing feature. However, this can lead to separation anxiety if your dog is left alone for long periods at a time.

Italian Greyhounds can be a little boisterous at times, which is an inherited trait from their parents. Since the breed is prone to barking, they will need to be taught, while still puppies, to curb this tendency. This breed does not make good watchdogs, even though they might love the sound of their voice a little too much.

Your Italian Greyhound will make it his mission in life to befriend any other furry friends who live in the same household. However, an Italian Greyhound will also not hesitate to chase off any cats he may believe are trespassing on his property.

Don't be fooled by your dog's small stature. He is a fast learner and eager to please.

These dogs also have other behavioral characteristics that every owner should be aware of:

Energy level

An Italian Greyhound's energy level can be high, especially when young. Since they're naturally fast runners with a compact muscle build that allows them to take off like a bullet, they enjoy zooming around and will need plenty of exercise. As they become older, they mellow out and become more laid-back.

Their hound instinct drives them to chase any prey they can find. This means they'll respond

Photo Courtesy of PeggyAnn C. Poss

well to outdoor games, like fetch, and love playing with toys (especially if they look like furry critters).

No yard? No problem! You can take your Iggy on a walk around the block or to a dog park. Walking outdoors is a great way for your dog to exercise. Be sure to use a collar and leash until you arrive at a safe, designated area. Walking with your Iggy off-leash can be dangerous. He may become spooked and run off or chase after a squirrel.

If you plan on hiking or traveling a long distance, you can carry your Iggy. There are various types of bags designed for toy dog breeds. They can come in handy when your dog becomes tired from walking.

Developing a good recall is essential because making IGs come back while they're chasing prey can be difficult, if not impossible. If your dog doesn't respond well to your recall commands, he should always be on a leash when in a public setting or outside a fenced yard.

Intelligence

Since Italian Greyhounds come from the sighthound family, they are quite intelligent. Their ancestors had an inquisitive nature, which helped them develop critical thinking skills that helped them find small critters and force them out of their hiding spots. IGs nowadays still carry these same instincts. It's not uncommon to see an IG trying to investigate a new sound or object.

Young IGs can get bored easily, so it's always a good idea to keep toy puzzles around. These types of toys will keep their brain stimulated. You can also play hide-and-seek with your dog's toys or teach your Iggy new tricks (handshake, lie down, roll over, dance, etc.). Use treats as a reward when your dog finds the hidden toy or completes a task.

Temperament

Even though Italian Greyhounds are known to be extremely friendly and loving with their owners, they may not respond well to new people or pets unless they have been socialized. If you're purchasing an Italian Greyhound from a responsible breeder, they should have already started the socialization process. After you bring your dog home, continuing to expose your new dog to friends and strangers will help reduce any timidness.

Italian Greyhounds are excellent at alerting their owners when someone is at the door, especially if it's a postal worker dropping off mail. Despite their small stature, they like to think of themselves as guard dogs and will become vocal to ward off any intruders. For this reason, some hard-of-hearing and elderly people use IGs as service dogs.

Stubbornness

Italian Greyhounds are known to be stubborn, especially when it comes to being forced to do something they don't want to do. They tend to have a "What's in it for me?" attitude. For this reason, they can be harder to train than other breeds.

It's possible to train an Italian Greyhound, but the process may take longer due to their stubbornness. There are experienced trainers who can assist you with correcting any problematic behavior. Most rescue organizations offer free training services. Remember to be patient; the end result will be worth it.

Common Behavior Issues

Like most dogs, the most common behavior issues are usually biting, barking, and jumping (especially if they haven't been socialized). However, Italian Greyhounds are notorious for being vocal, which may be problematic for some people. Once they start barking, it can be hard to get them to stop—especially if someone is at the door.

The best way to curb any undesired behavior is to start training your dog right away and be consistent. Keep in mind that IGs don't respond well to negative punishment, so you'll have to use positive reinforcements when training your dog. Later on in this book, we will discuss how to train your Iggy.

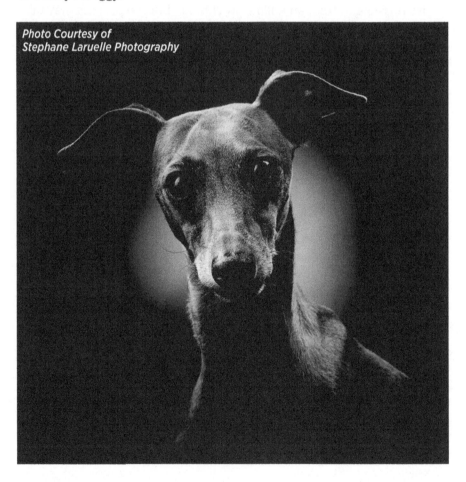

Photo Courtesy of
Stephane Laruelle Photography

Exercise Requirements for Your Italian Greyhound

As mentioned above, exercise plays a vital role in your Iggy's overall health and may even extend his life span. However, providing your pooch with adequate exercise goes beyond taking him out for an occasional walk or two.

All Greyhounds are considered to be moderate- to high-energy dogs and require at least 30 to 60 minutes of exercise each day to keep them healthy and keep boredom at bay.

Puppies – Puppies need several short exercise sessions throughout the day, but excessive exercise for puppies may be detrimental to their growth. Over-exercise refers to repetitive actions, such as walking briskly or running for an extended period of time, not typical playing in the yard or romping around the house. A good rule of thumb is five minutes per day for each month of age.

Adults – An adult Italian Greyhound is considered in his prime from one year old to seven years old, and requires, on average, 60 minutes of exercise split into two 30-minute or three 20-minute sessions a day. There will be days when the weather is bad, so you will need to offer other indoor alternatives.

Seniors – Do not make the mistake of assuming your elderly Italian Greyhound does not need exercise. Unless your pooch has serious health conditions that prevent him from exercising, you will want to continue with his daily walks. Regular exercise can relieve joint pain and maintain muscle mass. Plus, being out in the fresh air will put a little pep in your old pup's step.

Health exceptions – Some health conditions, such as patellar luxation (trick knee), may require strict bed rest while a dog is recovering to reduce swelling and manage pain. After that, a veterinarian may suggest doing strengthening exercises, such as walking uphill to build muscles around the knee.

Pregnancy – In general, pregnant Italian Greyhounds should be taken for daily walks and exercised as normal, except for the last week of pregnancy. Regular exercise will help the pregnant dog stay in shape, which will help in her labor and delivery. Exercise can gradually resume two to three weeks after the dog gives birth.

Is an Italian Greyhound the Right Fit for You?

Italian Greyhounds thrive in homes with families or individuals who can provide them with companionship and a moderate level of activity. They are well-suited for both apartments and houses, as long as there is enough space for them to move around and exercise. Families with older children or adults who can handle their delicate nature are ideal. Additionally, Italian Greyhounds' sensitivity to temperature makes them better suited to moderate climates or homes with climate control.

EVAN CONAWAY
azgreyhounds.com

Italian Greyhounds make wonderful, affectionate companion pets since they love people and are incredibly loyal to their owners. Ideally, this breed needs a fenced-in backyard to run and burn off excess energy and keep their bones strong. They also thrive in small places if you are able to regularly provide regular exercise.

If you are looking for a dog who wants to cuddle with you and enjoy living in an apartment or condo, then this is the breed for you!

Before you get an Italian Greyhound, here are some things to consider:

- Can I give him at least 30 minutes or more of quality time daily for playing, socializing, and exercising?
- Will I be able to spend five minutes a day brushing his coat and providing other grooming necessities, such as cleaning his teeth?
- Do I have time to take him for one or two short walks daily?
- Am I disciplined enough to train him to be obedient?

- Is there someone in the house most of the day to avoid him being left alone for extended periods?
- Can I reciprocate the unfailing love he will show me day after day?
- Do I have the time and commitment to socialize and house-train my Iggy? (They may take longer to house-train than other breeds.)
- Do I have enough funds in case there is a medical emergency?

Remember that Italian Greyhounds are pack dogs and view their human family as such, so they will always want to be in your presence where they can get plenty of affection. Since they develop a deep bond with their human family, it's important to make sure you are ready to commit to your IG for the rest of his life.

If you decide that an Italian Greyhound is the ideal choice for you and your family, you are not just getting a pet; you are gaining a new member of the family who will be dedicated to showing his new loved ones how much he adores them.

CHAPTER 2

Choosing an Italian Greyhound

It is easy to be won over by an Italian Greyhound puppy. His warm, dark eyes and floppy ears will beg you to bring him home.

Choosing the perfect Italian Greyhound may feel like an emotional roller-coaster ride because you do not want to make the wrong choice. There are so many details involved in picking out your puppy. In this chapter, we will discuss everything you need to know about choosing your new best friend.

Buying vs. Adopting

Some people prefer to get puppies from a reputable breeder, while others may opt for adopting an adult Italian Greyhound. Adoption fees are usually much lower than a breeder's price. The fees usually cover the costs of vaccinations, medical care, food, and boarding.

- Adoption: $90–$300
- Breeder: $1200–$3000

Buy or adopt? Most people contemplating getting a dog will ask themselves this question at some point. Neither option is better than the other, as there are pros and cons to both.

People can be passionate about both options, but ultimately, it is your decision and your decision alone. Nobody should pressure you to buy or adopt your new four-pawed companion. However, it is helpful to be well-informed about your options, so you can make the best choice for you and your family.

Adopting a Shelter Dog

There are quite a few negative stigmas surrounding shelter dogs. One is that they will have behavioral issues or that they will be unpredictable. The facts show, though, that the majority of shelter dogs have been surrendered to the shelter because of a change in the pet owner's circumstances, which have nothing to do with the pup's behavior.

THE BENEFITS

- The majority of shelter dogs are already neutered/spayed and microchipped.
- You are saving the life of the Italian Greyhound that you are adopting and making space in the shelter for another dog in need.
- The shelter will be able to give you a general idea of the dog's personality, so there should be fewer surprises once you bring your Iggy home.
- Many adult Italian Greyhounds are already potty-trained.
- The love and appreciation from a shelter dog are incomparable!

The costs of adopting can be considerably lower than buying a puppy from a reputable breeder. According to the Animal Humane Society, adoption fees for dogs and puppies can run from $90 to $300, depending on the shelter. On the other hand, buying an Italian Greyhound from a reputable breeder can cost anywhere from $1200 to $3,000. You can expect to pay even more if you buy a puppy with breeding rights.

THE CHALLENGES

- Since you are not raising your Italian Greyhound from puppyhood, you might not know his family history or where he came from.
- Many shelters have strict requirements for adopting one of their dogs to ensure the animal does not end up in a shelter again in the future.
- Since the Italian Greyhound is a relatively new designer breed in the United States, it can be difficult to find one in a local shelter.
- Finding a younger Iggy in a shelter can almost be impossible, and you may have to adopt an older pooch.
- Some dogs have been treated cruelly by their previous owners, which has left them with emotional scars and behavior issues.

Shelters and Rescues

Animal shelters throughout the United States are overburdened with millions of abandoned pets each year. By adopting your Italian Greyhound, you are making room for other dogs. You are giving your dog a second chance to have a loving home. Plus, the cost of adoption goes directly toward the shelter, so it can continue to help dogs in need.

Many Italian Greyhounds are patiently waiting for someone to adopt them and take them to their new, forever home. The majority of these dogs are loyal, devoted, well-trained pets who just got the short end of the bone for one reason or another and have no place to go.

If you are ready to take the leap and adopt an Iggy, then you need to do some prep work before you stroll into your local shelter. You will need to ensure that your new pet will mesh with your lifestyle and family and, among other things, realize that there are hidden costs that come with adopting.

Although you may want to adopt your Italian Greyhound from a rescue, it can be difficult to know where to begin. Start by phoning local veterinarian clinics to ask for recommendations. They often know of dogs who might need rehoming or of reputable shelters in the area that might have an IG up for adoption. Another option is to do a Google search online for shelters or rescues in your country or state.

Sadly, some rescue shelters are just out to make money and flatout lie to adopters, leaving them with aggressive, sick, pregnant, or even dying dogs. Adopting your Italian Greyhound from an unethical shelter can quickly turn into a nightmare for you and your family.

The majority of shelters are honest and great to work with, but here are some warning signs to watch for when adopting:

- The shelter refuses to let you meet your Italian Greyhound before adoption day. Most reputable shelters will let you meet with your dog as often as you like, even if you are still thinking it over. Just remember, though, someone else might adopt your Italian Greyhound while you are in the "thinking it over" stage.

- They refuse to take the adopted dog back. The majority of reputable shelters have a clause in the contract to allow you to return the dog within a specified time frame if something goes wrong. Hopefully, your Iggy will never have to return to the shelter.
- They adopt out Italian Greyhound puppies younger than eight weeks. By law, a shelter has to vaccinate and neuter/spay animals before putting them up for adoption. Also, it is unethical to spay or neuter a puppy younger than eight weeks, and it is also illegal in many states.
- The shelter provides no or little proof of vaccinations. Avoid any shelter that is unwilling to provide proof of vaccinations.
- The shelter staff reminds you of pushy used-car salesmen. A good shelter is more concerned about the dog's long-term care than about making a sale. They will give you the time you need with the pooch to make your decision without pressure.

Many shelters provide free pamphlets or information sheets regarding the adoption process, requirements, and information on how to care for your Iggy. Each shelter or rescue organization has different requirements before starting the adoption process.

The following is a general guideline. The requirements might vary for each shelter.

- Most shelters will require you to show a government-issued photo ID proving you are 21 years or older.
- You will need to fill out a straightforward application form or an in-depth questionnaire.
- In some cases, you will need to provide references, such as permission from your landlord, verifying you are allowed to have pets.
- Some shelters or rescues will send a representative to your home to make sure it is safe and suitable for a dog.
- The shelter will observe how you and your family interact with the dog during a meet and greet before taking him home.
- Adoption fees will vary depending on the institution. Generally, the fee covers basic veterinary care, food, housing, and care the dog received while in the shelter or foster care.

Once you start meeting different Italian Greyhounds who are available for adoption, your emotions will be running high. For this very reason, it is important that you do your research in advance. Be sure to read the adoption contract completely before signing, and always ask the following questions:

1. Is the shelter responsible for any immediate health issues? Some shelters provide two-week health coverage in case health conditions unexpectedly pop up, while other shelters expect the adopter to assume complete responsibility from day one.
2. Is your Italian Greyhound neutered or spayed? Many shelters automatically neuter or spay any dogs in their charge, but others will charge extra for the surgery.

3. Can the shelter provide you with copies of your dog's medical records or background information?
4. What is the shelter's return policy? Many shelters have rules in case the adoption doesn't work out. Many shelters require the adopters return the dog to them, even if it is years later.

If you are still on the fence about whether you should adopt your Italian Greyhound, here are a few common myths about adopting a dog:

I don't know what I'm getting – Often, shelters will be able to tell you, in detail, about the Iggy's personality traits and behavior. The shelter will inform you about the dog's history, such as why his former family surrendered him or whether he was a stray. Often, when shelter dogs are fostered, their foster parents will gladly share with you a wealth of information about your Italian Greyhound.

I cannot find a shelter that has Italian Greyhounds – Since Iggies are a purebred breed, it can be hard to locate a shelter with a dog that fits your criteria. Many shelters maintain a waiting list for specific breeds, so don't be shy to ask to be included on their list. Other excellent options are *Petfinder.com* and *adopt-a-pet.com,* as they will help you find an Italian Greyhound in your locality that is up for adoption. Simply enter your zip code and the type of dog you are seeking.

Shelter dogs have emotional baggage – Rescued dogs have a history, but their past may be a blessing in disguise as they will already be potty-trained and have a basic understanding of obedience training. All dogs, no matter their age, whether puppies or seniors, have a distinct personality. The shelter staff will help you find the ideal Italian Greyhound whose personality meshes with your lifestyle.

Shelter dogs were abandoned because they all have behavior issues – Quite often, dogs are given up because of an unexpected change of circumstances, such as divorce, allergies, moving into housing that doesn't allow pets, financial issues, or lack of time.

Buying from a Breeder

If you choose to buy a puppy, please do not support pet stores, as they sell dogs from puppy mills. Later on in this chapter, we will discuss puppy mills and how to find a reputable breeder you can trust.

THE BENEFITS

- You will know where your pooch came from and how he was cared for and socialized up to the point you brought him home.
- Raising your Italian Greyhound from the time he is just a puppy will give you complete control of his training and upbringing.
- Breeders often will help you choose a puppy whose personality matches your lifestyle.
- Reputable breeders will provide you with everything you need to know about your Italian Greyhound, including family background, genetic testing, and the personality traits of the dog's parents.
- Often you can pick the sex of the dog you prefer and the color of the dog's coat.

THE CHALLENGES

- Purchasing an Iggy from a reputable breeder is typically more costly than adopting.
- Often you will have to spend extra time researching to find a reputable breeder, and you might need to travel a considerable distance to pick up your puppy.
- Due to the Italian Greyhound's popularity, you might have to be placed on a waiting list for the next litter.
- Many responsible breeders will do a background check on the possible pet owner to ensure their pups are going to loving, caring homes.

As you can see, there are advantages and challenges to buying or adopting a puppy. Adopting a shelter dog is not for everyone, and the same goes for raising a puppy. Whatever you decide, the advantages will outweigh the challenges once you start sharing your life with your loving, four-pawed best friend.

How to Find a Reputable Breeder

> *Do your research to find responsible breeders that prioritize the health and well-being of their dogs. Ensure that the breeder conducts health testing on their breeding dogs to reduce the risk of genetic disorders. And don't hesitate to ask the breeder about a dog's history, socialization, and any specific care requirements.*
>
> EVAN CONAWAY
> *azgreyhounds.com*

Finding a reputable breeder is the next important step in finding your Iggy. Breeders not only connect you with your perfect puppy, but you can rely on them throughout your Italian Greyhound's life. Breeders are often likened to your own private guide as they provide invaluable information, from choosing the best puppy for you to how to care for it year after year.

When choosing where to purchase your Italian Greyhound, avoid pet stores or websites online, as the majority of these puppies come from puppy mills—inhumane, mass-breeding facilities.

Puppy mills are only concerned with churning out puppies for profit and completely ignore the needs of pups and their mothers. Often, puppy mills sell through social media, online classified advertisements, flea markets, and pet stores.

Mother dogs will spend their entire life in a cramped cage with little personal attention, and when they are unfit to breed, they will be dumped on the side of the road or killed. Due to a lack of sanitation and medical care, the majority of pups suffer from health issues and are prone to hereditary conditions like respiratory disorders and heart diseases. There are more than 10,000 puppy mills in the United States alone, and they sell more than two million puppies each year.

Photo Courtesy of Patti Bryan

Here are some warning signs that indicate the breeder is really a puppy mill in action.

- The seller offers more than one type of purebred or designer dog.
- They sell their puppies at less than eight weeks or younger.
- The breeder is located in another state but is willing to ship you the puppy without a face-to-face meeting first.
- The breeder refuses to show any potential clients where the puppies are bred and kept.
- The breeder doesn't ask any questions, and you can pay for the puppy without any previous screening.
- The seller makes no future commitment to you or the puppy. Reputable breeders always require you to sign a contract promising you will return the dog to them if you are unable to care for him in the future.

As with everything in life, it is important to do your research before signing a contract with the breeder. The best way to find a reputable Italian Greyhound breeder is to ask for a referral from a local veterinarian, friends, or shelters. Here are a few tips to help you find a reputable breeder.

Meet the breeder – The best way to get to know a breeder is by visiting their kennel or their home. If it is not possible to meet face to face, then organize a video-conferencing call to meet the breeder and their dogs. During the meet-and-greet session, observe the breeder and dogs. Does the breeder seem genuinely concerned about the well-being of their dogs? Are the dogs clean and well-fed? How do the dogs interact with the breeder and strangers?

Meet your Italian Greyhound's parents – The best way to get a glimpse into how your puppy will be as an adult is to observe his parents. This will give you an excellent sense of your Iggy's personality traits, behavior, size, and appearance.

Ask to see a FULL medical history – Any trustworthy breeder will proudly share Italian Greyhound parents' proof of health screenings. Also, the breeder will inform you of any health conditions that typically affect Italian Greyhounds and how to prevent them.

Be patient – A reputable breeder often will have one or two litters a year, meaning you might have to wait a few months before you can welcome your little pup home. Normally, the breeder will not let you take your Italian Greyhound home until after three months, so it can mature and learn to socialize with its littermates.

Be prepared to fill out an application form – Many reputable breeders will require potential pet owners to fill out an extensive application form to allow them to see if you are a good fit for one of their pups. This helps them ensure their dogs go to loving, forever homes.

Ask questions – When you meet with the breeder for the first time, be prepared with a list of questions about your Iggy. Reputable breeders will happily answer all your questions as they want to see their pups go to good, loving owners.

Once you've narrowed it down to one to three breeders, you can give them a call or email and ask plenty of questions. Don't hold back; there is no such thing as a stupid question! After all, this is a major decision, and you should be able to rely on the breeder for information throughout your dog's life. Take note of how the breeder reacts to your questions. They should be eager to share knowledge about their Italian Greyhounds. After all, reputable breeders want to see their dogs live in good homes.

Beware of parking lot deals or scams, especially online,

FUN FACT
Westminster Kennel Club Dog Show

Italian Greyhounds first entered the Toy Group at the Westminster Kennel Club Dog Show in 1877, nine years before the American Kennel Club officially recognized the breed in 1886. An Italian Greyhound won Best in Group for the first time in 1965. As of 2020, an Italian Greyhound has not yet won Best in Show at this dog show.

where clients are asked to deposit money without being able to verify the breeder or see the puppy in question. If they ask you to wire your money or buy gift cards, then it's most likely a scam.

Important Questions to Ask the Breeder

Before you can bring your Italian Greyhound puppy home, you will need to do some casual detective work to assess the breeder. Buying a puppy is a big investment and commitment, so logically, you want to make sure to get a healthy and happy Iggy from a breeder you can trust.

Here are a few questions to ask the breeder.

Have the Italian Greyhound's parents been checked for any inherited genetic conditions?

The Italian Greyhound is at risk for genetic health conditions, such as heart and hip problems. Make sure the breeder has tested and evaluated both parents and has the proper documentation to prove that neither parent has genetic diseases.

Can I meet the parents?

It might not always be possible to meet the father, but it is essential to see how the pup interacts with his mother and his littermates. Is the mother aggressive, shy, or well-adjusted? Are the puppies hyperactive or docile? Observe the size of the parents and their temperament. This will give you a general idea of what your puppy will be like.

How long have you been breeding Italian Greyhounds?

You want to find out how much experience the breeder has had with Italian Greyhounds. A reputable breeder should be knowledgeable about the Iggy's temperament, weaknesses, and strengths.

Will my puppy be vaccinated and dewormed before coming home with me?

You want to make sure the puppies are being supervised by a professional veterinarian. Many reputable breeders will provide you with their veterinarian information so you can do a quick background check. Be sure to ask what shots your puppy will receive before you pick him up and when he is due for his next round.

How do you socialize the puppies?

Puppies learn proper social skills from their mother and littermates. Ideally, the breeder is raising the puppies in a family environment, where the pups are exposed to adults, children, and a variety of noises.

Do you have any references?

Ask the breeder to send you a list of references. Call their clients and ask their opinions on the breeder, if they are happy with their Iggy, and if there were any problems, how they were handled.

What is the parents' family history?

A passionate breeder will love to share the history of their dogs with anyone who will listen. Most likely, they will share the history of the pure-bred parents, including registration details, which will allow you to check further into health tests and bloodlines.

How old is the mother, and how many litters has she had?

Make sure that the mother was not mated before two years of age, and she shouldn't be older than eight years old. During her lifetime, she should not have been bred more than four times, including this litter. If a C-section was required, she should not have had more than two in her lifetime.

Do you require a breeder's contract?

Most reputable breeders require a breeder's contract stating that you agree not to breed your Italian Greyhound and to have the dog neutered or spayed by a certain age.

Contracts and Guarantees

The number one thing you should expect from a breeder is a solid contract or guarantee in writing that the puppy they're selling is healthy and doesn't have any infectious diseases. In most cases, you'll be asked to bring the puppy to your veterinarian within 48 to 72 hours to confirm the puppy is in good health.

A breeder's contract is considered legally binding. However, if unreasonable demands are made, you can contact a lawyer to take a second look at the contract or find another breeder. As with all guarantees, you should ask for everything in writing. It's hard to prove verbal agreements in court if any legal problems arise.

What to look for in a contract

- Details of both parties
- The dog's registration and pedigree information
- Medical history
- Quality
- Price and payment specifications, such as a deposit to reserve your puppy
- Transaction information
- Returning the dog (rehoming procedures)
- Conditions of sale
- Valid signature and date

After signing the contract and paying the fees, you should receive pedigree papers and copies of the contract along with your puppy. These documents are important because they prove that your dog is a pure-bred Italian Greyhound.

Some contracts guarantee against certain genetic health issues like hip dysplasia, only if the pet owner takes certain precautions, such as not letting the Italian Greyhound run up and down stairs for the pup's first 12 months.

Your dog's pedigree papers will also provide assurances that any future offspring from your dog's bloodline will carry on quality traits known for that particular breed. If your dog came from parents that won awards at championships or dog shows, their scoring and value will be higher. The pedigree information can also be used to make sure your dog hasn't been inbred too much. Excessive inbreeding can lead to health issues.

Some people believe that it's unnecessary to obtain pedigree papers when purchasing an IG puppy as a family pet. However, it's always a good idea to treat these documents like you would a birth certificate. That way, you'll always have records on hand to reflect your dog's history.

Fostering an Italian Greyhound

The process of becoming a foster parent is similar to the adoption process, but you are not keeping the dog. Instead, you are giving him a temporary place to stay until a permanent owner is found.

Being a foster parent gives people a chance to help multiple dogs avoid the shelter environment, where they would be kept in cages. This also gives the Italian Greyhound a chance to work on its training in a home setting.

If you are curious about adoption or becoming a foster parent, there are rescue organizations and shelters in each state that can pro-vide you with more information. You can follow similar steps to find one in your area. You can also ask for referrals from local groups or clubs of like-minded people who devote their time to working with Italian Greyhound rescues.

Photo Courtesy of
Russell Tuncap

Male vs. Female

Some people believe male dogs are more affectionate, while female dogs are easier to train and more protective of their families.

According to veterinarians and professional dog trainers, when it comes to dogs, there is no superior sex. The sex of the dog shouldn't have a major bearing on your decision. Instead, you should make sure that the dog's personality and energy level is a match for yours. Whether your Italian Greyhound is male or female, its personality will be related to its surroundings and training.

It is worth mentioning that many of the biological differences between female and male dogs are related to their reproductive hormones, and the dog's behavior is affected by hormones. Once the dog is neutered or spayed, the hormonal behavior will disappear over time.

Even though both male and female dogs are excellent choices, there are a few physical, hormonal, and behavioral differences that you should be aware of.

Physical differences – Male dogs tend to be slightly larger in size when compared to their female littermates. Female dogs tend to mature faster than male dogs, making them easier to train.

Hormonal differences – Unneutered male dogs have a tendency to roam in search of a mate and to mark their territory by peeing on everything. Also, they will have an innate urge to mount anything that moves, even inanimate objects. Female dogs that have not been spayed will experience estrus (heat cycle) twice a year, producing a secretion to attract male dogs.

Behavioral differences – There are not many behavioral differences between female and male dogs. Your Iggy's behavior will be directly influenced by his training, upbringing, and surroundings. However, studies show that dogs tend to get along better with the opposite sex. If you are bringing a second dog into your home, create the perfect balance with a female or male dog.

Instead of focusing on the sex of the Iggy, choose a puppy whose personality, behavior, and demeanor will meld with your lifestyle.

Photo Courtesy of
Stephen Raymond

Choosing the Right Pup

> 66
>
> *Don't pick a dog just based on color or gender. Make sure the breeder or rescue matches the right dog to your family and lifestyle. Italian Greyhounds are not a one-size-fits-all breed, so be 1000% honest with the breeder or rescue about your needs and expectations and be willing to wait for the right dog.*
>
> LYNNE EZELL
> *Uwharrie*
>
> 99

Puppies can be weaned from their mother when they are eight to 12 weeks old. By then, their baby teeth and little tummies will be ready for eating solids. Before choosing your pup, there are certain things you should look for:

● Does the litter seem healthy?
● Are their eyes clear? Cloudy? Any discharge?
● Any dental problems? Missing teeth?
● Any vomiting or runny stool?
● How's their weight? Do they seem well-fed?
● Are they active or lethargic?
● Are their gums pink or white?

The pups should have clear eyes and seem active while awake, and there shouldn't be any evidence of vomiting or diarrhea. Their weight should be within the healthy range. Even though IGs are small dogs, they should have full bellies without any ribs showing. White gums are a no-no; it means the dog is anemic or has other underlying health conditions.

After you're sure that the litter seems healthy, you can start looking for emerging personalities. Watch the puppies while they interact with their siblings and people.

The goal is to pick a puppy that best matches your preferences. For example, are you looking for a laid-back, relaxed lapdog? Then choose the pup that is often found sleeping in the corner while his siblings are playing. Or do you want an energetic dog? Then go with a pup that is almost always playful.

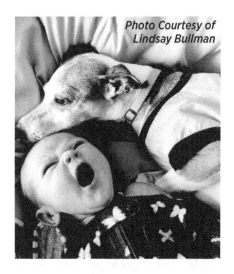

Photo Courtesy of Lindsay Bullman

Don't be surprised if you find yourself bonding with a pup that doesn't match your original criteria. Some people become attached to the runt of the litter or a pup with quirky characteristics. What's important is that you take your time and find the right dog for YOU.

The same goes for adopting. You can visit the rescue or shelters in person and take the dogs for a walk. As you interact with puppies, you'll be able to observe their personalities and behavior. If the IG is living with a foster parent, you can arrange playdates.

Avoid choosing the bold, pushy puppy, as he may grow up to be an aggressive dog who is difficult to train. Instead, befriend the quieter puppy who already has excellent manners. However, avoid puppies that tuck their tails under their legs or pull away from you when you try to pat them. Shy dogs often grow up into adult dogs who are easily frightened and may snap at younger children.

Watch how each puppy interacts with his littermates and how he acts when he is apart from them. Assessing the Italian Greyhound's reaction will give you a general idea of how he will act in your house when he is temporarily left alone.

Give the puppy a quick health check. Your Iggy's ears should be clean and odorless. The pup should be alert and aware of his surroundings. Even though it is typical for all dogs to have smelly breath, the pup's breath should not be offensive, and his curly coat should look soft, clean, and shiny. There should be no signs of fleas or ringworm.

If the puppies do not look healthy, then the best choice would be to walk away. Even though the thought of leaving those adorable puppies behind will be difficult, it will save you from heartbreak in the future.

CHAPTER 3

Preparing Your Home for Your Italian Greyhound

As the owner of a new puppy, you can expect your life to turn upside down within seconds. You can count on finding your leather shoes chewed apart and having to wake up at five in the morning to a barking dog only to find a variety of liquid and solid deposits on your living room carpet.

Considering some of the drawbacks of getting a new Italian Greyhound, you may ask yourself about the upside. The benefits of bringing home a new dog are limitless! Even though the first few months may be a challenge, thoughtful preparation and planning can give your bundle of energy a head start on settling into his new family. Any initial bumps in the road will transform into happy memories.

Puppy-proofing Your Home – Inside and Out

The big day has arrived!

Your cuddly Iggy is finally coming home. After months of searching for the ideal breeder or shelter, you finally found the perfect dog for you and your family. But before bringing your puppy home, you need to puppy-proof your home—inside and out.

Your Italian Greyhound will spend the majority of his time inside your house. So, it is extremely important that you take certain precautions and create a safe environment for him. You want to eliminate all dangers. All puppies are curious and will investigate every nook and cranny of a house and backyard. No matter how intelligent your pooch is, he will love chewing on your furniture and your favorite pair of shoes.

Before you bring home your Italian Greyhound, get down on your knees and crawl from room to room, looking out for any possible hazards at a puppy's eye level. The IG's personality is often compared to Velcro. This means that wherever you are, the puppy will be right by your side. For this reason, be sure to pay extra attention to rooms where you will be spending the majority of your time.

> **"**
>
> *If the dog is a puppy, you will need to watch out for furniture or stairs that might be hazardous to an Italian Greyhound until he gets adjusted to his environment. Because Italian Greyhounds are prone to breaking a leg, they will need to be protected (though after the puppy is two years old, the risk of breaking a leg is reduced to a normal percentage). Like any breed of dog, puppies should be kept away from electrical cords and toxic cleaning materials. They are very agile and good at finding ways to escape from yards, so look carefully for spots where there is too much space underneath a fence or places where they could climb up on something to get over a fence.*
>
> KAREN HAREN
> *Bethany Italian Greyhounds*
>
> **"**

In the kitchen

The kitchen is a fascinating place for your little bundle of fur. Your cabinets and drawers are ideal cubbyholes to crawl into and explore. You can buy childproof latches at the local hardware store that will help to prevent your curious pup from getting into trouble and, at the same time, keep him away from harmful cleaning supplies and foods. In chapter nine, you will find an extensive list of human foods that are considered toxic for all dogs.

If you have a garbage bin in the kitchen, make sure that it has a lid that tightly closes or, better yet, keep it tucked away under the sink with a childproof lock on the door. Italian Greyhounds love to eat, so never underestimate an Iggy left alone in the kitchen with food on the table. If possible, install a gate or door to keep your Italian Greyhound out of the kitchen as necessary.

In the living areas

Houseplants are another hazard for your Italian Greyhound. Many plants are toxic if consumed by your little puppy. Place any houseplants on a table, counter, or inside a spare room with the door shut. Common house plants that are poisonous to dogs include aloe vera, ivy, orchids,

Photo Courtesy of
Trevor Costello

Christmas cactus, lilies, and jade plants. You can find a more extensive list of toxic plants for dogs on the Animal Poison Control website.

If you have a fireplace, your Iggy can be harmed by flying ashes and flames. A simple solution is a protective fire screen. If you use fire-sticks to start your fire, be sure to place them up high and out of reach of your puppy.

Be vigilant in keeping living areas organized and tidy. Make sure that there are no small objects lying around, such as shoes, cell phones, or glasses—all of these items will tempt your curious and teething Italian Greyhound. Make sure that all blind cords and power cords are tucked away, out of sight, or placed inside a chew-proof PVC tube.

In the office

Your office is full of everyday items that will make your Iggy feel like he is inside of a candy shop with so many temptations—papers, magazines, paper clips, staples, power cords, and rubber bands, just to name a few. These items might be fun for your Italian Greyhound to play with, but if swallowed, they can cause serious injuries, even fatal in some cases.

Be sure there is nothing up high that can fall on your Italian Greyhound if he accidentally bumps into a piece of furniture. If your puppy accidentally displaces a heavy vase, for example, he may get seriously injured and/or damage your possessions.

In the bathroom

The bathroom can be a fascinating place for puppies. It contains all sorts of interesting places to squeeze in behind. However, if dental floss, medications, razors, cotton swabs, pills, or soap are left within your Iggy's reach, they can easily be ingested. Expensive emergency visits to the veterinarian's office are quite common for puppies. Be sure to place all shampoos, conditioners, tissue paper, etc., inside the bathroom cabinet or on a shelf out of reach.

Make sure the toilet seat is down at all times since your curious Italian Greyhound could accidentally jump into the toilet bowl and drown. Avoid automatic cleaning chemicals and keep the bathroom door closed. If you have a trash can inside the bathroom, make sure it has a locking lid or can be placed inside the cabinet. Tuck away any dangling power cords and place childproof latches on the cabinets.

In the bedroom

All canines, including Italian Greyhounds, are scent oriented and will gravitate toward anything that smells like you. If you don't want your clothing, socks, or slippers to quickly become chewing toys for your puppy, then put them away. If you use mothballs, place them somewhere that your Iggy cannot reach. These are very toxic for dogs if swallowed.

Place any small objects inside a drawer or up high on a shelf. This includes items such as jewelry, watches, hair clips, and hair bands. Dirty, smelly clothes are especially tempting for your Italian Greyhound, so be

sure to place them inside a laundry hamper. IGs love to squeeze their way into small spaces. If you don't want your dog crawling under your bed, then make a temporary blockade with boxes.

In the garage or basement

The garage and basement have many objects that can be a health hazard for your Italian Greyhound. Place pesticides, rodent poison, fertilizers, antifreeze, solvents, coolants, gasoline, and oils inside a closed cabinet or on a high shelf. Make sure that any screws, bolts, nuts, and nails are out of sight in a tightly closed jar or bag.

If you live in a colder climate, look for de-icing compounds that are safe to use around dogs, as many contain dangerous chemicals. Antifreeze has a sweet smell and taste that attracts dogs and can be fatal if ingested, even in small amounts.

In the laundry room

Your laundry is full of potential hazards—laundry detergents, cleansers, bleach, and fabric softeners can be dangerous for your Italian Greyhound if swallowed. While teething, puppies are tempted to chew and even swallow everything they can fit into their mouths, which can cause severe gastrointestinal issues.

Your washer and dryer can seem like a tempting place for your Iggy to crawl into for a little nap, so keep your appliance doors closed at all times. Do not leave buckets or bins waiting to be emptied anywhere near your pup. He could accidentally fall in and drown.

The stairs

Most breeders will recommend that you avoid letting your Italian Greyhound walk up and down stairs at all costs until he is at least 12 months of age. Iggies are prone to hip problems, as are the majority of smaller dogs. Using the stairs before their bones have fully matured can make any inherent problems worse. Also, smaller dogs can easily fall down the stairs, gravely injuring themselves. For these reasons, it is best to gate off the stairs until your Italian Greyhound is older.

In the yard

Your Italian Greyhound will love spending time outside with you and your family. If your yard is fenced, check to make sure that there are no holes that your pet can squeeze under and escape. If you have holes in your fence, block them off with boards or chicken wire. Your Iggy can squeeze through a space much smaller than you would imagine. Be sure your fence is high enough so your Italian Greyhound cannot jump over it.

Photo Courtesy of Viviana Randolph

Walk through the grass in your bare feet, looking for any objects that could potentially harm your puppy and removing any rocks, nuts, or pinecones.

As noted earlier, certain plants can be poisonous to your dog or cause diarrhea and vomiting. This includes both common indoor plants and outdoor plants such as daffodils, foxglove, tulips, birds of paradise, and lupines. Be sure to block off access to your plants while your puppy is roaming the yard. You can find a more extensive list of toxic plants for dogs on the Animal Poison Control website.

If you have a swimming pool, spa, or pond, be sure to block off access. Even though your Italian Greyhound can swim, he could still drown if he falls in and is unable to get out. Also, many of the chemicals used in maintaining swimming pools, spas, and ponds are toxic. If your Iggy drinks the water, it could cause an upset tummy or diarrhea.

Heatstroke prevention

Avoid leaving your dog outside for long periods of time during extreme weather, even if it doesn't seem that hot outside. And always make sure your dog has access to water. It's important to keep your dog hydrated, even if he will only be outdoors for a short amount of time.

Having a shaded area in the yard will reduce the chances of your dog getting heatstroke. If there are no trees in your yard, set up a canopy or some type of shelter to provide shade.

When heat waves happen during the summer, try to limit outdoor activities to morning or evenings when the temps are cooler and keep your Italian Greyhound indoors most of the time.

Watch for symptoms of heatstroke, such as excessive panting, lethargy, vomiting, diarrhea, or loss of consciousness. If you see any of these symptoms, move your dog to a cool area and seek medical attention immediately. Pouring cool water over an overheated dog can help, but make sure the water is not too cold to avoid shock.

Better safe than sorry

By taking the time to puppy-proof your home before you bring your Italian Greyhound home, you are giving your dog a head-start in settling into his new future home. As your Iggy settles in and gets older, he will learn basic obedience training and what is expected of him, so you won't need to be so vigilant with him.

Set up a feeding area

Your dog will need a spot for his food and water bowls, preferably on hard surfaces like the kitchen floor. It's much easier to clean up spilled food or water on a hard floor than carpet. But if you don't have any hard surface available, you can place a waterproof mat over the carpet to prevent stains.

Make sure you keep the water bowl full at all times. Even though your dog is small and only needs small amounts of food, he can become dehydrated if he doesn't have access to water. If you are worried about nighttime accidents, you can remove the water bowl an hour before bedtime and put it back first thing in the morning.

Food can be given once daily or split into two intervals a day. Food serving recommendations can be found on the back of your dog's food can or bag. Try to avoid giving your dog human food, although your dog will try his best to beg for it!

Set up a cozy corner

Even though your Iggy may prefer to be glued to your side, a soft dog bed will provide another place where he can lie down. If you have a crate, you can place the dog bed inside. This will also give your pup a safe space to retreat to if he feels stressed out when guests come over to your house. It wouldn't hurt to have more than one dog bed in your house.

IGs have a thing for blankets, so make sure they always have one nearby to burrow under. Why? If they could speak, one of the first things they'd tell you is that they hate the cold! (Don't be surprised if your Italian Greyhound argues with you about going outside while it's raining or snowing.)

Since their fur is so short, they become cold easily. Wearing sweaters can help Italian Greyhounds stay warm when they're not under blankets. If you don't have a doggie sweater on hand, a toddler-sized sweater can be a good substitute.

Photo Courtesy of
Kerry McGuire

Prepare for potty accidents

Placing pee pads inside the house will prevent accidents in undesired areas and make clean-up a breeze. You can put the pee pads on any hard floor. Or you can put a pee pad on the carpet, but you may want to enlarge the area by adding more pee pads.

The pads use the same type of technology as a baby diaper. The material will absorb all the liquid as your dog pees on it. Then you can simply fold it up and throw it away. You can also put pee pads inside the crate or travel carrier to keep it clean and dry.

Provide plenty of toys

There's no such thing as too many toys when it comes to Italian Greyhounds, especially puppies. Some IGs enjoy hoarding their toys and will hide them under their blanket.

IGs mainly use toys for stimulation, while others may cuddle with them for comfort. It's always a good idea to get different types of toys (plush, squeaky, puzzle, etc.) so your dog will have plenty to choose from. Over time, as your dog's personality appears, you may see a preference for a certain type of toy.

FUN FACT

Italian Greyhound in the White House

President John Tyler, the 10th president of the United States, gifted an Italian Greyhound to his wife Julia in 1844. The dog had been ordered from the consul of Naples and was named Le Beau or "the beautiful one" in French. Le Beau had a reputation for being spirited but was described by Julia as "...perfectly well and hearty and has the most unfailing attention."

Remember to throw away any broken or torn pieces; they can be a choking hazard.

Other Accommodations

Doggie steps are optional; they can be used as an aid for small dogs and senior dogs. The steps provide easier access to elevated areas, like the couch or bed. There are other things you can add to make your home more comfortable and accessible, like a window perch or a doggie sofa.

Establish Puppy House Rules and Daily Routines

Before your Italian Greyhound first sets his paw in your house, you will need to establish certain house rules and your pup's daily routine. These steps will ensure your puppy will quickly adapt to his new life with less conflict.

Your Italian Greyhound might seem carefree and without a concern in the world, but his new routine will help him feel secure in his new environment. Remember, you have just taken your puppy away from the only world he has ever known, leaving his mother and littermates behind. Your dog just had a frightening car ride and has now arrived in a strange new world with new smells, sounds, and people.

Building a routine for your Italian Greyhound and establishing house rules will help your puppy understand what is expected of him. Also, it will reduce any surprises that may cause additional stress during the transition to his new family.

Have a family meeting

Before you bring your Iggy home, have a family meeting to decide who is going to be the primary puppy parent. Below are a few topics to discuss with your family to make sure everyone is on the same page.

Where will he sleep?

For small dogs, it is preferable to place the crate inside or near someone's bedroom for the first year or at least until the dog is house-trained. In chapter six, you will find more information regarding crate training.

Is he allowed on the furniture?

Your Iggy is a lap dog, so he will love spending hours each day cuddling with his family on the sofa. Will your dog be allowed on all the furniture or just the couch, but not the bed?

Where and who will be with him during the day?

Italian Greyhounds are very sociable pups and cannot handle being alone for long periods of time. If someone works from home, then place your pup's crate and playpen near the main workplace.

Are there any areas or rooms in the house that will be permanently off-limits?

Too much freedom can be an overwhelming temptation for your Italian Greyhound. As your puppy grows to understand house rules, you can give him more freedom. Too much free roaming early on will lead to potty accidents, chewed-up furniture, and extra stress.

Where will his designated potty area be?

Whether you are training your Italian Greyhound to go to the bathroom inside or outside, each member of the family needs to know the procedure and where to take him.

How will you train him?

Italian Greyhounds respond favorably to positive training methods, which will be discussed in Chapter Seven of this book. Choose the Iggy's main trainer, and have the entire family reinforce the new behavior.

Establishing a routine and house rules is essential for your Italian Greyhound, even more so if there is more than one person living in the house. This will help maintain consistency. Your Iggy will be eager to adapt to his new family and to understand what is expected of him. The more consistent the entire household is at following rules, the sooner your dog will figure everything out.

Preparing Your Current Pets and Children

As the day draws closer to bringing home your little bundle of fur, you will need to prepare your current pets and children for the arrival. First impressions have never been more important, so plan ahead for a smooth transition.

Before bringing home your Italian Greyhound, teach your children how to pick up the puppy and pat him. It is highly effective to use a stuffed toy when teaching your children how to do this. Explain to younger children that even though your Iggy looks like a little toy, he isn't. Even though they will want to play constantly with the new puppy, tell them that he will need time to explore his new surroundings and rest.

Children tend to yell when they get excited, which can frighten the new puppy. Do practice sessions with your children, helping them to use softer, indoor voices to avoid startling your Iggy.

If you have any cats or dogs already, be sure to assure them of your love. Before leaving to pick up the new dog, take your current dog(s) for a walk and give them a few yummy treats. Allow them to have access to all the areas where they were previously allowed; otherwise, they will think you are punishing them. If you have a cat, ensure he will have access to high areas so as to observe the new dog from a comfortable distance.

Create a new puppy sanctuary, which includes a crate and an enclosed puppy pen. Allow the resident pets to explore the area freely before bringing home the new dog. If possible, ask the breeder to give you a piece of cloth that has the new puppy's scent. Let your current pets smell the scent, as this will help them embrace your Italian Greyhound quicker.

Supplies

Before you bring home your new four-pawed best friend, there are several must-haves to have on hand. Once your puppy is home, you will not want to leave your adorable dog home alone to go shopping, so make sure you get these items beforehand. The following list is only a suggestion. You might discover you need to add more items later on.

Puppy toys – It is essential to give your puppy lots of different options for mental stimulation and teething. Chew toys teach your pooch to chew on certain objects instead of your furniture or shoes. IGs especially love squeaky/crinkly toys and puzzle toys that contain a treat.

Crate – You need to find a suitable crate for your Italian Greyhound. There is no need to buy a puppy-sized crate and then another crate when he is adult-sized. Instead, save some money and time by getting a crate that is designed for your Iggy when he is fully grown. The crate should provide enough room for your pooch to stand up, turn around, and stretch. In Chapter Five of this book, we will discuss everything you need to know about crate training.

There are two basic types of crates—plastic and wire. Plastic crates are quite popular for bigger dogs and for traveling.

However, I personally prefer metal crates for the following reasons:

- Wire crates can easily be collapsed and can take up less space in storage. Plastic crates only come in two pieces, and they take up more room.
- Some puppies can feel claustrophobic in a plastic pen, as there is less visibility. Wire crates provide a clearer view, allowing your pup to see everything around him. When he needs quiet time, you can easily place a blanket on top.
- The majority of wire crates come with a divider that allows you to adjust the size of the crate as your puppy grows.

• The plastic tray on the bottom of the crate makes for easy cleanup as it simply slides up. Plastic crates will need to be taken apart to thoroughly disinfect them.

Clicker – A handheld device that makes a clicking noise, used in positive-reinforcement training. It is an essential training tool that you will start using from day one.

Poop bags – Being a responsible dog owner means picking up after your puppy. Look for poop baggies that are made from durable material and are easy to dispose of. It's even better if they are made from biodegradable materials.

Appropriate food – This includes whatever food your puppy has been eating (the breeder should provide a few days' worth of the food they were feeding your Iggy) and what you have decided to feed your dog. To avoid stomach upset, make a gradual transition to the new food by mixing the two foods together.

Food and water dishes – Avoid brightly colored plastic food and water dishes as the dyes can seep into your pup's food and water. Italian Greyhounds tend to be sensitive to these harmful dyes, which can cause eye irritation (teary eyes) and skin allergies. Instead, opt for stainless steel dishes that can be washed and disinfected in the dishwasher.

Photo Courtesy of Jamie Wilson

Pee pads (if you are pad training) – Pee pads are essential for indoor potty training, even if you are planning on training your Italian Greyhound to go outside. In the beginning, your puppy will have a hard time not urinating everywhere, so you can place the pee pad in an area close to his crate and slowly move it toward the designated area.

Puppy bed or blanket – The crate will provide a sense of security for your pooch, but a soft, warm blanket will make it feel like home. Look for an orthopedic mattress designed for the crate size and your pup's comfort. Also, your puppy will greatly appreciate having a soft, fluffy bed to relax on while watching television with his new family.

Toothpaste and toothbrush – You will need to get your Italian Greyhound used to having his teeth brushed from the very first week of bringing him home. Never use human toothpaste on your puppy. It contains an artificial sweetener called Xylitol, which is extremely toxic for dogs. Instead, look for toothpaste specifically designed for toy-sized dogs.

Training harness – A no-pull harness will protect your Iggy's tiny trachea. It also teaches your pup not to pull while on his walk. Trust me—your Italian Greyhound will love his harness just as much as you do!

Leash and collar – Keep your Iggy safe by using a durable collar and leashing him whenever you take him outside. I prefer a six-foot leash as it keeps my IG close to me but still gives him some freedom. The collar also is a place for your pup's identification tags, etc.

Stain and odor remover – Your Iggy will have accidents before he is trained. Look for stain and odor removers that destroy pet urine enzymes. These enzymes are like a red flag calling out for your dog to return to the exact same spot to urinate there.

Doggy treats – All dogs love treats, and your Italian Greyhound will not be the exception. Plus, treats are an essential part of training your pooch. There is a wide selection of doggy treats available.

Nail trimmer – Look for a pair of nail trimmers that are designed for toy-size breeds. They should be good quality, as they need to last a long time. Check out the reviews online to make sure the trimmers are easy to use.

Hairbrush – The Italian Greyhound's fine and glossy hair will need to be brushed daily to prevent it from becoming tangled and matted. The best brush for your Iggy is a small-sized comb and bristle brush, as it will quickly smooth out any knots. Also, stainless steel combs with round tips will brush your dog's hair without pulling or tugging.

Puppy gate and playpen – You are bringing home a new dog who doesn't have a clue about the boundaries and limits in your home. Placing him in a playpen or blocking access to stairs with a puppy gate will keep him safe, happy, and properly contained.

Besides everything that you need to do to make your Italian Greyhound feel like a member of the family, do not forget to capture your memories together through your camera or phone. Also, the best thing you can give your puppy is your unconditional love!

Kennel or No Kennel?

Some people believe kennels or crates are necessary, while others don't. The truth is it depends on your situation and preference.

If you have other pets in the house and want to provide your Italian Greyhound with a safe space, or your Iggy has frequent accidents at nighttime, an enclosed area like a crate would be a good idea.

Playpen fences (also used for babies and toddlers) are good substitutes when visiting a residence that doesn't have a fence. They will keep your dog contained in the yard. The playpen is not an ideal permanent solution because your IG will need room to run and exercise.

CHAPTER 4

Bringing Home Your Italian Greyhound

N ow that you've done your research and made preparations, it's time to bring your new dog home! It can be an exciting time for the family, but keep in mind that it may also be scary for your Italian Greyhound. Leaving its previous home can cause some anxiety. This chapter will prepare you for the first few days with your new puppy, so you and your dog can have a great start to your new life together.

Setting Up a Plan

Setting up a plan will help keep things organized when picking up your puppy. It'll also help you prepare for any possible mishaps. Here are some examples of what you'll need to take with you when you pick up your new dog:

- Leash and collar
- Blanket
- Dog treats
- Pee pad (optional)
- Dog carrier

The collar and leash will prevent escape so you can safely walk your new dog to the car and your new home. Having a blanket will keep your dog cozy.

You'll most likely receive documents from the breeder or rescue center regarding your dog's personal information and records of any vaccination or medication it has received. Hang onto these documents

Photo Courtesy of Russell Tuncap

and put them up in a safe place once you get home. You'll need these documents again, such as when you bring your dog to the vet.

If you have other pets at home, you'll need to make accommodations to keep them separated while your new dog becomes used to his new home. You can put the other pet(s) in a different room, with their own water and food bowl, prior to picking up your new dog. Or you can install a baby gate between different areas. That way, the animals can acclimate and get used to each other's presence.

The Ride Home

For special occasions, it does not get much more exciting than bringing a puppy home for the first time. For you and your new best friend, this is a once-in-a-lifetime experience, so you want to make it memorable.

Most dogs are anxious during their first car ride. They may pant a lot, get carsick, or have accidents (this is where the pee pad comes in handy). If your Iggy seems nervous on the ride home, offer comfort and speak soothing words. You can try to offer treats. If dogs associate treats with car rides, it may help them develop a positive response.

The first car ride home should not be taken lightly. It is an opportunity to get off on the right paw and start bonding together. Before you head out to pick up your bundle of fur, make sure you are well-prepared by bringing along a blanket, a few chew toys, a leash and a collar, plus any cleaning supplies in case he has an accident in the car.

Upon arriving at the breeder's house to pick up your dog, any final paperwork will be dealt with outside before going inside to pick up your Italian Greyhound. The breeder probably will give you a small bag of the current dog food your puppy is eating to wean him onto the new food you are planning to feed him.

No food should be given to your pooch two to three hours prior to travel to prevent car sickness. If the trip home is longer than three hours, be sure to bring along his food dish to give him a handful of food in case he gets hungry. Iggies love to eat, and when they are hungry, they will clearly let you know by whining or barking.

Before hopping in the car and driving off with your new Italian Greyhound, take him for a short walk away from his mother and litter-mates so he can get used to being close to you. This will also give your puppy an opportunity to relieve himself before getting into the car. Let your Iggy explore the car at his own pace by giving him a chance to smell his new blanket and crate. Leave the doors open and turn the car on so he won't be frightened by the engine noise.

But how should you transport your new dog home? Should he be placed inside a cardboard box on the floor or in a traveling crate? Or should he sit on your lap and be allowed to roam about the car freely?

Is it better for him to sit in the back seat versus the front seat? Here are some common concerns:

Your safety – All puppies are curious by nature, and if they are not secured inside of a crate, they can easily and dangerously become wedged under the pedals while you are driving.

Your Italian Greyhound's safety – Younger pups lack coordination, and if allowed to wander around on the seats while the car is moving, they could possibly fall to the floor and hurt themselves. In addition, if you have to come to a sudden stop or swerve around a corner, your Iggy could be thrown off balance and be seriously injured.

*Photo Courtesy of
Bethany Shaker*

Front or back seat? – In the United States, children who are seven years old and younger are not permitted to sit in the front seat due to the impact of airbags. In the case of an accident, the airbag is instantly activated, releasing a punch that could seriously injure or kill a child. In the case of your itsy-bitsy Iggy, the force would, without a doubt, be fatal.

Crate or carried? – Many people, understandably, just want to cuddle with their adorable little bundle of fur on the drive home. Some have a small cardboard box that they plan to place on the floor of the car, but this will not prevent a dog from climbing over the edges and gallivanting around your car. Your best choice is to use a travel carrier/crate.

You want your Italian Greyhound to associate good memories with his crate as you will be using it for training, so take the crate out of the car and place it on the ground with a few yummy snacks inside. Let your

WHEN CHOOSING A TRAVEL CARRIER, CONSIDER THE FOLLOWING POINTS

- **Find the correct size** – A 12-week-old Iggy weighs approximately one to one and a half pounds and should be slightly smaller than a soccer ball. A full-grown Italian Greyhound will weigh between seven to 15 pounds and range from nine to 15 inches in height. The carrier or crate should be big enough for your pup to stand up in and turn around.

- **Design matters** – Look for a dog carrier that has passed third-party crash tests and comes highly reviewed. A poorly designed dog carrier can be hazardous in an accident.

- **Choose a style** – There are two basic styles of travel carriers for dogs—hard and soft cover. Hard covers offer superior protection for your dog and are preferable if traveling long distances. Soft covers offer less protection for your dog but are easier to carry than heavy, cumbersome hard-covered carriers.

puppy go in on his own terms so he feels safe. Place a soft blanket and chew toy inside.

Bathroom breaks – Puppies haven't learned to control their bathroom urges, so if the drive home is longer than two hours, you may have to make a bathroom stop. Avoid spots that are frequently visited by other dogs. This is because your Italian Greyhound puppy hasn't received all his vaccinations yet, and you do not want to risk him picking up a disease.

Even if your puppy doesn't go to the bathroom, it gives him a good opportunity to stretch his legs. Be sure to put the leash and collar on your Iggy before you let him out of the car for any rest stops.

Two is better than one – Ask a friend or family member to go with you to pick up your Italian Greyhound, as they can drive the car while you sit in the back seat next to your puppy. Iggies tend to bond quickly with people they encounter early on. Plus, remember this is the first time he has been for a car ride and separated from his family, so being alone can be a terrifying experience.

Car sickness – Many puppies and older dogs suffer from car sickness. Watch for your dog pointing his nose toward the floor, lips wrinkled up, drooling and heaving. Lay a towel under him to facilitate cleanup. Cover his crate with a blanket to help him feel more secure, or open the window a crack to let in fresh air.

Climatic considerations – Puppies have a difficult time regulating their body temperature and are prone to hypothermia and hyperthermia. Make sure the inside temperature of your car is comfortable, and never leave your dog alone in the car.

Psychological well-being – Come straight home. This is not a time to stop and grab some groceries or stop off for a quick visit with friends. Keep the entire trip quick, smooth, and simple. Remember that your pup is already having an incredibly stressful day.

Make it a positive experience and avoid creating emotional scars that could resurface later on in the dog's life, such as separation anxiety. Talk to your Italian Greyhound in a soft, calming voice to make him feel safe. If you play music in the car, choose relaxing tones.

The First Night Home

For the first few nights, even weeks, you are going to be sleep deprived. Puppies tend to sleep between 16 to 20 hours a day, but they have near-hourly bathroom needs. When your Italian Greyhound wakes up, he will start whining or crying to let you know that he has to go to the bathroom. You will not have much time to get him to his designated potty spot. So, have a spot close by and run!

Place your Iggy's crate in the area where you want him to sleep. Some new puppy owners prefer to put the crate inside their bedroom so they can hear when their puppy wakes up. Once you pick a sleeping place for your puppy, don't change it until he is potty trained.

Scent is one of your Italian Greyhound's strongest senses. On his first night sleeping without his littermates, he will feel overwhelmed. If the breeder gave you a small piece of mama-scented towel or blanket, place it inside the crate to soothe your anxious little puppy.

Looking for a few other tricks to calm your new friend to sleep on his first night away from his mother?

Try hiding an old-fashioned alarm clock under his bedding. The steady tick-tock sound resembles the sound of his mama's heartbeat. Or try placing a hot water bottle under his blanket to keep him toasty warm at night.

From the very first night, you need to start teaching your Iggy bedtime is sleepy time and not playtime. If he barks to go to the bathroom, take him to the designated bathroom area. Once he goes to the bathroom, reward him with a treat, then take him back to his crate to go back to sleep.

Do not be fooled by those big brown eyes! He needs to learn nighttime is for sleeping, not for playing.

Your new pup's bladder has not built up enough control to get through the entire night without needing to go to the bathroom. It will take a number of weeks before you will be able to sleep through the night without having to rush him to his bathroom spot. Expect to get up at least five to six times, the first few nights, to take him to the bathroom.

Photo Courtesy of
Frank and Carol Rizzo

The First Few Weeks

> *During the initial weeks with your Italian Greyhound puppy, establishing good habits and routines is crucial. Start house-training immediately, providing frequent opportunities for your puppy to relieve himself outdoors and rewarding successful elimination. Begin socializing your Iggy early, exposing him to a variety of people, animals, and environments in a positive and controlled manner. This helps build the dog's confidence and reduces the likelihood of fear or aggression later on. Begin teaching basic commands such as sit, stay, and come using positive reinforcement techniques, and introduce your Iggy to crate training, making sure the crate is a safe and comfortable space. This will help with house- training and provides a secure resting place.*
>
> EVAN CONAWAY
>
> *azgreyhounds.com*

Potty accidents are bound to happen the first night (and the next couple of weeks), so make sure you place pee pads on the floor nearby and let your IG out frequently. Go to Chapter Six for more information on house-training.

If you decide to crate train your Iggy, nighttime would be a good time to start. After a while, your dog will get accustomed to the schedule and anticipate when it's time to go inside the crate. Don't forget to let your Iggy go potty outside one more time before going inside the crate.

Since Italian Greyhounds have small bladders, they may still need to be let out for potty breaks once or twice throughout the night. It may take some time for your new dog to adjust to his new home and routine. At first, it will be like an overload of stimulus for your dog, and he may act excited or anxious.

Loud noises and sudden movements may make your dog nervous for the first few weeks. Your Italian Greyhound may try to hide under furniture or in corners if he's not in your lap, constantly seeking reassurance and comfort. (On a positive note, if you're going through a cold season, a clingy Italian Greyhound will keep you warm!)

There WILL be potty accidents. Remember to take your dog out and repeat the reward system each time. With time, your Iggy will settle down and become confident enough to roam around the house on his own.

One of the most common questions an owner may ask is, "How long does it take for my shy dog to open up? Will it always be like this?" The answer is it usually takes about one to two months for a dog to fully open up and get used to its new surroundings, especially if it's adopted from a shelter environment.

Giving your Italian Greyhound plenty of love and affection may help him come out of his shell faster. However, if your dog prefers to be left alone at first, don't worry. Like some people, dogs need to learn that they can trust their new owners. You can sit near your IG and drop treats on the ground between you and your dog.

First Introductions

Have your family offer treats to create a positive experience. If the dog loves toys, then encourage them to try and gently play with the toy and see if your Iggy responds.

Children are usually very excited when a new pet arrives and will want to be involved. You can suggest that they participate in feeding and taking care of the dog or play gentle games, like catch, with a plush toy.

Establishing rules with children will help them understand that your Iggy has boundaries. Since Italian Greyhounds can be fragile, have kids ask for an adult's assistance when it

FUN FACT
Popularity Ranking

As of 2020, Italian Greyhounds are ranked the 73rd most popular breed out of 196, according to the American Kennel Club (AKC). Breed popularity is determined by AKC registration statistics for the current year.

comes to picking the dog up, and you can also show them how to apply a "soft touch."

Remind your family members to be gentle, rather than petting or playing with the dog aggressively, and to avoid loud sounds when the dog is nearby. It's always a good idea to show people (including strangers) how to respect a dog's space by letting the dog sniff their hand first before petting.

Introducing Your Italian Greyhound to Your Resident Dog

One of the biggest mistakes pet owners make when introducing their new dog to their resident dog is simply tossing them together and hoping for the best.

Your older resident dog has already declared your house his territory. When you bring a new dog into the older dog's territory, he may respond with aggression to defend what he feels is rightfully his. Depending on your new Iggy's energy level and personality, he may be submissive, act fearful, or even fight back.

According to the Humane Society, more than 40 percent of US households that have pet dogs have more than one dog. The majority of those dogs in a multiple-pet household did not arrive at the same time. So, if you are bringing your Italian Greyhound into your pack, what are the dos and don'ts of the first introduction?

 DO

Choose a neutral area – Ask a friend or family member who knows your older dog for assistance. You, your new Iggy, your helper, and your current dog should meet in a neutral area, such as a place where you do not walk your resident dog often and that is not familiar to your new dog.

Go for a walk together – Go for a long walk together, as it will drain both dogs' energy levels and allow them to become familiar with each other in a place that is neither of their territories. Once the dogs walk together side by side, tolerating each other, then you can go home. First, enter the house with your current dog, and then bring the new dog inside your house. By doing this, your resident dog is essentially inviting the new dog into his territory as his guest.

Use a leash – Introduce your new Iggy to your current dog while on the leash. This will allow the older dog to feel as if he is in control of the situation. Also, if there are altercations, you can quickly pull your puppy out of harm's way without causing a huge commotion.

 DON'T

Do not place the dogs in the same crate – This is a recipe for disaster. Do it this way, and you will wind up with one or both dogs being injured and some very hurt feelings. Instead, close off a small part of the house with either a dog gate or a playpen with the new dog's crate inside.

Do not get involved – Once your dogs are both inside the house together, there may be altercations between the two of them, but do not become irritated or annoyed with your older dog. It is natural that the older dog will try to put the new dog in his place. Stay calm and let them establish a hierarchy among themselves.

Do not forget to show affection to your older dog – Small puppies can be quite annoying for older dogs, and they can feel a bit jealous of the attention you are giving the new dog. Do not forget to cuddle your older dog with extra love and attention to reconfirm that you still love him. Do not expect the dogs to embrace each other instantly; often, it can take up to six months before the new addition to the household is accepted or tolerated.

Helpful suggestions to ease the tension between your dogs.

- Confine your Iggy to an established part of the house, which is far away from the older dog's crate and feeding area. Be sure to make any changes at least a week before bringing home your new dog and allow your older dog to sniff out the new dog's area.

- After your dogs have finished eating or having playtime, place your new puppy inside his crate and close the door. Ask your older dog to come over and investigate the new dog on his own terms.
- Give your older dog the royal treatment! This will prevent his feelings from being hurt. Never let the new dog push past him for your affection or praise. Your older pet deserves and needs to feel he is still loved as much as he was before.

Here are some tips for a successful introduction:

- Females vs. females or males vs. males may cause some tension and may require more time to acclimate. The males will end up bickering until they establish who's alpha. Introducing a female to a male, or vice versa, is easier than introducing a male to another male.
- Have someone help you take both dogs out for a walk on separate leashes. Keep them both at a distance and reward them with treats if they see each other without being provoked. Start walking them (still at a distance) and continue to give treats and positive remarks for good behavior. For example, say "Good dog!" each time the dog looks at the other dog. As time goes on, the dogs will start becoming more comfortable walking side by side.
- If your puppy hasn't had its vaccinations yet, continue to keep it separate from other animals that may carry disease or exhibit symptoms of illness. Avoid taking your puppy to dog parks until after the vaccinations are completed.
- Don't leave toys or food lying around; it could start a fight between your pets. You can bring out the toys and food when you're able to closely monitor the situation, then put them away.
- Cats may be challenging because IGs may view cats as small prey that they can chase indoors. You'll need to change their perspective of the cat from prey to companion. You can use positive reinforcement methods while petting the cat and invite your IG to join. The same goes for other small pets, like rabbits or guinea pigs.
- If your IG responds aggressively to the other pet, remove it from the situation and place your dog in a small time-out. (Either in the kennel or behind a baby gate.) After repeating this several times,

your Iggy will learn that he needs to leave the other pet alone if he wants to stay by your side.

- Some people rush to rehome the other pet or the new dog if they are having difficulty getting along, but that can cause trauma and anxiety for the

FUN FACT
First AKC Italian Greyhound

The first Italian Greyhound to be registered with the American Kennel Club (AKC) was named Lilly and was registered in 1886, two years after the AKC was founded.

animal. Instead, try contacting an experienced trainer first. They can do video sessions or home visits to remedy the situation.

Cats and Dogs

Typically, cats are more aloof and distrustful, while dogs are generally more sociable and territorial. However, these differences do not indicate that dogs and cats cannot share the same space—they simply need a little help from you.

With some simple training techniques, love, and a whole lot of patience, your Italian Greyhound and cat may eventually become friends or at least learn to tolerate each other.

Here are some suggestions to help your Italian Greyhound and your cat get along.

Use positive reinforcement – Never yell at or hit your cat or dog, as it will just make the situation even more uncomfortable, tense, and stressful. Instead, reinforce any type of positive behavior between them, such as tolerating each other from different sides of the room. Offer treats for any type of good behavior around each other. Reinforcing good behavior when the animals are relaxed will lead to them wanting to be around each other, as they will learn that this means receiving praise, treats, and affection from you.

Play games together – Never underestimate the power of playtime, especially if it encourages your beloved pets to play together. Play games with each pet separately, with the other pet observing within close proximity to observe. Once your cat and dog appear to tolerate each other, even if it is from a distance, play games with each one simultaneously, such as playing with a string, hide-and-seek, or scavenging games. Just a word of caution—be careful not to play any games that may get either pet overly excited.

Give them their space – Even though you want your Iggy and cat to be best buds, it is never the best decision to force them together. Instead, keep your cat and dog separated if there is any sign of aggression, fighting, or stress. Cats and dogs need some time and space apart from each other during an argument.

Keep them safe – While teaching your Italian Greyhound and cat to like each other, you need to take into consideration their physical safety. For first introductions, you will want to play it safe, as you do not really know how either of your pets will react. Provide high places for your cat to run to, and for your dog, use two levels of safety, such as a leash and

Photo Courtesy of Stacey Lawson

a baby gate. If your pup gets too excited, ask him to lie down or distract him with his chew toy.

Use sensory cues – Cats and dogs are both highly scent-oriented. Swap out beds, blankets, or towels to help your dog and cat get used to each other's scent without the pressure of seeing one another. Another helpful sensory cue is to let them listen to each other's sounds from a safe, comfortable distance so that when they are closer together, a bark, growl, or hiss will not frighten the other pet.

Give your cat his own territory

Cats need to feel safe and protected.

Set up a "base camp" by making a refuge that your Iggy cannot access. Create several safe spots for your cat around the entire house to allow your cat to confidently navigate the shared space without crossing paths with his canine roommate.

All cats are natural climbers, so take advantage of your home's vertical space to create an escape route for your cat. Install shelves, buy tall cat trees, or place a cat bed on top of a bookcase. By doing this, you give your cat an opportunity to observe your Iggy from a safe distance of his choice.

Make sure your Italian Greyhound cannot access your cat's litter box. Cats enjoy privacy while doing their business, plus some dogs enjoy snacking on cat feces, which is a bad habit for your Iggy because he can contract intestinal parasites. These parasites can cause a long list of health problems, such as vomiting, diarrhea, anemia, and weight loss.

Baby gates are an excellent option to keep your Iggy out of your cat's base camp, but since Italian Greyhounds are known for being escape artists, keep the litter box in an open space and use an uncovered box. This way, your cat will not be surprised and cornered mid-squat.

To prevent disastrous mealtime encounters, schedule regular meal-times for your cat and dog. In other words, no free feeding. Place bowls at separate ends of the house or place your cat's food dish up high on a table or a countertop where your Italian Greyhound cannot find it.

Keep a close eye on your cat's toys. Dogs tend to love the scent of catnip even more than cats, which can prompt competitive fighting and bickering.

The following steps will maximize the chances for success.

- Before you bring home your Iggy, make sure your cat is up to date with vaccinations and is parasite-free. Plan to keep your pets separated for at least three days after the new arrival. The goal is for your cat to get used to your dog's presence without face-to-face contact. Even though they cannot see each other, they can smell and hear each other.
- Feed your cat and dog on opposite sides of a closed door. This will help your cat to associate the presence of the new dog with something pleasant, such as eating. If your cat seems skittish about eating close to the door, then place her food dish a few feet away and slowly move it closer each day or until your cat is comfortable eating next to the door.
- Begin face-to-face meetings in the common area of your house. Keep your Italian Greyhound on a leash and distracted with a chew toy, and let your cat come and go as she wishes. Do not restrain either pet, as that could result in injury. Reward your cat with treats and praise. Then do the same with your dog. If either pet shows signs of aggression, redirect your pet's attention by tossing a toy, etc.
- Be prepared to supervise your pets' interactions for at least the next few weeks, perhaps even longer.

Do not be surprised if there are altercations. If the cat growls or bats her paws at the dog, it is her way of communicating her boundaries to the dog. With time, the cat will learn to coexist with the new dog.

Just as you would with an older resident dog, reassure your cat that you love her by patting her and giving her some favorite snacks. Cats like to do things on their own terms, so never force your cat to meet and greet the new dog, as it will not end well.

Realize your cat has a personality. If she acts like she just barely tolerates the new dog, then that means that she probably has accepted your Italian Greyhound. Remain watchful to ensure all of their interactions go smoothly—especially when your Iggy hits his rambunctious "teenage" stage.

Options if Your Pets Don't Get Along

Every pet owner's dream is to come home and find their pets cuddled up together on their blanket. Yet, the sad reality is pets do not always get along, especially if they are different species. If you find your two pets cannot be friendly, they may need to be separated for a few days, then reintroduced to each other.

Reasons why your pets may not be getting along:

Hormonal – Often, disagreements between your pets are related to hormonal changes. An easy fix for this problem is to make sure all your resident pets are spayed or neutered, as this will keep any unwanted aggression at bay.

Food – All animals, no matter their species, have a built-in instinct to protect their food. If you notice aggression around mealtimes, place your pets' food dishes in separate parts of the house and feed them at the same time.

Jealousy – All pets need to feel loved and cherished. An easy solution for this problem is to designate quality time with each of your pets alone, without the other pets watching. This will ensure each pet that you love it and are never going to replace it.

Dominance – Rivalry among pets is normal, especially if you bring a new pet into the household. Only one pet can be the leader of the pack, and this is something they need to figure out on their own terms and time schedule. Once your pets have established which pet is the leader, respect their decision by feeding the boss first.

Fights will happen, especially during the first few weeks, as they determine who will be the dominant leader in the house. When this happens, never attempt to separate them, as you will end up injuring yourself. The best solution is to douse the animals with water, causing them to back off from each other instantly. Be sure to keep them separated and under close supervision until they learn to get along.

Photo Courtesy of
Leah O'Brien

A good relationship between your pets may only take a few days to build, or it could take a couple of years. Managing their environment and using positive reinforcement will help your pets to get along and is an essential part of the process.

If you fear your pets' behavior may cause harm to each other, you, or another person, it is not unreasonable to think about giving up one of your pets. Some pets cannot and will not tolerate other pets and are happier living in an "only child" environment.

But before you consider such a drastic decision, there are lots of behavior specialists out there who are willing to extend a helping hand to encourage your pets to get along. A certified dog or cat trainer or a board-certified veterinary behaviorist will be able to diagnose and treat your pets' stress, anxiety, phobias, aggression, and reactivity toward each other. Often extreme misbehavior occurs because the pet is suffering from an underlying medical condition, so be sure to check with your vet.

Talk to friends and family members.

Maybe you have decided to give up one of your pets, but perhaps your cousin would love to adopt him. Or a colleague could be searching for a furry companion. If you just ask around, you will be surprised how many people would be thrilled to give your pet a new forever home. Just be sure the home is suitable for your pet by visiting ahead of time.

Seek out rescue groups.

Most localities have active rescue groups dedicated to "fostering" pets in a caring home until they can find them their forever home. One of the main advantages of a rescue group is you are assured that your pet is going into the home of someone who not only loves pets but understands how to take care of them. There is also the option of looking for rescue breed–specific groups.

Find a "no-kill" organization or shelter.

If you are considering surrendering your pet to a shelter, you absolutely need to confirm that it is a no-kill facility. These types of shelters have the goal of helping your pet find a new loving forever home as soon as possible.

Ask around.

If you did not have luck with the above alternatives, then think outside of the box and contact dog trainers or your veterinarian to see if they know of any good homes that are searching for a good pet. For anybody who genuinely cares about their pets, the pound is not even an option.

The First Vet Visit

In most situations, you will be advised to bring your dog in to see the vet 24 to 48 hours after you pick him up. That means you'll need to choose a vet and make an appointment ahead of time.

The first vet visit will most likely be a wellness check, where your vet will weigh your dog and examine him from head to toe. If they find a medical issue, you can contact the breeder or adoption center for a resolution—especially if there is a contract or guarantee involved.

If your dog is a puppy, he may be due for some vaccines to prevent diseases like parvo and rabies. This is where the breeder or adoption documents come in handy. You can give them to the vet, and they will determine if your dog is up to date with his vaccines or if he needs another round.

What should you expect during the first vet's visit?

You will be allowed into the examination room with your Iggy. Be sure to bring along some of his favorite treats. Be calm and relaxed, while talking to your pooch; use an upbeat, happy voice, praising his good behavior.

The veterinarian will weigh your Italian Greyhound, check his temperature, and examine his eyes, ears, mouth, paws, teeth, genital region, and fur. Then, the vet will listen to your dog's heartbeat and lungs using a stethoscope. The veterinarian will palpate your dog's lymph nodes and abdominal areas. Once the general examination is finished, the vet will administer any vaccinations and dewormers required.

The vet will most likely discuss any future medical procedures your Italian Greyhound might need, such as spaying or neutering and micro-chipping. If you have any questions regarding your pup's general health, now would be a good time to ask. Your vet's knowledge and experience can help you learn more about the breed and its needs. For example, this would be a good opportunity to ask about grooming and how to avoid allergies since IGs tend to have sensitive skin.

Your veterinarian will give you a vaccine schedule for your Italian Greyhound. Be sure to place future dates on your calendar so you don't forget.

CHAPTER 5

House-Training

> "
>
> *Potty training should be one of the first things you do once you bring your Iggy home. Puppies respond to scent, location, and timing, so new owners should be diligent about when it's time to go potty. A gentle reward goes a long way, and punishment can sometimes make the puppy afraid to go potty at all, so use positive reinforcement. Some Iggies don't want to go outside when it's raining or cold—if so, know that they can be trained to use a litter box.*
>
> KAREN HAREN
> *Bethany Italian Greyhounds*
>
> "

ouse-training your Italian Greyhound requires consistency, patience, and plenty of positive reinforcement. The goal is to train your pooch by instilling good habits and building a loving bond with him.

Typically, it will take four to 10 months to completely house-train your Italian Greyhound. Since Iggies are a smaller breed, they have smaller bladders and faster metabolisms, which means more frequent bathroom breaks. Do not be discouraged by setbacks. Accidents are part of house-training. By being consistent, you can get your pooch on the right track in a few months.

Whether you are teaching a puppy or an older shelter dog, this chapter will answer all your housebreaking questions.

First Things First

Not being house-trained is usually the number one reason why Italian Greyhounds are surrendered. This is due to the fact that Italian Greyhounds are particular about certain things, like going potty outside while it's raining, and they don't typically let their owners know when they need to go.

House-training 101

Choosing a potty spot is important, especially for Italian Greyhounds, since they can be picky about where they do their business. If you have a fenced backyard, you can let your dog roam freely. In the city, it can be harder, so walk around with your IG and take note of specific places that the dog favors and return to these spots.

IGs, like most toy breeds, have small bladders. That means they need to do their business often. Try to establish a schedule or a routine so they can learn to anticipate when they are going to go outside next. You can start with 30-minute intervals, then one hour, and so on. Most adult IGs will need potty breaks every three to four hours, but every dog is different, so what may work for one dog may not work for another.

Watching for cues can help you spot when your dog needs to go, and you may notice a pattern:

- whining at the door normally used to go outside
- sniffing the floor and circling or squatting
- trying to hide behind furniture or searching for corners in a closet.

When you see these cues, take your dog to the designated potty site and give him a reward and plenty of praise if he succeeds.

If you're training a puppy or a dog that's prone to having accidents, using a pee pad in a designated area inside your home will make clean-up a breeze, BUT there is a chance using a pee pad frequently may cause your dog to become accustomed to it rather than going outside. So, continue taking your IG outside and reward him each time he goes.

Your IG will most likely argue about going outside when it is raining or snowing. You can put a square piece of board on the grass in your yard before it rains or snows and pick it up when it's time for your Iggy to go. That way, your IG will always have a "dry" spot. Or, you can try putting on doggie boots so his paws don't get wet. (You can also bribe him with his favorite treats!)

Photo Courtesy of
Whitney Buettner

Crate Training Basics

Some Italian Greyhound owners may feel guilty to be crate training their four-pawed best friend, but for your dog, the crate is his own private bedroom for resting and sleeping. All dogs instinctively search for small spaces to shelter themselves. A crate is more than a simple tool for potty training your Italian Greyhound. It will be your dog's safe haven and a lifesaver during emergencies.

Crate training is widely accepted by professional trainers and veterinarians as the most effective method to teach dogs desirable behaviors and prevent separation anxiety. Your Italian Greyhound will naturally accept his crate as his sleeping quarters and sanctuary, and most dogs avoid soiling their bedrooms.

When properly and humanely used, crate training provides many advantages for you and your Iggy:

Advantages for you ...

- You will have peace of mind when you have to temporarily leave your Italian Greyhound home alone, knowing your pup is comfortable and safe in his private bedroom instead of running unrestrained throughout your house and destroying who knows what.
- By temporarily confining your Iggy to his crate, you can effectively establish a regular bathroom schedule and prevent unwanted accidents during the night or when your pooch is left alone.
- Crate training will allow you to confine your Italian Greyhound when he becomes overly excited by guests or children running around. Another advantage is that you can temporarily place your dog inside his crate during dinnertime, which helps to prevent him from begging.
- You will be able to travel with your Iggy safely and be assured that your dog will quickly adapt to any new situations or strange surroundings, as long as he has his familiar "security blanket"— his crate.

Advantages for your dog ...

- Your Italian Greyhound will love the privacy and serenity of having his own den, which he can retreat to whenever he is tired, not feeling well, or stressed out.
- Your dog's crate will spare your Italian Greyhound from feeling isolated, lonely, and frustrated from being placed alone in the basement or laundry room. The crate will only restrict him from certain things for his own safety and will not keep him away from his family surroundings.
- Your Italian Greyhound can be included in any family outings and trips instead of being left home alone.
- Since your Iggy will avoid soiling himself inside his crate, he will learn to control his bowels faster and associate elimination only within a specified location.

Since Italian Greyhounds are highly social dogs, it is important that they are with you as much as possible, even if you are busy and cannot interact with them. Your Iggy needs to feel that he is part of your family. That comes from being included in family activities.

Although crate training is a fantastic training tool, it can be abused. Never leave your Italian Greyhound locked inside the crate all day long. Leaving a dog locked inside for long periods at a time is inhumane and cruel. This can cause emotional distress or destructive behavior, not to mention physical harm. If your dog spends large amounts of time confined to his crate, he will start to exhibit problematic behaviors, such as barking, chewing, and jumping.

If your schedule requires you to leave your Iggy home alone all day, hire a dog sitter

HELPFUL TIP
Litter Box Training

When house-training your Italian Greyhound, you may struggle with finding a convenient place for your pet to relieve himself in your home when he can't make it outside. A litter box with a puppy pad or kitty litter can be a viable option for Italian Greyhounds because they are so small. If you choose to use a litter box, make sure that the container is large enough for your dog to enter and turn around comfortably.

or ask a close friend to drop by every three to four hours to let your dog out of his crate. This will help him to stretch his legs, go to the bathroom, and play.

If your Iggy is under 12 months of age, he should never stay inside his crate for more than two to three hours at a time. This is because your puppy cannot control his bladder and bowels for long periods of time.

Your Italian Greyhound's crate requires regular maintenance; otherwise, it can become soiled and become a breeding ground for bacteria. You will need to regularly wash your Iggy's bedding in hot water and disinfect his crate using pet-friendly cleaning supplies.

Be sure to remove any dangling ID tags, harnesses, or collars, which could easily get caught on the crate doors, causing injury or accidental strangulation.

How to Crate Train

Even though dogs are considered den animals and prefer having a small space that's all theirs, Italian Greyhounds often will not automatically take to their crate, as they prefer spending time with their families. If you do not handle crate training properly, your Italian Greyhound may even come to fear his crate. First introductions have never been more important!

If you follow the suggestions below, your Iggy will love his crate and may even start to go into the crate on his own whenever he needs some quiet time or rest.

First introductions

One of the worst ways to introduce your dog to his crate is by forcing him into it and locking him inside. You would not like to be trapped inside a small, confined room, and your dog does not either. The goal with the crate is for your Italian Greyhound to view it as his own private bedroom, which he can enjoy whenever he wants.

For the first introduction, place a soft, fluffy bed or blanket and a couple of chew toys in the crate and leave the door open. If you have a piece of blanket with your pup's mother's scent, be sure to place it in the crate, as it will be reassuring for your dog. While your puppy is watching, throw in a few treats, then back off and give your Iggy the space he needs to explore his crate on his own. Most Italian Greyhounds will immediately go into the crate after the treats and start sniffing around.

If your Iggy is wary of entering his crate, try enticing him by placing his food dish, treats, and favorite toys near and inside the crate. Your ultimate goal is to help your Italian Greyhound feel comfortable with going inside his crate. This could take a few days. Be patient with your puppy throughout the entire process.

Use during mealtimes

Once your Italian Greyhound freely enters and leaves his crate, your next goal is to get your dog comfortable with staying in the crate for longer periods of time. Use your Iggy's love of food to your advantage by creating a positive association with the crate by feeding him inside the crate. Try placing the food dish far back in the crate so your Italian Greyhound has to go all the way inside. If your Iggy is not willing to go all

the way back, place his food dish toward the front of the crate. Each time you feed him, slowly move it back.

Closing the crate

Once your Italian Greyhound is happily eating his meals inside his crate while standing with his back toward the door, it is time to start closing the door. While he is eating, close the door without locking it. Once your pooch is finished eating his food, immediately open the door. Each time you feed your dog, leave him inside with the door closed a bit longer, adding a minute or two each time.

If your Iggy begins to whine, open the door immediately and be sure not to leave him inside as long the next time. However, if he whines the following time, do not open the door until he stops whining; otherwise, you will teach him that whining equals an open door.

Extending crate time

Once your Italian Greyhound loves his crate, then it is time to start lengthening his time inside. Entice your Iggy inside with a few treats and a favorite toy. Once he is in the crate, close the door. Spend a few minutes hanging out near the crate, then move out of sight by going into another room. This will get your Italian Greyhound used to being alone inside the crate with the door shut. When you return, do not open the crate immediately; instead, sit beside the crate for a few minutes. Slowly increase your dog's time inside the crate, being sure to reward him after each crate training session.

FUN FACT

Frisbee Meyers

American comedian and host of an NBC late-night talk show Seth Meyers has an Italian Greyhound named Frisbee. The adorable pup appeared with Meyers in a Chrysler ad, as well as on Late Night with Seth Meyers, where he took part in a lighthearted competition with a champion Italian Greyhound. Frisbee has his own Instagram account with over 22,000 followers (@thefrisbeemeyers).

Leaving and returning

Once your Italian Greyhound has mastered all of the above steps without whining, then he is ready for you to leave him for short periods of time. The key to this step is to avoid any excitement. Entice your dog into the crate with a treat and a favorite chewing toy. Once he is inside, quickly praise him for being such a good boy and close the door. Go about your business in the house, then go outside, shutting the door to the house behind you. When you come back inside, keep a low-key attitude and ignore any excited behavior your dog may be displaying.

If your Iggy starts to whine or paw at the door of his crate before being released, ignore him until he stops, then let him out. Otherwise, you are just reinforcing bad behavior that will develop into a habit.

Crating your Italian Greyhound at night

Be sure to take your Iggy to his designated bathroom spot before bedtime. Place the crate in your bedroom, hallway, or somewhere near where you are sleeping. If your Italian Greyhound is still a puppy, he will need to go to the bathroom every two to three hours, so you want the crate close enough to you to hear your dog when he starts whining. If your Italian Greyhound is older, you should place the crate close to you so your dog doesn't associate his crate with being socially isolated. Once your Iggy sleeps through the entire night without disturbances, then you can move the crate to another location.

If your Italian Greyhound whines or cries from inside his crate during the night, it might be difficult to discern if he is whining to go to the bathroom or whether he wants to be let out of the crate. Ignore him for a minute or two, and if he continues whining, use the word or phrase your dog associates with eliminating himself. If he gets excited, then take him to his designated bathroom spot.

If you are convinced that your Italian Greyhound is only whining so that you let him out of his crate, do not give in. Ignore him until he stops whining; otherwise, you are teaching him that by whining loudly, he can get what he wants. Never yell at your Iggy or tell him to stop whining and pound on the crate, as this will only make things worse.

Once your dog is comfortable being left in the crate for 15 minutes at a time, you can start leaving him inside for longer periods. If he is still a puppy and not housebroken, never leave him inside his crate for more than 30 minutes at a time. A full-grown dog that is house-trained should never be left inside of his crate for more than four hours at a time.

Dos and don'ts of crate training

- Never punish your dog while he is inside the crate; otherwise, he will associate his crate with negative experiences.
- Never leave your dog inside the crate for more than four hours at a time. Crates are NOT substitute dog sitters. Leaving your dog locked inside for an extended period of time can cause separation anxiety and depression.
- Do not make a big show of your departure. Place your dog inside the crate a few minutes before leaving, and make sure he is occupied with a toy or treat before you leave.
- Do take your dog to the bathroom as soon as you get home, as this will help your dog realize potty time comes after crate time.

House-training Basics

House-training your Italian Greyhound takes time, patience, commitment, and vigilance. Your Iggy will most likely have accidents in the house. This is a normal part of bringing home a puppy. However, by following the suggestions below, you will learn how to minimize potty accidents.

Try to maintain the routine below for two to three weeks. If your dog stops having accidents in the house, you can start giving him a little more freedom each week. Reinforce good behavior by continually rewarding your Iggy for going in his designated spot.

Establish a routine and be consistent in sticking to the following suggestions.

Set a schedule

Puppies thrive on a regular schedule. Plan on taking your Italian Greyhound outside or to his designated bathroom spot inside the house frequently, at least every two hours, and as soon as he wakes up after his nap and after eating or playing. If your dog does not seem interested in going potty, restrict his access inside the house and try again in 15 minutes.

Reward good behavior

Generously praise your Italian Greyhound every time he relieves himself in his designated spot. Be sure to praise him and give him his treat immediately after going to the bathroom; do not wait until you are back inside.

Establish a location

Choose a convenient location inside your house or outside to be your Italian Greyhound's bathroom spot. If you clean up an accident inside of the house, after disinfecting the area correctly (as discussed in the next section of this chapter), take the soiled paper towels and rags to the bathroom spot. The scent will help your Iggy recognize the area where you want him to eliminate. Below you can find more information about cleaning up after your Iggy.

Use a verbal cue

Before and while your dog is relieving himself, be sure to say the command word for bathroom—go potty—to remind him of the task at hand. Do not play with your dog until after he has relieved himself, as puppies get easily distracted and may forget they had to go to the bathroom until they go back inside the house and have an accident.

Regular feeding times

As soon as possible, get your Italian Greyhound on a regular feeding schedule. Depending on the instructions from the breeder, your Iggy may need to be fed two to four times a day. By feeding your dog at the same time each day, he will relieve himself more consistently, making house-training easier on both of you.

Bedtime

Just because it is bedtime, it does not mean that you can take a break from house-training. Take turns with a family member to get up every hour or two to take your puppy to the bathroom. Remember, his bladder is not fully developed yet, and he will not be able to hold it all night.

Supervise, supervise, supervise

Until your Italian Greyhound is fully house-trained, avoid letting him roam about your house freely, as it will reduce any opportunities to have an accident inside.

Do not acknowledge bad behavior

If your Italian Greyhound has an accident, simply take him to his pad or litter box. Never yell at him or tell him he is a bad dog or give him another type of punishment. This can worsen the problem and cause your dog to feel anxious about going to the bathroom in front of you, causing him to search for hidden spaces to potty and making it even harder to break bad habits. Remind yourself that the reason your dog had an accident is that you were not paying attention to his signs when he needed to go to the bathroom.

Cleaning up after doggy accidents

Puppy accidents can be a pain in the neck. However, they can easily be avoided if you clean up those accidents quickly, efficiently, and correctly.

Contrary to common belief, dogs do not relieve themselves in the house out of spite or because they are impossible to train. The majority of potty accidents happen for one of the following reasons.

1. Your Italian Greyhound does not yet understand where he is supposed to go to the bathroom.
2. You are not giving your puppy ample opportunities to go to the bathroom in his designated spot.
3. Your pup suffers from a medical condition, which will be discussed below.

If you do not thoroughly clean and deodorize where your puppy had an accident, it will lead to more accidents in the same area. Simply wiping up the mess might satisfy your eyes and nose, but there is an enzymatic scent only your dog can smell that will lure him back to the same spot later on.

Follow this three-step cleaning process to deter any future potty accidents:

STEP 1

Protect your own paws: Before cleaning up your dog's mess, make sure to wear gloves to protect yourself from potential urine and fecal pathogens, especially if your Italian Greyhound cat is not fully vaccinated yet.

STEP 2

Remove the mess: For any type of accident, pick up any solids with a paper towel or baggie and blot up (do not rub) any excess liquid. Once you have removed the bulk of the mess, follow up by using damp towels or rags to gently blot away the rest of the smaller residue.

STEP 3

Use a good enzymatic neutralizer for pet accidents: Avoid using any ammonia-based cleaning products as they may enhance the urine smell, which will make the spot irresistible for your puppy. The best cleaning products will not mask the scent or simply clean up the accident, but they will neutralize the enzymes that entice your dog to pee or poop in that same spot. Look for products that are specifically designed for cleaning up after dogs.

There WILL be potty accidents. Remember to take your dog out and repeat the reward system each time. With time, your IG will settle down and become confident enough to roam around the house on its own.

When House-training Relapses

It can be frustrating to discover your well-behaved Italian Greyhound regressing to bad bathroom etiquette. However, there may be a good reason for your pup's behavior.

Medical problems

Bathroom accidents can often be associated with physical issues such as urinary tract infections or parasite infections. Be sure to check with your veterinarian to rule out any possible physical problems.

Submissive/excitement urination

Some Iggies, especially younger ones, may temporarily lose bladder control when they become overly excited. Often, this occurs during greetings or playtime. Involuntary urination or defecation is not a house-training issue, as your dog simply has no control over it and is unaware that he just soiled himself.

Hormonal behavior

As your Italian Greyhound matures, he will have hormonal changes. Marking territory is a common behavior trait for both male and female dogs. If your dog is marking inside the house, then return to the first steps of house-training. If the problems persist, you can consider using a bellyband designed to prevent him from marking.

A bellyband for dogs looks like a big Band-Aid or diaper that wraps around your Italian Greyhound's rear girth. Often, the bellyband has a waterproof shell with an absorbent liner which prevents any unwanted accidents in your house. Most styles are reusable and machine washable.

There are also absorbent diapers made for female dogs, with an opening for the tail. These bands and diapers are a great option for senior IGs that struggle with bladder leakage.

And who said diapers had to be ugly? There are many customized washable diapers for toy breeds. The wraps are usually geared toward boy dogs who like to spray or mark indoors. They usually have snap buttons or Velcro and are easy to use. Even if your Iggy is considered

Photo Courtesy of Leah O'Brien

house-trained, having a diaper can be handy, especially if you're planning on traveling.

Fear or anxiety

If your Iggy is afraid of loud noises such as fireworks or thunderstorms, he may lose control of his bladder and/or bowels. If this happens, try to isolate the sounds that frighten him and help him learn to associate good memories with those noises.

Climate changes

Be proactive by observing your pup's bathroom habits. During the warmer summer months, he may spend more time outside. But on the other hand, during the colder winter months, your pup may need to be reminded of proper indoor bathroom etiquette.

New environment

Just because your dog is housebroken in your house does not guarantee that he will know how to act when placed in a new setting. If you are traveling or visiting a friend's house, go back to the basic house-training methods until you can trust your Iggy again.

Tell-tale signs your Italian Greyhound needs to go to the bathroom

Young puppies—under the age of four months—do not have enough muscular control to hold their urine or feces. The instant they have to go to the bathroom, often they have already gone. If you wait for any tell-tale signs that your little puppy has to go, you will be too late. Instead, you need to anticipate your puppy's needs.

As mentioned before, your baby Iggy will need a bathroom break as soon as he wakes up or after munching a few treats. Puppies also will need to relieve themselves after a few minutes of playtime. You are much better off giving your Italian Greyhound too many potty breaks than too few because the more often he has accidents inside, the harder it will be to house-train your puppy.

No matter how old your Iggy is, he will need frequent bathroom breaks until he is fully housebroken. As your dog ages, there are some tell-tale signs that indicate he has to go to the bathroom. By learning to read your dog's body language, you can learn to tell when he needs to relieve himself. Watch for the following tell-tale signs to prevent accidents:

Sniffing the floor – Dogs will sniff out an area to go potty and will look for a familiar scent. If your Italian Greyhound starts sniffing the floor or around your furniture, immediately take him to his designated area and praise him for going potty there.

Turning in circles while sniffing the floor – Sniffing the floor might just mean your pup is searching for something to eat. If he starts turning around in circles while sniffing, however, then he probably has to poop. Pick him up as fast as you can and get him to his bathroom spot. Again, praise him for a job well done.

Barking, scratching, or standing at the door – Puppies generally are very vocal about when they need to go. If your Iggy starts barking and staring in the direction of the door or his pee pads, then take him to his spot immediately.

Whining – If whining is combined with any of the above behaviors, your dog most likely needs to go potty. Younger dogs who still have not mastered housebreaking will often just sit and cry to tell you they need to go really badly.

Potty Pads vs. Litter Boxes

Although most Italian Greyhound owners prefer to train their dogs to relieve themselves outside, sometimes it is necessary to teach them to have an indoor bathroom spot. Perhaps, this is due to living on the seventeenth floor of an apartment building or having mobility issues that prevent you from taking your puppy outside constantly for bathroom breaks.

Generally, indoor potty training is recommended for owners whose Iggies will permanently be trained to go indoors, as it can be difficult to train your dog to go outside once he has been taught to go indoors. Other owners opt to partially indoor house-train their Italian Greyhound—or at least until he is old enough to control his bladder or bowels.

If you decide to house-train your Italian Greyhound to go indoors, you will need to be very consistent and clear with your pup so as to prevent confusion as to where his designated spot is. Outdoor potty training often is easier because dogs can clearly observe the distinction between indoors and outdoors. Plus, with indoor house-training, your Iggy may have difficulty distinguishing the difference between the carpet and the potty pads.

Your Iggy will not automatically know that he is supposed to relieve himself on the potty pads, etc. The general rules for house-training methods using litter boxes, potty pads, newspapers, or grass pads are the same.

How to use potty pads, grass pads, or litter boxes to house-train your Italian Greyhound.

This is one of the easiest indoor house-training methods and can be combined with outside potty breaks.

1. Create a small area inside of your house using gates.
2. Place your dog's crate inside the area with his bed, food, water dishes, and any chew toys.
3. Place your Iggy's potty pads in a corner.
4. As your dog becomes more reliable about using his potty pads, you can gradually increase his area until you can trust him to relieve himself on his potty pads.

Litter boxes

Litter boxes resemble cat litter boxes. The difference is that they are filled with odorless doggy litter. The raised sides create a clearly defined area, preventing spillage, just in case your Iggy tends to miss his target. Litter boxes are relatively easy to clean up. It is preferable to use litter designed specifically for dogs as it is made of larger bits and absorbs more urinary volume.

One of the main disadvantages to doggy litter boxes is that smaller dogs may be hesitant to crawl into the box, making house-training more of a challenge. Other dogs may decide to eat the litter or fling it all over the room.

Potty pads

Potty pads are super absorbent, disposable, and/or washable. These pads will protect your flooring and carpets. Some pads come with a built-in scent to entice your Iggy to use it as his bathroom spot. The lack of edges means there will be occasional spillage. One of the main disadvantages is the pads can be messy if you do not replace the old pad with a new one before saturation occurs.

If you choose to use potty pads, you can increase your chances of success by placing them inside a tray with a low edge instead of putting them directly on the floor. This will prevent the potty pad from sliding around and will help your dog make the distinction between the floor and his bathroom area. Another advantage to placing a tray under the potty pad is it will eliminate a common problem with dogs who place their front paws on the pad while their back end is off the pad, making a mess, of course.

Grass pads

Grass pads resemble a litter box but with artificial turf that mimics the outside. Like litter boxes, they have raised sides to prevent urine from leaking on the floor. This option can be helpful if you are house-training your puppy to go outside, as it will help reinforce appropriate bathroom surfaces. The grass pads need to be regularly cleaned; otherwise, they become quite smelly.

Whether you choose a litter box, artificial turf, or potty pads, you will need to train your dog to use it by literally taking him to the designated spot. Reinforce good behavior by praising him each time he goes in the right place. Be patient and never punish him.

Playpens and Doggy Gates

Raising your Italian Greyhound is a full-time job, but nobody expects you to be able to watch him 24/7. Playpens and doggy gates are excellent tools to keep your Iggy safe, secure, engaged and close to you at all times!

A playpen or doggy gate will confine your Italian Greyhound to a small area of your house and will prevent him from roaming freely about the house and getting into trouble. They can also be used to separate pets who have trouble getting along and to protect your furniture against damage from your teething puppy. Plus, they are a huge asset in house-training your curious Iggy, but there are a few points to consider before you buy a playpen for your pup.

- **Durable materials** – You want a pen or gate that is durable enough to withstand some chewing and strong enough to prevent your puppy from pushing his way out.

- **Size and height** – The pen or gate should be tall enough so your dog cannot jump or crawl out of it. If it comes with interlocking panels to expand or change the shape of the pen, that will factor in the full-grown size of your Iggy and allow you to use the playpen or gate throughout his life.

- **Your Italian Greyhound's escape abilities** – Your Iggy is from the Greyhound family, so he is highly intelligent and perhaps a real Houdini in disguise. For this reason, you may need to consider a more heavy-duty gate or playpen with taller sides.

- **Easy setup** – You will be moving the playpen or gate from room to room when you are house-training your Italian Greyhound, so it needs to be portable and easy to set up.

While choosing a playpen or doggy gate for your pooch, take into consideration the layout of your home. The majority of outdoor playpens can be used inside, but the opposite is not always possible. Consider portability if you plan to travel with your Italian Greyhound's playpen or doggy gate or use it outside during the warmer months.

What To Do If All Else Fails

There may be some underlying reasons why your Iggy can't "hold it." It could be because he's dealing with a UTI or some other underlying health condition.

A trip to the vet can provide some answers. They'll run basic tests and tell you if there's an infection present. If the tests come back with no abnormal findings, then it's possible your dog has some anxiety associated with going potty outside. In that case, you can explore other options discussed earlier, like a band or diaper.

CHAPTER 6

Basic Training for Your Italian Greyhound

Children need to learn the alphabet before learning to read, as it will become a foundation that will set them up for success throughout their lives. Similarly, your Italian Greyhound will need to learn the ABCs of basic training and boundaries, as it will become the foundation upon which all future training will be built.

Your primary job is to introduce your little puppy to his new world in a positive way. In this chapter, we will discuss how to avoid common training mistakes and how to nip bad behavior in the bud.

Proper training requires time and patience, but there are many benefits—it will help you build a relationship with your dog and make it easier to take your dog out in public. It'll also improve communication and reduce any future problematic behavior.

Disobedient or Bad Parenting?

There is an old saying— *"To err is human,"* which means we all make mistakes whether we want to or not. That saying could not be truer than when it comes to puppy training. Often, these training errors are not life-threatening, and they can be amended. But they definitely will slow down the entire training process, causing irritation on both ends of the leash.

Photo Courtesy of Marcy Ringer

Here are some of the most common mistakes people make while training their puppies. This is to help you avoid making them:

Waiting too long to start training – Training your Italian Greyhound should begin the minute he comes home with you, regardless if he is a puppy or an older dog from a shelter. Avoid the temptation to wait until he outgrows his puppy stage, as he will develop bad behavior and habits in the interim.

Younger Iggies might not be able to learn advanced commands due to a lack of agility. They will, however, be able to start learning potty training and basic commands like "come" and "stay."

Lengthy training sessions – Longer training sessions are impractical for many reasons. Puppies and adolescent dogs have short attention spans. They tend to become bored or distracted quickly. Instead of one long training session each day, break the classes up throughout the day to keep your pooch interested in learning. Keep training sessions short and sweet—aim for five to 10 minutes for each session.

Not enough practice – There is an old proverb, *"Repetition is the mother of learning,"* which means repetition is the key element in learning. Through repetition, a skill is practiced and rehearsed until it becomes easier. Remember, when it comes to your Italian Greyhound, practice makes perfect!

Many dog owners make the big mistake of assuming their dog has learned everything in his obedience classes. But fast forward a few weeks, even a few months, and the dog has forgotten everything he has learned. What happened? Dogs, just like us, get rusty. Be sure to reinforce your dog's skills daily; all you need is a few minutes each day.

Rewarding negative behavior – Many dog owners do not realize they are rewarding their pup's bad behavior. For example, they might comfort their puppy because he was frightened from being left alone for a few minutes or by letting their puppy bark at the neighborhood cat because it is cute. This leads to repetition of the same unwanted behavior.

Italian Greyhounds are very sociable dogs who thrive on their owner's attention. Whenever you give your pup attention, he understands that you are pleased with his current behavior, and therefore, it should continue. If your dog's behavior is undesirable, like jumping up, barking, whining, or begging, then the best thing you can do is to completely ignore your dog until the behavior stops.

Inconsistency – Inconsistent training will confuse your Iggy. For example, let's say your pooch is not allowed on the couch. Occasionally, you make the exception for your dog to come cuddle with you on the couch. But then you turn around and discipline your pup for sitting on the couch. He will not understand what he did wrong, as one minute, he is allowed on the couch, and the next, he is not.

Strive to be consistent with your Italian Greyhound. For example, every time you come home, do not give your fuzzy ball of fur any attention until he is sitting on the floor and not jumping up. This can be difficult, especially when you have had a bad day at work. Consistency will prevent your Iggy from becoming confused and, in the long run, will make the training process easier for both of you.

Impatient – Training your Italian Greyhound takes time, and you need to remember that every dog learns at a different pace. Avoid getting frustrated while training your dog, as he will pick up on your negative vibes. Training sessions should be upbeat and positive, so make sure your attitude is in the right frame of mind first.

If your Iggy is struggling to learn something, instead of becoming frustrated with him, stop and consider whether this is a good time or if the session has gone on for too long.

HELPFUL TIP
Where Can You Go?

Italian Greyhounds need early and frequent socialization to avoid becoming skittish and overly sensitive. But where can you take your Italian Greyhound to expose him to a variety of stimuli? Pet stores often allow leashed pets who are vaccinated. You may also be able to bring your dog to restaurants, particularly those with outdoor seating, and some hardware stores. It's always a good idea to ask ahead if you're unsure about whether your pet will be welcome, and don't forget to pack some paper towels and baggies in case of accidents. Be flexible with your plans if the new scenario proves to be too stimulating for your dog.

Remember, training sessions should be short and sweet (about five to 10 minutes) and end on a positive note. If you are impatient and getting irritated with your pup, stop the training session by doing an easy action that your puppy already knows, such as "sit" and end with a reward.

 JUST A WORD OF CAUTION: *never ever train your Italian Greyhound when you are in a bad mood. This is a recipe for disaster. You could easily take your frustration and anger out on your poor, defenseless dog if he makes a mistake. Instead, make a cup of tea and snuggle up with your Iggy on the couch until your mood improves.*

Lack of daily routine – Italian Greyhound's love routine. During the first few months with your dog, he will learn where to eat, play, sleep, and go potty. By establishing a specific routine and schedule when these things happen, you will promote proper behavior and confidence for your dog. Italian Greyhounds are eager to please their new family, so use this to your advantage!

An inconsistent routine can lead to potty accidents and an increase in undesirable behaviors, such as barking or biting. Be sure to establish a manageable routine for your Iggy before you bring him home. This will help to avoid unnecessary stress and get your pup on the right track as soon as possible.

Harsh discipline – Studies have proven that using harsh discipline in dog training is counterproductive. In general, Italian Greyhounds respond better to training when combined with positive reinforcement like praise and treats. Harsh discipline involves yelling, hitting, use of physical force, leash-jerking, grabbing at the scruff of the neck, and staring down. All these negative actions will seriously affect your dog in the following ways:

- They may cause your Iggy to become aggressive, even violent, around strangers, putting you and others in danger.
- They may cause your Iggy to become fearful and suffer from separation anxiety later on in life.
- These methods teach your dog to distrust humans.

When you hit or yell at your dog, you are teaching him to fear you, you break his trust and weaken his confidence. There is no place for any type of harsh discipline in training your dog.

How to Train an Older Shelter Dog

If you have adopted an older dog from the shelter, congratulations! Shelter dogs make excellent family pets. No matter the reason why your Iggy ended up in the shelter, with a little tender loving care, he can become a happy, well-adjusted member of your family.

Most likely your adopted Italian Greyhound already has received some obedience training and just needs a little refresher course. Or perhaps his past has triggered some behavioral issues. That is why your older Iggy will need a little extra time and patience to learn his new boundaries and what is expected of him.

Adjustment period – As you know, adopting a dog means it comes with a history. The stress of being abandoned at the shelter and away from his previous family can make your pooch wary of his new surroundings. Be sure to give your Iggy time to adjust to his new home, family, and other pets. Your Italian Greyhound may need only a few hours to get used to his new place, or it could take a few weeks. During the adjustment period, be sure to follow a regular routine to keep things predictable and consistent.

Establish boundaries – Training begins from the very first minute you bring your Iggy home. Avoid the temptation to pamper your pooch the first week or two to make up for the time spent in the sterile, cold shelter. Older Italian Greyhounds are wise beyond their years, and they know how to use those big, dark eyes to get away with bad behavior.

Be aware if you let your Iggy get away with unacceptable behaviors when he first comes home, then it will be much harder to train him to stop doing it later. For example, this could be chewing on the furniture, relieving himself on the carpet, or climbing up on the furniture. Be sure to establish your Italian Greyhound's boundaries from day one and make sure the entire family is aware of them and enforces them.

Be patient – Your Iggy's life experiences can make him nervous about his new surroundings. Be patient and give him time to adjust. Once your Italian Greyhound realizes he has found his forever home, he will quickly settle in.

If you need to correct your Italian Greyhound's bad behavior, redirect his attention to a more appropriate behavior. For example, if your Iggy tends to chew on the furniture, then give him a chew toy. Once he starts chewing on the toy instead of the furniture, praise him and reward him with a treat. It might take a few weeks or months to erase years of bad habits, but with patience, he will improve.

Stick to a schedule – Shelter dogs need a routine. Your adopted Italian Greyhound has spent the last couple of days or weeks in an unpredictable and stressful kennel area. By establishing a schedule for feeding, walking, training sessions, playtime, and bedtime, you are giving your Iggy peace of mind and stability.

Challenges When Teaching Older Dogs

The saying *"You can't teach an old dog new tricks"* has been around for decades. The truth is, you *can* teach an old dog new tricks, and it is not that much different from teaching a puppy.

Actually, there are quite a few advantages to teaching older dogs, compared to puppies, due to their longer attention span. However, your older Iggy might need a little more motivation than a puppy, especially if his previous owners mistreated him. Even though your Iggy might not be as agile or mentally sharp as a puppy, he still has a built-in desire to please you.

One of the most common mistakes that pet owners make while training a shelter dog is assuming that all dogs have the stamina of a puppy. Older Italian Greyhounds get tired faster than younger dogs, perhaps because of health problems.

Here are some suggestions to consider when training an older dog.

- Keep training sessions upbeat and positive. If you or your Iggy become agitated, anxious, or nervous, then it is best to take a break.
- Old joints do not like doing the same movement over and over again. Avoid asking your Italian Greyhound to "sit" 20 times in a row without taking a break. Doing so may cause your pooch pain and may make him slow to respond.
- Keep training sessions short and sweet.
- Recognize and take into consideration your Italian Greyhound's limitations.
- Use verbal and hand signals. Older dogs may be hard of hearing, so the hand signals will help.
- Positive reinforcement is your secret weapon, especially treats. If you are worried about weight gain, chop unsalted, boiled, skinless chicken breast into small pieces.
- Be aware of the temperature. Older dogs are more sensitive to heat and cold than younger dogs.

- Train on soft surfaces. Choose soft surfaces such as carpet, grass, or a yoga mat to make training sessions more comfortable for your elderly Iggy.
- Practice one trick at a time, as multiple tricks may be confusing and frustrating for your elderly dog.

Remember that training sessions should be fun and give you moments to bond with your Iggy. If your dog's health and age prevent him from learning a new trick, concentrate on making him feel comfortable, loved, and cared for.

Obedience Classes

Whether you have a puppy or a shelter dog, obedience classes can help your Iggy learn to behave correctly at home or while out and about. Typically, obedience classes teach the pet owner how to teach their dog basic commands, such as lie down and sit. Also, your Italian Greyhound will learn socialization skills required to interact with different people and other dogs.

Before your Iggy begins any type of obedience or socialization classes, be sure your dog has received all his vaccinations at least seven days before.

Beginner obedience classes for dogs often will be divided into age groups and will teach your Italian Greyhound the following:

- Basic commands, such as sit, lie down, come, and roll over
- Not to pull on the leash while going for a walk
- Not to jump up on other people or dogs
- Not to chew on your furniture
- How to socialize with new people, dogs, and places

Obedience classes are designed to teach basic training. So do not expect them to resolve any major issues such as aggression, separation anxiety, depression, and excessive barking.

The majority of obedience classes will meet for approximately one hour each week for a period of eight to 10 weeks, depending on the

*Photo Courtesy of
Cheryl Serra*

program. The success of each course will depend entirely on the pet owner having daily training sessions with their dog, putting into practice what they learn each week. Here are some suggestions to consider when choosing the right obedience course for your Iggy.

Ask for referrals – The best place to start is by asking fellow dog lovers, friends and family, and of course, your veterinarian, for recommendations on obedience classes in your locality. In addition, you can also look online for reviews on the obedience course you are interested in.

Check their credentials – Look for an instructor who has credentials from one or more of the following associations: the National Association of Dog Obedience, the Association of Pet Dog Trainers, the National K-9 Dog Trainers Association, and the International Association of Canine Professionals.

Visit a free class – Most obedience classes will let you observe a class or two before signing up for the entire course. If they do not allow you to sit in on a class for free, even without your dog, then that is a warning sign to look for another course. Transparency is essential for the well-being of you and your dog. Be patient in searching for the best choice for you and your Italian Greyhound.

Watch out for red flags – Obedience classes are not only about teaching your Iggy new commands but also about socializing your dog with other people and dogs. The class should be fun and enjoyable for your dog. Never accept an instructor who encourages pet owners to yell or hit their dogs or use potentially harmful techniques or devices. Dogs are very intuitive. If you notice your Italian Greyhound is uncomfortable around the instructor, there probably is a good reason.

Pick the right fit – The best dog obedience course should be a good fit for your budget. Also consider driving distance, quality and content, and of course, your overall first impression of the instructor. Be sure to take into consideration any referrals you received to help choose the best obedience course for you and your Iggy.

When to get professional help

It can be a challenge to figure out if your Italian Greyhound is simply misbehaving or if he has behavioral issues. If your Italian Greyhound does have a behavioral problem, normal training tactics may not be enough. There are a few extreme cases where you might need help:

Biting – It is normal for a puppy to go through a biting stage while he is teething. However, when a dog viciously bites and snaps, that is unacceptable. Aggressive behavior cannot be fixed by common obedience

Photo Courtesy of
Tina Hordyk

classes. In this case, the dog will need professional help from a dog trainer who specializes in behavioral issues.

Separation anxiety – Italians often suffer from separation anxiety, but the problem can often be resolved by working one on one with your pooch. But if you have tried and tried to reprogram your Italian Greyhound's bad behavior and he still goes into a destructive panic mode every time you leave the house, then he may need specialized training and medication.

If you need professional help for your Iggy, the best place to turn to is your vet for recommendations.

Obedience classes can be a great place to start, especially for beginners who are doing this for the first time. They can provide plenty of resources and access to experts that have been working with dogs for years. You can ask the trainers in the class multiple questions or request one-on-one sessions.

Most of the time, the classes will start with basic obedience commands that you'll use often:

- Sit
- Come
- Stay
- Down/off
- Heel

The trainers in these classes will show you how to ask your dog to perform these tasks and also teach you how to say "no" without being excessive. They will explain in more detail about positive reinforcements and using the reward system, then show you how to use it. In most cases, they will do demonstrations with markers (clickers).

Even if you feel like you can train your dog without obedience classes, it would still be a good idea to give it a try or at least contact a trainer for future reference in case there are any problematic behaviors.

Ask your vet or local rescue organization for obedience class recommendations. They are usually in contact with professional trainers who work with adoptable dogs to prepare them for new homes and have plenty of experience hosting obedience classes or personal sessions.

What Is the Reward System?

The best approach, as many trainers and Iggy owners will tell you, is consistent training with positive reinforcements, also known as the reward system. It basically means you're praising the desired behavior rather than focusing on punishments.

This method is effective with Italian Greyhounds because they are sensitive (and stubborn), so they don't respond well to negative reinforcements. Actually, it can make the situation worse.

Photo Courtesy of
Sarah Evans
Divine Kennels

As with any training, it takes practice. Try to find out what works best for your dog. Here are some examples of positive reinforcements:

- Praise using words and happy voice/tone
- Toys
- Treats
- Something your dog likes

Keep in mind what may work for one dog may not work for another. For example, some dogs LOVE yummy dog biscuits, while others may not find them appealing. You can try different things and see which one your dog becomes excited about.

The key is to reward good behavior and give your dog motivation to continue repeating it. If you are out in an environment with plenty of distractions, it may be more challenging to maintain your dog's attention long enough for him to learn a new trick, so try to start at home first and work your way outside.

Give the reward as soon as possible after your dog completes the task. Don't wait too long to deliver. If your dog has to wait too long before receiving his reward, he may lose interest or become confused.

Some trainers use a clicker or whistle (also called a marker) to go along with the reward to help create a stronger connection between the action and the result. For example, if your dog has become used to receiving a reward every time he hears a click, and he hears one at the exact moment he's going potty, he will associate it with a reward.

Unacceptable Behavior from Day One

Many dog behaviors that we consider to be inappropriate are actually an instinctive part of their canine personality, such as digging, barking, or rolling on a dead animal. For your pooch, these activities are innate behaviors, but you can train your Iggy to at least minimize these habits.

Here are some helpful strategies to nip bad behavior in the bud.

- **Burn off excess energy** – A tired dog is a well-behaved dog. If your Italian Greyhound is not getting adequate exercise, he will channel his energy into another activity, like chewing your furniture or digging up your flower garden.

- **Prevent bad habits from developing** – Keep any objects, such as toys and shoes, out of sight. Make sure houseplants are off the floor, and electrical cords are tucked away, etc. It is easier to prevent bad habits from happening if there are no temptations in the first place.

- **Reward desired behaviors** – Anytime you notice your Iggy is behaving correctly, be sure to pat his head and tell him what a good boy he is. Examples of good behavior are if he is walking beside you on the leash without pulling or he is sitting quietly, waiting to greet you instead of jumping.

- **Be consistent** – If you do not slip your Italian Greyhound a piece of turkey from the kitchen table, but your husband does, the dog will learn to beg. Or if you make him sit on the floor by the couch, but your children let your dog hop up on the couch, guess what he will do? Everyone needs to be consistent in following the same rules.

Chewing

Dogs naturally chew on objects for a number of reasons. In the case of puppies, chewing is a way to relieve pain caused by teething, and older dogs chew on bones to keep their jaw strong and teeth clean. However, this behavior can quickly turn into a habit if they are not taught what objects are appropriate for chewing and which are not.

 SIMPLE SOLUTION: *If you catch your Iggy chewing the wrong thing, instead of scolding him, quickly distract him by clapping your hands. Then replace the object with a chew toy. Never use old shoes or socks as chew toys.*

Barking

Your Iggy may vocalize in one way or another by barking, howling, whining, or more. Barking is considered normal behavior for dogs unless it is excessive. Your Italian Greyhound might be barking out of excitement, boredom, fright, or to alert you that something is out of the ordinary.

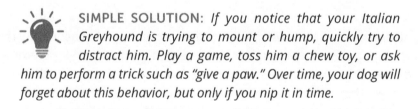

SIMPLE SOLUTION: *If your Iggy is barking for your attention, simply ignore him until he stops barking, then praise him for being quiet. Do not even look or speak to your Iggy while he is barking, as he will think you are encouraging him to bark even more. If your pooch is barking at a stranger, such as the pizza delivery guy, tell him it is okay and introduce him to the new person, reassuring him there is no reason to be scared.*

Mounting

Mounting and humping are normal behaviors for both male and female dogs. Your Italian Greyhound may attempt to mount both moving and inert objects, such as people, other animals, dog beds and toys, or he may just lick himself. Neutered and spayed dogs may continue mounting or humping because this behavior feels good.

SIMPLE SOLUTION: *If you notice that your Italian Greyhound is trying to mount or hump, quickly try to distract him. Play a game, toss him a chew toy, or ask him to perform a trick such as "give a paw." Over time, your dog will forget about this behavior, but only if you nip it in time.*

Digging

If given the chance, all dogs will love to dig up your flower garden. It is just part of their natural instinct. Your Iggy is prone to digging because of his parents' hunting heritage. Dogs generally dig to burn off excess energy or due to boredom, hunting instinct, a desire to conceal a bone or toy, to cool off, or to escape.

SIMPLE SOLUTION: *Try to determine the reason why your Italian Greyhound is digging up your backyard, then work to eliminate the cause. For example, if your dog is digging out of boredom, then spend more time with him exercising each day. If your pup is digging for no apparent reason, dedicate a small part of the garden or sandbox where he can freely dig. Teach your Iggy that it is only acceptable to dig in a certain spot.*

Separation Anxiety

Separation anxiety is one of the most common behavioral issues with Italian Greyhounds, and it occurs when your dog is left alone for a short period of time or for a few hours. Your Iggy can exhibit one or all of the following destructive behaviors: excessive barking, whining, chewing, inappropriate urination, and defecation. Often a dog suffering from separation anxiety will follow his owner around constantly. In the following chapter, we will go in-depth about how to prevent separation anxiety.

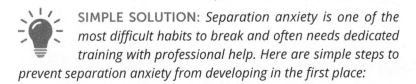 SIMPLE SOLUTION: *Separation anxiety is one of the most difficult habits to break and often needs dedicated training with professional help. Here are simple steps to prevent separation anxiety from developing in the first place:*

- Ask a family member to hide near your Iggy's crate but out of sight.
- Place your Italian Greyhound inside his crate with a chew toy and a few treats. Avoid making a big show about leaving.
- Text the family member who is hiding to ask how your pup behaved. If he behaved, calmly greet him and reward his good behavior.
- Each time that you leave, slowly increase the time away until your Italian Greyhound learns how he is supposed to act when he is left home alone.

Running away

Your Iggy's heredity genes are programmed to sniff out a small animal or rodent, so his little nose is going to get him in trouble!

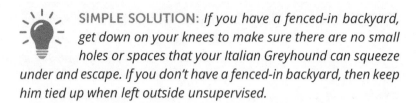 SIMPLE SOLUTION: *If you have a fenced-in backyard, get down on your knees to make sure there are no small holes or spaces that your Italian Greyhound can squeeze under and escape. If you don't have a fenced-in backyard, then keep him tied up when left outside unsupervised.*

Jumping Up

Puppies naturally jump up to reach and greet their mother. Even after being separated from their mother, puppies will continue jumping up on people as a way to greet them. But jumping dogs may be annoying and can be dangerous as they can knock over an elderly person or child.

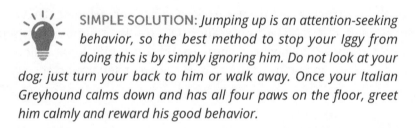 SIMPLE SOLUTION: *Jumping up is an attention-seeking behavior, so the best method to stop your Iggy from doing this is by simply ignoring him. Do not look at your dog; just turn your back to him or walk away. Once your Italian Greyhound calms down and has all four paws on the floor, greet him calmly and reward his good behavior.*

Begging

Begging is a bad habit often encouraged by pet owners. All dogs love food, especially table scraps. The best way to prevent your Italian Greyhound from begging in the first place is by never giving him food from the table.

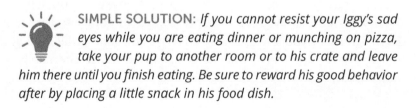 SIMPLE SOLUTION: *If you cannot resist your Iggy's sad eyes while you are eating dinner or munching on pizza, take your pup to another room or to his crate and leave him there until you finish eating. Be sure to reward his good behavior after by placing a little snack in his food dish.*

Positive Reinforcement

> *Italian Greyhounds can be intelligent but may also exhibit independent and stubborn traits. They can be sensitive to harsh training methods, so positive reinforcement techniques tend to work best. New owners should expect that training an Iggy may require patience, consistency, and finding motivating rewards. Keep training sessions short and enjoyable to maintain the dog's interest and prevent boredom.*
>
> EVAN CONAWAY
> *azgreyhounds.com*

Positive reinforcement is one of the most effective ways to train your Iggy. When using this method, you will give your pooch a reward to reinforce good behavior. For example, you ask your Italian Greyhound to *"sit,"* and he immediately does it, so you give him a treat. You are rewarding his good behavior.

Positive reinforcement teaches your dog that positive actions equal rewards. This reward can be in the form of verbal praise, affection by scratching behind his ears, a game of fetch, or a delicious treat. Your dog's brain observes the cause and effect. Your dog's brain is saying, "If I sit, I get spoiled! Wow, I need to sit every time they ask me!" And practice makes perfect.

It might take a few practice sessions for your Italian Greyhound to notice the pattern of COMMAND + OBEDIENCE = REWARD. If you want to get the most out of positive reinforcement training, there are a few Dos and Don'ts to follow:

DO

Immediately reward your Italian Greyhound's good behavior

Your Iggy has a short attention span and lives in the moment, so your response to his good behavior should be immediate. You can reward your dog, using both praise and treats, whenever his behavior pleases you. For example, if you are house-training your pooch, be sure to reward him every time he does his business outside.

Keep sessions short and fun

The goal is to teach your Iggy that good things happen when he obeys you. Make training sessions short, fun, and positive, leaving each class on a good note. For example, if your puppy has difficulty learning a new command, end the session by asking him to perform a command he already has mastered.

Wean from treats

Treats are an excellent tool to motivate your Italian Greyhound in the beginning, but you will eventually want to wean him off all those extra treats and switch to more praise and affection. Over time, your dog will forget about those high-calorie treats and just want to please you.

 DON'T

Make it complicated

Keep commands simple and clear. Instead of teaching your Italian Greyhound to "*sit down here*," simply say, "*Sit.*" Choose specific and simple commands.

Be inconsistent

As discussed earlier, it is useless to reward your dog for staying off the couch but then later let him come on the couch for a cuddle. This type of behavior will confuse your Iggy, and he will not be able to decipher what you actually want. Additionally, everyone in your household needs to understand and abide by the rules for your dog. Otherwise, he may run himself ragged trying to figure out how to behave with each member of your family.

Stop correcting your Italian Greyhound

Many pet parents assume that positive reinforcement means they cannot say no to their dogs. This is not true. If your Iggy is acting out of sorts, a firm NO is one of the best ways to correct his bad behavior. Of course, you should never yell, scold, hit, or hurt your Italian Greyhound in any way.

Photo Courtesy of Leslie Teed

How to reward your Iggy

Knowing which rewards to give your Iggy can make training sessions more stimulating and fun for both you and your dog. Here are several ways to reward your pup's good behavior:

Treats

Treats are one of the most popular rewards for positive reinforcement, as they are fast and easy to dispense. Plus, it is gratifying to see our little four-pawed companion happily devour his snack. Treats are ideal for training sessions with your Iggy when you are teaching him to learn a new behavior or command. However, the downside to treats is they are high in calories, which can be an issue if your Italian Greyhound has a weight problem.

Games

Often pet owners forget that games are another fun way to reward your Iggy. Initiate a game your dog enjoys immediately after he does something which pleases you. Games stimulate your dog's brain in the same way as yummy treats. For example, ask your pooch to sit, and once he sits, offer him the ball and start playing fetch. During the game, you can teach him the command *Leave It* or *Drop It*. Once he drops the ball, tell him to sit down again, and when he does, start playing fetch again. Your Italian Greyhound will love this method to reinforce proper behavior.

Praise and attention

There is nothing your Italian Greyhound loves more than being praised and getting attention from you. A pat on the chest or a scratch under the ears is just as rewarding for your dog as a handful of treats. Instead of giving him your undivided attention, make him work for it first. For example, ask him to sit down. Once he does what you have requested, then give him some cuddle time. If he does not do what you requested, then walk away, and when you return, try again. This exercise teaches your pooch that certain actions either get him attention or don't.

Clicker Training – It Really Works

Clicker training began in the late 1990s as an effective alternative to negative training methods that relied heavily on pain, fear, or intimidation to bully a dog into being obedient. Clicker training is often combined with positive reinforcement methods and is considered to be a highly effective teaching option.

A clicker is a small, handheld device that has a thin metal strip inside that makes a distinctive clicking sound whenever you push down on the button. You can find a good-quality clicker at most pet supply stores; an added bonus is they are quite inexpensive. If you prefer, you can download an app on your phone that duplicates the clicking sound.

In positive reinforcement, we use a short marker word(s) to show our approval. The clicking sound is faster than you can say "good boy," and much more effective than training with treats and healthier for your dog's waistline. The clicker allows you to communicate effectively to your dog by showing him exactly what you liked about his behavior. It also solves the problem of having to dig a treat out of your pocket in time to reward him.

In clicker training, the clicking sound, over time, will replace your "yes" of approval. When you ask your Iggy to sit down, the instant his butt hits the ground, activate the clicker, followed by a reward as quickly as possible.

How to use a clicker

1. Choose a calm area for training without any distractions, such as your backyard. Choose a moment when your dog is hungry, preferably before meals, to start clicker training. Be sure to have a handful of treats in your hand or pocket.
2. First, you need to teach your Italian Greyhound the meaning of a click. Click the device in your hand and immediately give your dog a treat and praise him generously.
3. Repeat this activity five to 10 times each day until he associates the sound with the yummy reward.

4. Start using the clicker in training sessions to reinforce good behavior. Once your Iggy learns the positive effects of the clicking sound, the noise starts acting as a reward in itself.
5. Once you and your dog have mastered clicker training, you can move on to more complicated commands and tricks.

A clicker creates an unmistakable, distinctive sound that only occurs when you are actually holding the clicker and training your dog.

An advantage to using a clicker over a marker word is that the click doesn't convey any emotional tone, such as happiness or sadness. Neutral sounds such as the clicker eliminate the stress or confusion your Iggy may feel around trying to figure out your mood.

How to use the clicker for basic and advanced commands

1. At the exact moment your Italian Greyhound completes the desired action, press the clicker. Then reward him with a treat and with praise.
2. Be aware that if you are not able to click at the exact moment your dog performed the new behavior, he might not associate the new action with the treat.
3. For more complicated commands or tricks, you can click and reward for small steps toward the desired behavior. For example, if you are teaching him to fetch the ball and bring it back to you, click for fetching, then again when your Iggy brings the ball back.

The clicker does not replace yummy treats, but over time you will be able to slowly wean your dog off those high-calorie treats as the sound of the click becomes the reward. You will still need to give him an occasional treat. Otherwise, the clicker will lose its effectiveness.

If you have an older Italian Greyhound with teeth or weight issues, a healthier option to doggy treats is to give him a few pieces of unseasoned cooked chicken or turkey breast during the clicker training sessions. Remember, your dog lives in the moment, so when you click the clicker, immediately give him a treat, so he can learn to associate the clicking sound with a treat.

Test your Iggy when he is playing or distracted by clicking the clicker. If he immediately stops whatever he is doing and looks at you, then you know he is ready to start being weaned off treats. If your pooch does not acknowledge the sound, then you know you need to spend extra time training with the click-treat combination.

One of the most common mistakes with clicker training is that pet owners forget to give their dogs verbal praise. Your pooch will associate the clicker sound with a yummy reward, but he still needs your verbal approval. Never ignore your pup's need for love and affection from you. Remember, your Italian Greyhound thrives on your praise and smile of approval.

Tips for successful clicker training

- Try using a clicker with a wristband, as it will stay tethered to you and prevent you from accidentally dropping it.
- Place the treats in a baggie. You only have two hands, and a baggie allows you to keep the treats close.
- Keep all of your clicker-training sessions short and sweet. Greyhounds learn better in bursts of five to seven minutes than in long 30-minute sessions.
- The clicker is not a remote control to cue your Iggy into doing something. The clicker only marks the moment your dog does something worth rewarding, not the other way around.
- Keep the clicker in a safe place, out of reach of mischievous children who think it is a toy.

CHAPTER 7

Socializing and Mental Stimulation

I n this chapter, we'll discuss socialization in depth because it's important to socialize your Iggy, or he won't be friendly to new people or pets, which can lead to problems down the road.

Socializing your Iggy is the key to ensuring you will have a happy, confident, and well-adjusted dog in the future. Also, it helps your pooch learn to be comfortable within his society, which includes many different types of people, environments, buildings, sounds, sights, smells, animals, and other dogs.

Properly socializing your Iggy early on in life ensures he does not spend his life jumping in fright at anything that moves. Adult dogs who have not been properly socialized during their younger years often will be fearful or aggressive when exposed to something new.

Importance of Good Socialization

The idea behind socializing your Italian Greyhound is to help him become acclimated to different types of sights, sounds, and smells in a positive, memorable manner. Proper socialization will prevent your pooch from being fearful of the mailman, children, car rides, etc., and help him develop into a well-mannered, happy companion.

Younger Greyhounds naturally accept everyday things they encounter in their environment until they reach a certain age, then they start to become suspicious of things they haven't experienced yet. After the first few months, it will become more of a challenge to get your Iggy to accept new situations that may frighten him.

Photo Courtesy of
Kerry McGuire

In general, well-socialized dogs are more enjoyable to be around. This is because they feel more comfortable in a wide variety of situations than poorly socialized dogs. They are less likely to be aggressive or fearful when presented with something new. Poorly socialized dogs can be a headache, as they often react with fear or aggression when they meet unfamiliar people, animals, dogs, or even new experiences.

On the other hand, Italian Greyhounds who are well-socialized feel calm and relaxed around cars, honking horns, other dogs, crowds, veterinary clinics, etc., and are a joy to live with as they adapt quickly to every situation. Often, well-socialized pups have fewer health issues than dogs who are constantly stressed out by their surroundings.

The more positive new experiences your dog is exposed to, the better!

Socializing your Italian Greyhound is a big project and requires planning. It requires exposing your Iggy to a wide variety of sounds, animals, dogs, places, people, and experiences to help him be comfortable later on in life. Take into consideration the type of lifestyle you plan to give your Italian Greyhound and make a list of any sights or sounds he might encounter on a regular day. For example, consider some experiences such as trains, garbage trucks, crowds, cats, crying infants, a schoolyard full of screaming children, and more. While it might be impossible to expose your pooch to everything he might encounter in his lifetime, the more bases you cover, the better.

When socializing your Iggy, try the following.

- Introduce your Italian Greyhound to one new situation at a time. This will help to avoid overwhelming him. For example, if you plan a puppy playdate, organize it in your backyard or a park your dog is already familiar with.
- Immediately after a new experience or meeting a new person, reward your Iggy with a few treats and generous praise.
- If your Italian Greyhound seems uncomfortable or wary of the new experience, such as hearing a group of children playing in the playground, move further away and distract him by playing catch, moving gradually closer each time.
- Always follow any new socialization experiences with praise, patting, a fun game of catch, and of course, a special treat.

Socializing your Italian Greyhound is not optional. It is an essential part of your Iggy's training. It will help him grow up into a relaxed and happy companion. The more well-adjusted your dog is to his surroundings, the easier it will be for you to share your life with him.

What is the best age for socializing your Italian Greyhound?

The best age to socialize your Iggy is between three and 16 weeks old. After that age, your dog will become more wary and cautious of situations and things he has not encountered yet. From about 16 to 20 weeks old, the opportunity to smoothly socialize your Italian Greyhound gets harder and harder. After 20 weeks old, it is more difficult to socialize your dog, but not impossible.

Since your Italian Greyhound has not received all his vaccinations at this age, you should be careful when exposing your puppy to unknown animals or even walking in areas where animals might have been.

Photo Courtesy of
Gill Eastland

However, if you wait to socialize your dog until he is old enough to be vaccinated, you might miss out on vital training opportunities.

If you have adopted an older Iggy, even though you may have missed out on the crucial puppy socialization period, it is not too late to teach an old dog new tricks. The key is slowly reintroducing your older Italian Greyhound to sights, sounds, smells, people, and animals with careful supervision and a huge dose of positivity in the form of praise and treats. With patience, you can help your Italian Greyhound overcome all his fears.

Socializing Your Italian Greyhound with the Neighborhood Dogs

Since your puppy has not received all of his vaccines yet, you will need to be extra careful when exposing him to unknown dogs or walking in areas where other animals may have been. But if you wait until your Iggy is old enough to be vaccinated, you will miss out on crucial training opportunities.

By taking the following precautions when socializing your puppy, you almost completely eliminate the risks of him becoming sick:

- Before socializing your Iggy with another dog, ask the owner if their pup's vaccinations are up to date and if he is parasite-free.
- Avoid socializing your Italian Greyhound in dog parks or other areas. Organize a meet-and-greet with dogs in a controlled environment, such as your backyard or an area that can be easily disinfected.
- Sign your Iggy up for puppy training that specializes in socializing puppies.
- Taking your Italian Greyhound for daily walks is an excellent opportunity to burn off excess energy and expose him to other dogs in a neutral setting.

Socializing your older Italian Greyhound with other dogs

As mentioned before, the best time to socialize your Iggy is while he is still a puppy. Unfortunately, it is not always possible to socialize your dog within this short time frame. This is especially true if you have adopted an older Italian Greyhound, and he never had a good opportunity to be socialized in the past. Or perhaps your Iggy was sick when he was a puppy, and the veterinarian recommended keeping him away from other dogs.

Even if your Italian Greyhound was not taught how to behave around other dogs when he was younger, that does not mean he is a lost cause. The key is slowly reintroducing your older dog to sights, sounds, smells, people, and animals with careful supervision and a huge dose of positivity in the form of praise and treats. With patience, you can help your Iggy overcome any fears.

Here are some tips on how to socialize your adult Iggy.

Introduce your dog to other dogs while walking – Walking your older Italian Greyhound is an excellent opportunity for your dog to observe and possibly meet other dogs and also to practice proper behavior when out and about.

Use a muzzle if necessary – If your Iggy typically barks and growls at other dogs, then maybe you want to consider placing a muzzle on him. The muzzle will prevent your dog from biting or attacking another dog, and it will also help both dogs stay calmer and more receptive to meeting each other.

Expose your Iggy to different social activities – Instead of taking your unsocialized Italian Greyhound to the dog park and hoping for the best, expose him slowly by walking your pooch on the leash around the outside of the park, letting your dog observe the dogs play inside. Take your time, introduce your Iggy to a new situation each day, and be sure to generously praise and reward him for any good behavior.

Socializing with Other Animals

Do you have smaller pets, such as hamsters, rabbits, guinea pigs, gerbils, geckos, etc.?

While dogs usually consider small animals and rodents to be prey rather than buddies, the two species can live together peacefully. Before you introduce your Italian Greyhound to your small critters, it would be helpful if your dog has previously learned some basic commands, such as *sit, come*, and *stay*. These commands will guarantee your Iggy will be well-mannered and make a good first impression with your small critter.

Prior to their first introduction, take your Italian Greyhound out for an invigorating walk and a game of fetch to tire him out. An overly excited dog can frighten your small pet.

After your Iggy is worn out from playtime, confine your small critter to its cage, which is its safe space. Bring your Italian Greyhound close while on a leash. Command him to *sit* and *stay* next to the cage and reward your dog for any calm, non-aggressive behavior. Allow him to sniff at your small critter through the cage, then reward him once again for any good behavior. If your dog tries to snap or bark at the small critter moving freely in its cage, walk away with your dog and try again later.

After the initial introduction, continue having your pets meet for a few minutes at a time, lengthening the time of each meeting. Always keep your Iggy on a leash and your small critter confined until your dog shows no sign of aggression. Once this happens, let your small critter run about its enclosure freely while your Italian Greyhound observes on his leash. When your dog neither shows any interest in chasing after the critter nor displays any signs of aggression, then you can try letting him off his leash. Never forget to praise and reward your dog's good behavior.

Iggies are sighthounds, who were originally bred to hunt small animals, so a small rodent, such as a rabbit, guinea pig, or hamster, is an almost irresistible temptation. Even if your dog shows no signs of aggression or prey drive around your small critter for an extended period of time, he could still harm it, even by accident. Never leave your Italian Greyhound unsupervised with your small critter.

Italian Greyhounds and Strangers

Even the friendliest dog can become aggressive if he is not properly socialized. To avoid this happening to your Iggy, you will need to expose him to as many different types of people as possible. But the quantity of those experiences is not as crucial as the quality of each of these encounters. Your pooch needs to associate each encounter with a positive, fun-filled experience.

Socializing your Italian Greyhound involves exposing him to as many different people as possible, including men, women, children of all ages, men with beards, people in wheelchairs, and so on. You should also plan on introducing him to people wearing different styles of clothes, such as uniforms, raincoats, hats and gloves, etc.

If your Italian Greyhound only spends time with you and your immediate family, over time, he can become wary of anyone who is not his

family. For this very reason, it is crucial you diversify your pup's social calendar and organize a meet-and-greet.

When you take your Italian Greyhound out of his comfort zone, make sure you are relaxed and calm, as your dog can read your emotions. If you are nervous, then your pooch will be nervous too and perhaps even afraid of the new situation.

Remember, Rome was not built in a day—take your time introducing your Iggy to everyone on your list. Start off slow, first with friends and family, then integrate a stranger, such as the mailman. Avoid taking him to busy public areas too soon, as he may become overly excited or fearful of strangers in general.

Before introducing your Italian Greyhound to somebody new, inform them ahead of time that you are bringing your dog over for a brief socialization session. Ask them to be ready to pamper him with love and affection, and be sure to slip them a treat or two to give your dog.

Start off with meeting people in neutral, familiar environments, not a music festival or a parade, which can be overwhelming for you and your pooch. Instead, plan your meet-and-greet while on your walk together, in your yard, at a dog-friendly café, or in a small store. Once your Iggy has acclimatized to these situations, you can try standing outside a busy supermarket with more people.

Here are some helpful suggestions to help your Italian Greyhound become acclimated to all sorts of people.

- Stay calm and confident during meet and greets, even more so if your Iggy is frightened. If your dog is skittish or agitated, don't make a big deal about his behavior, as it will cause him to become more upset.
- When asking strangers to pat your Italian Greyhound, ask them to pat him where their hands can be seen, such as his chest or under his chin.
- Use treats and praise to give your Iggy a positive association with meeting strangers and experiencing new situations.
- Enlist a different dog walker or dog sitter each week to expose your Italian Greyhound to a variety of caregivers during the day.

Your Italian Greyhound should be exposed to the following people within his first few months with you.

- Neighbors
- Family and friends
- Groomer and vet
- Unfamiliar people wearing different styles of clothes (hoods, jackets, face masks, sunglasses, uniforms, hats, and so on)
- Mailman
- Anyone who regularly comes to your house

When arranging these different encounters, be sure to choose a variety of different environments for each one, such as shopping centers, parks, inside a store, etc. Your Italian Greyhound will want to investigate any foreign objects, such as wheelchairs, bicycles, skateboards, and benches.

Follow your Iggy's cues. Interactions should be long enough to make a positive impression but not so long that you wear your buddy out. Even simple new experiences can be overwhelming for your puppy, so keep them short and sweet!

Italian Greyhounds and Children

Italian Greyhounds adore children of all ages. Plus, your Iggy's high energy can keep up with the energy of children. Italian Greyhounds are very loving and gentle, making them an excellent fit for families with children. However, remember that first impressions make lasting impressions, and this statement could not be truer than when introducing your dog to children. Italian Greyhounds are very fragile and can easily be hurt by a child's rough handling.

There are several benefits for children to be raised in a household with a dog, from improved social skills to teaching them responsibility. Studies have shown dogs can improve a child's mental health, and many children view their pet dog as their best friend in whom they can confide.

Similarly, your Italian Greyhound can benefit from the enthusiasm and energy of a younger playmate to keep him busy throughout the day. But even if you do not have children living in your house, your Iggy will need to learn to behave around kids.

Dogs and children need to be properly prepared for first introductions and taught proper manners. If adequate training and supervision

do not take place, it may create a dangerous situation for both the dog and child, as an overly enthusiastic child can easily injure your tiny Italian Greyhound. Likewise, a scared or overly excited puppy could bite and seriously hurt a child. However, these tragedies can be easily avoided if you are willing to put in the time to properly socialize your Iggy with children.

Educating children on proper behavior around your Iggy

Before introducing your Italian Greyhound to small children, sit down with them to establish a few ground rules about how to behave around your dog. It might be a challenge to get them to concentrate as children may have difficulty focusing when they are excited, so you might need to repeat the rules a few times. Good rules to teach them include:

- They should pat the dog gently.
- Never force attention on the dog; instead, let the dog come to them.
- The dog's crate is not a play toy or a place for hide-and-seek. It is strictly off-limits. If the dog goes inside, leave him alone.
- Do not approach the dog while he is eating or chewing a bone.
- Leave the puppy alone while he is sleeping.

Make sure there always is an adult around to supervise interactions. Young children should never be left unattended with your Iggy.

Children can often mistake your adorable Italian Greyhound for a cuddly, stuffed toy, so it is important to remind them how to properly handle your dog. A general rule of thumb is to teach them to treat the puppy as they would another child; do not pull his ears or tail, climb on him, or engage in rough play. Here are some suggestions to consider when socializing your dog with children:

Create a positive environment – Before first introductions, make sure everyone is in a good mood. Never encourage a grumpy, cranky child to meet your Iggy or vice versa, as it is a recipe for disaster. Also, if the child is overly excited or rowdy, wait until he calms down—otherwise, your Italian Greyhound will be scared.

Take it slowly – Children tend to have jerky movements and high-pitched voices when they get excited, which can easily frighten your Iggy. Before first introductions, show the children how to walk, talk, and approach your puppy. Tell them to use their inside voices and use gentle hands while patting the dog. No poking, grabbing, pulling, or squeezing the puppy. Keep introductions short and sweet!

Supervise – The first few introductions will be brief, but over time the dog and the children will adjust to each other's presence and be able to play together for longer periods. No matter how well they get along, never leave small children alone with your dog without proper supervision. Accidents happen quickly, and it is crucial you are there to prevent them.

Let your Italian Greyhound set the pace – If your Italian Greyhound is nervous around children, let him set the pace. Instead of handing your puppy to the child to hold, ask the child to sit on the ground and place your Iggy near him. Ask the child to play with something, and your curious Italian Greyhound will come and investigate. As your Italian Greyhound's confidence grows, let the child pat him and eventually hold him.

Keep it positive – One of the best ways to build a good relationship between your Iggy and small child is by using positive reinforcement. When your pup is behaving properly around small children, generously

Photo Courtesy of Stephen Raymond

praise him and give him lots of treats. This will teach your dog that good things happen whenever children are around. Soon he will seek out the children and be on his best behavior.

Safe spaces calm fears – One of the disadvantages of children and puppies is that they can easily get excited, which may cause misunderstandings and hurt feelings. It is important to teach your children that your Iggy's crate is his private place; if he goes there, it is because he wants some downtime. Place your dog's crate in a secluded area of the house where he can retreat from rambunctious children if he feels overwhelmed.

Steps for a successful first encounter with small children

For the best success with his first encounter with a small child, choose a moment when your Italian Greyhound is tired, perhaps after a walk or playtime.

1. Ask the child to sit on the floor with his legs crossed. Place your Iggy nearby and have the child place his hand out with a treat for the puppy.

2. Once the puppy sniffs out the little person, you can gently pick up your puppy and place him on the child's lap. Remind the child to use his inside voice and to talk softly. Generously praise your Italian Greyhound and give him a reward. Instruct the child to gently pat the puppy using soft, gentle strokes.

3. Your Iggy most likely will curl up and go to sleep. If not, he will decide to move on and explore his surroundings. If the latter happens, tell the child not to grab or pull the puppy back to his lap. Doing so could frighten and maybe even hurt your small Italian Greyhound.

4. If your puppy decides to explore his surroundings, let him do so for a minute or two, then direct his attention to the child by repeating steps one and two. If the dog runs away again, be sure to reassure the child that the puppy likes him, but he is very curious.

5. Do not forget to praise and reward your puppy every time he sits and plays with the child. Positive reinforcement is the key to laying a foundation for a healthy relationship between your Iggy and children of all sizes.

Socializing your Iggy is a lifelong process that will need to be reinforced throughout the years. Never force interactions with strangers, other dogs, or animals and children. Always let your dog establish his own terms for discovering and accepting new situations, environments, and people.

Leaving Your Dog Home Alone

Leaving your Italian Greyhound home alone for the first time can be nerve-wracking for everyone involved, and your IG may exhibit some separation anxiety behavior. The good news is, with time, IGs can get used to it.

How To Reduce Separation Anxiety

First, let's talk about separation anxiety—it's when a dog acts out from the stress of being alone. Usually, the behavior lasts from the time you leave until you come back. In some cases, it may only last 20 to 30 minutes until your dog tires and retreats to its safe spot in your home.

Each dog has its own way of expressing anxiety symptoms. Here are some examples.

- Being vocal – Howling, barking, whining
- Destruction – Destroying or chewing on items around the house
- Relieving themselves – Going potty on the floor (or on furniture)

If you return home after a couple of hours and see some pillow stuffing strewn around the room or some poop on the floor, try to restrain yourself from punishing the dog. It won't do any good and only adds to the anxiety and stress your Italian Greyhound is already going through.

Instead, start working on training by doing "dry runs." This means you're not actually leaving; you are just getting your Iggy used to being alone.

Start by leaving the room where your Italian Greyhound is and shut the door for a short time, then open the door again and let your dog see you. This will teach your dog that you will come back. Repeat this several times.

When you are ready for the next step, pretend you are leaving to go somewhere (but you're not really going anywhere). Put on your jacket and your purse, grab the keys, and head out the door. But wait by the door for a while, then come back inside. Repeat this process until your IG becomes bored or used to it.

When your dog seems used to you leaving and coming back, try to stretch out the time you are gone. You can start with five-to-10-minute intervals and work your way up to 20 minutes, then an hour, etc.

If you are worried about your dog while you are gone, you can install a camera inside your house to monitor him from your phone or tablet. Some camera systems come with a treat dispenser, but try to avoid talking to your dog through the microphone unless your IG is well-trained because it may confuse him more and increase any separation anxiety symptoms.

> Don't stay away for too long. Iggies are clingy and shouldn't be left alone for more than four to five hours. If you are going to be gone most of the time, then this may not be the right breed for you.

To make your dog's alone time more fun, leave him a safe toy (without any small parts he might choke on). A good toy would be a Kong with a treat inside. Don't forget to also lay out his favorite snuggly blanket and stuffed plushies.

Physical Exercise

> 66
>
> *Exercising an Italian Greyhound involves both mental and phys-ical stimulation. Provide daily walks to fulfill their exercise needs. Although Iggies are small, they still require moderate exercise to maintain their health and prevent obesity. If you have access to a secure and enclosed area, allow your Iggy to run and play off-leash. They have a natural instinct to chase, so make sure it's a safe space.*
>
> EVAN CONAWAY
>
> *azgreyhounds.com*
>
> 99

Being a good puppy parent means providing your pup with daily physical activity. The benefits of regularly exercising your Iggy are end-less. Regular physical activity helps your pup to sleep better at night. Just a slight case of sleep deprivation for your dog can cause all sorts of behavioral issues. You will notice your pup's overall mood will improve with daily exercise.

Another reason to regularly exercise your Italian Greyhound is that it helps keep his weight down. In the United States, more than 50 per-cent of dogs are considered overweight or obese. Like in people, excess weight leads to a long list of health problems.

A few health benefits for dogs derived from regular physical activity

- Maintains and builds muscle mass, which can reduce the risk of injury.
- Helps to prevent canine diabetes and certain cancers.
- Decreases the risk of urinary tract infections, as exercise stimulates frequent urination.
- Helps to reduce the risk of arthritis.
- May increase your Iggy's life span.

Italian Greyhounds have an extensive history, dating back more than 2,000 years. But the breed gained huge popularity with the nobility during the Renaissance, especially in Italy. This extreme popularity is what might have led to the name "Italian Greyhound." The breed can be spotted in countless Renaissance paintings, during which time dogs were artistic symbols of loyalty.

There are other benefits derived from providing your Italian Greyhound with a regular exercise regime. For example, just sticking to a walking schedule can combat many common behavioral problems.

Exercise gives your Iggy an opportunity to burn off his energy in a healthy way. If you exercise your dog randomly and without any structure, you will not see any improvement. However, if you follow a strict exercise schedule, you can eliminate or reduce the following:

- **Aggression** – Italian Greyhounds can develop the canine equivalent of cabin fever. Regular exercise helps your pooch to release his tension, meaning he will be much calmer when he gets back home.

- **Destructive behavior** – If your Italian Greyhound does not have a regular energy release, he will focus his energy by chewing on your furniture, digging, scratching, and other destructive behaviors.

- **Barking** – One of the main reasons for excessive barking is related to a lack of exercise and can easily be eliminated by a few rounds of fetch in the backyard each day.

Tips on how to exercise your Iggy

Taking your Iggy for a walk around the block is a great way to begin, but there are countless opportunities to give him more exercise and have fun at the same time. If you have any questions about whether or not your particular type of exercise is safe for your puppy, check with your veterinarian.

Walking – Your Italian Greyhound lives for going on walks, but remember to stop and let him sniff out his surroundings. Walking is an excellent form of physical activity, but exploring his surroundings can also be quite stimulating and exciting.

Swimming – Iggies love water, and swimming is a fantastic exercise, especially for an older dog who is suffering from joint problems, as it is a low-impact exercise. If you are taking your Italian Greyhound out on a canoe or a boat, do not forget to put a life jacket designed for dogs on him.

Hiking – Your Italian Greyhound loves the great outdoors just as much as you do. Take your pooch along with you on your next adventure to explore a new park or trails in your city. Always keep an eye on your Iggy for fatigue, and make sure your dog has access to cold water and shade anytime he is exercising.

Fetch – Fetch is never boring for your Italian Greyhound; in fact, he could play for hours. Switch up the ball with Frisbees or your pup's prized chew toy to keep him on his toes. Exercise of this nature will release endorphins, which will have an overall calming effect on your pup's behavior.

Games – Inclement weather may dampen your outdoor plans, but there are plenty of games to help your Iggy burn off excess steam. For example, hide-and-seek or chase gets your pup moving. Tug-of-war can build muscle and a special bond with you. Greyhounds love a good game of tug.

Nip Boredom in the Bud

66

Engage your Iggy's mind with puzzle toys, interactive feeders, or obedience training sessions. Mental stimulation is important for his overall well-being. You can also provide interactive play sessions with toys and games that encourage chasing, fetching, or problem-solving.

EVAN CONAWAY

azgreyhounds.com

99

Just like humans, dogs may get bored with their same old everyday routine. One of the main factors behind behavioral issues is boredom. Bored dogs develop destructive behavior and may start chewing on furniture, digging up the garden, or trying to escape from the yard.

Here are some creative ways to stimulate your Iggy so that he does not get bored and start misbehaving.

Teach him a new trick

Engaging your Iggy in training sessions not only teaches him a new command or trick but it provides him with a mental challenge. Once you move past the basic commands, then move on to more advanced commands. Even older dogs will benefit from training sessions, which often help them become less anxious and calmer around other dogs.

Play together

Purchase a board game such as canine cards or dominos, which allows you to place one or two pieces of kibble or yummy treat in some of the game parts. Give your dog one of the many toys with a hidden treat, and let him try to figure out how to work it out. Another option is to play hide-and-seek or treasure hunt. Your pup will love the challenge, and it will be a wonderful opportunity to bond together.

Run errands with your Italian Greyhound

Even a quick errand to the mailbox, grocery store, or friend's house will leave your Iggy feeling quite stimulated. (Remember, you should never leave your dog alone in the car, even for a few minutes.) Your Italian Greyhound will absorb the new sounds, scents, and situations. By the time you get home, your pup will fall right asleep, even though the activity was not physically taxing.

Give him a task to do

Dogs were originally bred for hunting, herding, and retrieving. In the case of your Italian Greyhound, he is a sighthound and was originally bred to retrieve or sniff out birds and rodents. A hearty game of fetch or Frisbee will leave your Iggy feeling satisfied. He will not tire of bringing you back the ball over and over again like it is his job.

Switch up your pup's toy collection

Nobody wants to play with the same old toy day after day. Give your puppy a toy to play with, and when he becomes bored with it, replace it with another one. Keep all his toys in a box and rotate them out. Your pup will love it when you switch up his toys, just as if he is getting a brand-new toy.

CHAPTER 8

Expanding on Basic Training

Training your Italian Greyhound will teach him basic good manners, such as politely greeting guests when they arrive, walking properly on the leash, and coming when called. By teaching your dog these basic commands, you are setting him up for a happy and safe life. Plus, a well-mannered dog is loved by all!

Many of the misunderstandings between dogs and humans are related to a communication gap. However, obedience training takes time; think of it as a marathon and not a short sprint. Some commands your pooch may learn in a day or two, and others may take a few weeks to master.

Benefits of Proper Training

A well-trained Italian Greyhound will bring you years of companionship, joy, and a sense of pride. When a dog is constantly disobedient or exhibits behavioral issues, it can be a source of stress for both you and your dog. Training your dog is your responsibility—not just for your dog's best interests but for your own peace of mind as well.

Your Iggy's behavior reflects directly on you as his owner. No matter your dog's age or temperament, he can benefit from a little extra instruction. Here are five reasons why you need to train your Italian Greyhound.

Training benefits both you and your Iggy – When you train your dog, he is not the only one reaping the benefits. Regular training sessions with your pooch help you to understand your dog's needs and personality, making you an even better owner.

Training keeps your Italian Greyhound safe – The more easily you can control your Iggy by using basic commands, the better you can protect him when unrestrained. A dog who bolts when he is off the leash is likely to run in front of a car and get hit or even escape out the front door before you are ready to leave.

Training helps your Iggy to be more sociable – Obedience training teaches your Italian Greyhound his limits, boundaries, and how to behave in social situations. As a result, other people and dogs will enjoy being around your dog.

Training makes traveling a breeze – Nobody enjoys being around a disobedient dog. A well-trained dog will obey your commands but also those of others. Training will make boarding easier, either at the kennel, a close friend's house, or a relative's home.

Because you can teach an old dog new tricks – Old dogs *can* learn new tricks. It is never too late to improve your Iggy's education. With a little extra patience, an older dog can learn just as well as younger dogs.

A well-behaved dog experiences less stress and anxiety, interacts better with others, and over time will form a stronger bond with you. Some of the best gifts you can give your dog are your time and energy to train him, which will make him a happier and healthier dog in the long run.

How Do You Become the Alpha?

Wild canines and wolves operate as a social hierarchy, with one leader and his or her followers. Often, the alpha leader is the strongest of the pack and makes the majority of the decisions for the rest of the pack. Just because your Iggy is domesticated does not mean that his hierarchical instinct has disappeared.

If you have more than one dog in your house, you may have noticed how one of the dogs seems to set the tone over the rest. Regardless of how many dogs you have in your house, there should only be one alpha in the home—YOU!

Being the alpha leader does not give you or anyone the right to punish or physically hurt your dog. By being the leader, you are simply establishing that your rules protect your dog. A word of caution: if you lose your patience and get visibly upset with your dog, in the eyes of your Italian Greyhound, you have already lost your position as the alpha leader.

Smaller breeds, like the Italian Greyhound, tend to gravitate toward whoever is in charge. However, you should be aware that during your pup's adolescent years, he will test your dominance before he decides to be a submissive, obedient dog.

Photo Courtesy of
Rebekah Niland

Establish the rules and limitations – Italian Greyhounds are scent dogs, so their intelligence will urge them to test out limitations and challenge your authority. Never punish your dog; instead, firmly correct any bad behavior, such as jumping up on the couch or grabbing a piece of food from your hand.

Smaller dogs like your Italian Greyhounds will whine until you pick them up. Do not pick him up until he stops whining or you have distracted him with another unacceptable behavior.

Stay calm yet assertive – In nature, the leader of the pack, or alpha dog, shows his dominance by taking charge of every situation. He is not nervous or doubtful. Your dog can sense your emotions. If you are uncertain or fearful, your Italian Greyhounds will interpret it as a sign of weakness. He will think he needs to protect you and become your leader.

If he starts chewing on your furniture, say a firm NO. Then distract him with a more appropriate chew toy. Once he is chewing on the toy, praise and reward him.

Set a routine – Iggies love routine! The structure of a well-established routine teaches them what to expect each day. Be consistent in feeding, walks, playtime, bedtime, and bathroom breaks. Your pup will benefit from an established routine, as he will not need to worry about what is or is not about to happen next.

Sticking to a regular bathroom schedule while house-training will prevent accidents in the house. If a dog feels a certain urgency to go to the bathroom, he is more likely to "hold it" if he knows and trusts that you are going to be giving him an opportunity soon to relieve himself.

Picking the Right Rewards/Treats

Picking the right treat to motivate and encourage your Italian Greyhound is essential. Enticing treats for dogs come in a wide assortment of flavors, sizes, textures, and shapes. Some training sessions require a more appetizing reward with a stronger scent, such as meat and cheese.

However, many treats your Iggy loves are often high in fats and sugars. These fats and sugars may be a hidden cause of weight gain, health issues, or even dental problems.

It can be easy to lose track of the number of treats you hand out throughout the course of the day. Depending on your Italian Greyhound's activity level, a 10-pound dog may burn only 300 calories each day. If one medium-sized doggy biscuit contains roughly 30 to 50 calories, just two or three of these can become an overindulgence.

- Choose treats that are specially formulated for dogs, as they are designed to please their palate without causing tummy upset.
- Choose treats that have added nutrients or benefit your dog's teeth.
- Keep track of the calories you give your dog each day in treats and subtract these from his total daily caloric intake.
- Try to keep treats under 10 percent of your dog's daily intake.

Due to the wide variety of treats available, try to make wise choices. Be sure to read the ingredient label and check for fat content. Ask your veterinarian for recommendations about the best type of treats to use for rewards for your Italian Greyhound. Here are some useful tips to help you choose the best reward for different training situations.

Small-sized treats – Smaller-sized treats can quickly be gobbled up, making them ideal for keeping your Iggy motivated and attentive during training sessions. If your dog spends too long chewing a treat between repetitions, cut the treat in half.

Soft and smelly treats – Soft, smelly treats will be your Italian Greyhound's favorite treats. These treats are better suited for training your dog to do more complex commands, such as *roll over* or *leave it*. Or if you have stepped up your pup's training sessions to a public area with more distractions, this type of treat will keep him motivated.

Chewy treats – Some training sessions will need the treat to last a little longer, such as crate training or learning to stay still on the couch. For these occasions, a chewy treat is ideal as it keeps your dog distracted for a longer period of time.

Switch it up – Dogs can become bored with the same old treat. For training, mix a bunch of different treats together in a baggie to keep your Italian Greyhound intrigued, especially if he is struggling to learn a new command.

Photo Courtesy of Jennifer Thompson

Basic Commands

> *I suggest that a command word should be connected to a specific action. For example, if the dog wants to chew on your favorite shoe, I like the command 'That's mine' instead of 'No.' The word 'No' is just too vague—same for any other command you have for the puppy. If you want him to stay, have one command word rather than confusing the puppy with 'Wait,' 'Don't come,' or 'You can't come out.' The command word isn't important, but consistency is essential.*
>
> KAREN HAREN
> *Bethany Italian Greyhounds*

Your Iggy will love learning these basic commands, as it means spending time with you and having your undivided attention. It is fundamental to start teaching your dog these commands as soon as possible because it will help him grow into a well-behaved dog who is a pleasure to be around.

If your Italian Greyhound is adopted, he most likely knows most of these basic commands already but may need a refresher course. Just be more patient with your older dog because he may be dealing with mobility issues. Training your dog, no matter his age, is an excellent way to spend time together and have fun!

Your Italian Greyhound is a fast learner, and he is eager to please you, so use that to your advantage. With kind and gentle guidance, you should be able to teach your pup to sit, come, stay, etc., in a few weeks' time.

As we noted earlier, keep commands simple. Say *sit* instead of *sit down here*.

When training your Italian Greyhound, pay close attention to the tone of your voice. Never yell at your dog, as he has exceptionally good ears and can hear you very well. A loud, angry voice is not going to teach him anything except the fact that you are upset. Patiently show your dog what you expect of him, speak in a soft, kind voice, and praise him affectionately.

Sit

Teaching your Italian Greyhound to sit is one of the most important commands, thus making it the best choice to start with. Once your dog knows this command, he will be much calmer and easier to control. Plus, the *sit* command is the foundation for other commands, such as *stay* and *come.*

Here is how you teach your Iggy to sit.

1. Hold a treat near your dog's nose.
2. Slowly move your hand upward, allowing his head to follow the treat, which will cause his bottom to lower to the ground.
3. Once your Italian Greyhound is in a sitting position, say *sit*, and give him the treat and affectionately praise him.

Repeat this sequence a few times a day until your Iggy has mastered it. Then start asking your dog to sit before dinnertime, going for walks, or any other situation you want to teach him to be calm.

Stay

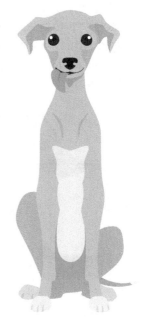

The *stay* command is similar to the *sit* command as it makes your dog easier to control in certain situations. This command is handy for moments when you need your pooch to stay out of the way as you clean your house or if you do not want him to overwhelm your houseguests.

Here is how to teach your Italian Greyhound to stay.

1. Tell your Iggy to *sit*.
2. Once he is sitting, then open the palm of your hand in front of you and say, *"Stay."*
3. Take a few steps back. Reward him with a yummy treat and affection if he stays sitting.
4. Gradually increase the number of steps you take backward each time before rewarding your dog.
5. Always reward your Italian Greyhound for staying still, even if it is only for a few seconds.

This command teaches your dog self-control, so do not be discouraged if it takes a little longer than you thought. Most dogs, especially Italian Greyhounds, prefer to be on the move, exploring their surroundings instead of simply sitting still and waiting.

Down

This can be a challenging command to teach your Iggy, as it requires him to get into a submissive posture. Be sure to keep the training sessions for this command fun, upbeat, and positive. Also, never forget to praise and reward your dog once he successfully follows through on the command.

Here is how to teach your Italian Greyhound to get in the down position.

1. Tell your dog to sit.
2. Use a particularly delicious-smelling treat and hold it out in front of you in a closed fist.
3. Place your closed fist in front of your Iggy's snout. When he sniffs it, slowly move your hand toward the floor so he follows the treat.
4. Slide your hand along the ground in a vertical line toward you to encourage his head to follow.
5. Once he is in the down position or lying down, say "*Down*," give him the treat in your hand, and generously praise him.

You will need to practice this command daily until your dog has mastered it. If your pooch tries to lunge toward your hand, say a firm "*No*," and take your hand away. Never push him into a down position; instead, encourage him every step of the way until he figures out how to please you.

Come

This command is a godsend for times when you lose your grip on the leash or accidentally leave the door open. This command is quite easy to teach and will keep your Iggy out of trouble.

Here is how to teach your Italian Greyhound to come to you.

1. Put a leash and collar on your Iggy.
2. Get down to your dog's level and say, "*Come*," while gently tugging on the leash.
3. When your pup comes to you, be sure to reward him with treats and affection.

Once your Italian Greyhound has mastered coming to you with the leash on, then attempt the same sequence without the leash in a safe, enclosed space.

Off

Off can easily become confused with *down*. The off command is used to teach your Iggy not to jump on people or to climb on certain furniture. The goal is for your dog to keep all four paws on the ground.

Here is how to teach your Italian Greyhound *OFF.*

1. When your dog jumps up, say a firm *"Off"* and point to the floor. Once he is standing with all four paws on the ground, reward his good behavior.
2. If you found your Iggy on the couch, and he is not allowed to be there, say a firm *"Off"* and encourage him to come to you. When he comes, reward him with a treat and praise.

Another way to avoid this bad behavior is by simply ignoring it. When he jumps up on you, turn around and act like you are leaving. Wait a few seconds, and then try again. Reward your dog when he does not jump up on you.

Leave It

This command can keep your Italian Greyhound safe when his curiosity gets the better of him, such as when he smells something on the ground that may be potentially dangerous for his health if he eats it. The goal of this command is to teach your dog he will get something even yummier if he ignores the other item.

Here is how to teach your Iggy to leave it.

1. Place a treat in each of your hands.
2. Open one of your hands with the treat inside and say, *"Leave it."*

3. Close your fist again; ignore any behaviors such as licking, sniffing, pawing, or barking at your hand to get the treat.
4. Once he stops, give him the treat from the other hand.
5. Repeat until your Italian Greyhound moves away from the fist when you say, *"Leave it."*
6. Next, only give your Iggy the treat in the other hand when he looks up at you and away from the closed fist.

It is vital to maintain constant eye contact with your Italian Greyhound during this command session. Make sure in your second hand you always have a yummy, smelly treat and, in the other hand, just an ordinary piece of kibble.

How to Introduce the Leash and Collar

Some Italian Greyhounds are quick to embrace their collar and leash, while others tend to shy away from them.

Whether you live in an urban or rural setting, your Iggy is going to need to learn to use a collar and leash. Often, the breeder will introduce

FUN FACT
Italian Greyhounds in Film

The 2003 film Good Boy!, based on the book Dogs from Outer Space by Zeke Richardson, featured an adorable Italian Greyhound named Nelly. Voiced by Brittany Murphy, Nelly played a supporting role in the film. Viewers sometimes mistake Nelly for a Whippet, a dog breed that is slightly larger than the Italian Greyhound but smaller than the Greyhound.

your Italian Greyhound to a collar when he is only a few weeks old. The first thing you need to do is make sure you have all the right equipment for training your pooch to walk on a leash.

Below is just a short overview of the different types of collars and leashes available and their uses:

Standard collar – This is your basic collar often used to place your dog's ID tags, etc. Italian Greyhounds are expert escape artists, and they will easily slip their heads out of a standard collar.

Muzzle harness – This type of collar is not popular, and its general idea is to keep your dog from following his nose instead focusing on you. Often, this type of harness is used for training sessions for show dogs.

Back harness – This style of harness is great for smaller breeds such as your Iggy. This style of collar prevents their airway from being damaged from pulling on the leash. Also, it prevents your four-pawed friend from sliding out of his collar.

Martingale collar – This collar option is for dogs who have the tendency to pull on the leash. It is a double-looped collar, which tightens when your dog pulls on the leash. There is no need to worry about choking, as it only tightens enough to be uncomfortable.

Standard leash – This classic leash can come in a variety of styles and lengths. It can be a rope style or a flat band.

Retractable leash – A retractable leash has a coiled-up compartment, allowing you to let out as much length as desired or lock it so that your Italian Greyhound cannot go any further.

The following steps will help you train your pup to use a collar and a leash.

Step 1. Go to a neutral space, such as your living room or backyard, and let him sniff the collar. Put the collar on your dog when he is distracted. Once he is used to the collar, attach the leash and let him run around with it behind him while in the house. Just keep an eye on him to make sure he doesn't get the leash caught on anything and possibly hurt himself.

Step 2. Take your Italian Greyhound for a walk around the block or to a neighbor's house. This will allow your pooch to get used to the leash and collar while in a safe environment. If your Iggy walks without pulling, give him praise and treats.

Step 3. Now you are ready for a real walk. When you start walking, if your Iggy pulls or tugs on the leash, do not painfully pull back on the leash. Just stop walking and say, *"No."* When your dog stops pulling on the leash, give him a reward and affection.

Advanced Commands

Now that you have mastered all the basics, you can consider moving on to more advanced commands. These tricks will keep your Iggy active, fit, and mentally stimulated. Plus, they will strengthen the bond you share with your four-pawed pal.

Remember that obedience training is an ongoing process. You will never be completely finished. You will need to keep working with your Italian Greyhound throughout his lifetime. For example, people who learn a second

Photo Courtesy of Jennifer Conrad

language at a young age but later stop speaking and using the language may eventually forget much of it as they grow older. The same goes for your Iggy. Do regular practice sessions to reinforce commands and tricks he has already learned, so they can stay fresh in his mind. Plus, it is an excellent way to bond and spend time with your dog.

Look

Teach your Italian Greyhound to pay attention to you or something in particular.

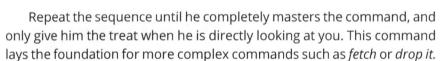

1. Hold a treat between your thumb and pointer finger, so your Iggy can see it.
2. Bring the hand holding the treat up to your nose and hold it there.
3. Say the command, *"Look."*
4. Hold the treat there for a few seconds, then give him praise and the treat.

Repeat the sequence until he completely masters the command, and only give him the treat when he is directly looking at you. This command lays the foundation for more complex commands such as *fetch* or *drop it.*

No

This might seem like a basic command, but dogs tend to quickly forget it because they hear it so often in day-to-day conversations. You will need to constantly reinforce this simple yet crucial command. This command will teach your Italian Greyhound to stop whatever he is doing when he hears the *no* command and look at you.

1. Ask your Iggy to sit.
2. Place one of his all-time favorite treats in front of him on the ground so he can see, but it is still out of reach.
3. When he lunges forward to grab the treat, say, *"No."* Raise your hand in the stop sign. Your hand will be the barrier between the treat and your dog. Do not raise your voice or yell at your dog.
4. You need to pay constant attention while practicing this command, as your pooch will try to sneak in a few treats.

The goal of this command is to teach your Italian Greyhound to look at you when you say *"No"* and not at the treat. He should look to you for permission to eat the treat. Once your dog looks at you, then pick up the treat and give it to him. Repeat this command until he has mastered it and can wait a minute or two when he hears the *"No"* command.

Roll Over

This is a difficult command to teach because it is physically difficult to guide your dog through the movements without having to help him roll over.

1. Tell your dog to go into the *down* position.
2. Hold a treat between your thumb and pointing finger, so he can easily see it. Place it close to his nose.
3. Do a backward circle with the treat in front of his gaze, causing him to follow the treat. The movement should result in him flopping over on his side while trying to roll over.

The first few times you practice this, you might have to help your Italian Greyhound roll over, so he can follow the treat. Say the command, *"Roll over,"* as he is in the process of rolling and give him the reward at the end.

CHAPTER 9

Traveling

According to a recent survey, more than 68 percent of US households own a pet dog, and about 37 percent of pet owners regularly travel with their dogs every year.

When making travel decisions, choose the safest and most comfortable option for your Italian Greyhound. For instance, unless you will be able to spend the majority of your time with your pooch, he will most likely be happier left at home than tagging along with you on your journey. But if you have decided to bring your pet along, follow the suggestions and tips below and have a safe, stress-free trip.

Preparing Your Iggy for Travel

Whether your Italian Greyhound is a seasoned traveler or you are planning your first big trip together, there are several things you can do beforehand to help make the trip less stressful for both you and your furry friend. Avoid travel drama by preparing your pup for travel as soon as possible.

- Food – Be sure to pack enough dog food for the duration of the entire trip, as switching your dog's food may cause him to have an upset tummy. If you are planning on traveling for a longer period of time, research ahead of time whether your Italian Greyhound's regular dog food is available in your final destination.

- Water – Throw in a bottle or two of clean drinking water to keep your dog hydrated throughout the journey. Never allow your dog to drink water from an unfamiliar source, such as a creek, puddle, or pond.

Photo Courtesy of Kelsey Cook

- **Food and water dishes** – Do not forget to bring your pup's food and water dishes along. Be sure to place them in an area where you can easily reach them throughout the trip. If you are tight on space, look for a set of pop-off food dishes.

- **Crate or carrier** – Depending on your method of travel, you might need either a hard-cover crate or a soft-cover carrier. Make sure to choose a comfortable traveling case, as it will most likely be used as your Iggy's personal bedroom when you reach the final destination. How to choose an appropriate travel crate is discussed in the following pages.

- **Toys** – Be sure to bring along a few of your Iggy's favorite toys for the journey, as this will keep him distracted during long-haul trips and also help to relieve stress.

- **Blankets and doggy beds** – A nice, fluffy blanket will keep your Italian Greyhound warm during the journey, plus the familiar scent will keep him calm. If you have space in your luggage, bring along his doggy bed so your dog can use it at the final destination.

- **Collar, leash, and ID tags** – Be sure to place your dog's collar and ID tags on him before leaving the house, and do not remove them until you return home. If your Italian Greyhound is an adventure-seeker, he may suddenly escape to explore his new surroundings, so you may want to invest in a GPS dog tracker tag.

- **Cleaning supplies** – Traveling with dogs can get messy. Be prepared by bringing along potty pads, baby wipes, paper towels, disposable garbage bags, and of course, a pet-friendly stain remover.

- **Medications** – If your Iggy is taking any type of medicine or supplements, make sure you have enough for the duration of your trip.

- **Health and vaccination certificates** – Do not forget to bring along your Italian Greyhound's medical information when traveling in case of an emergency.

Traveling by Car

Whether you are taking your Iggy on a short trip or a long journey, you will want to ensure your pup is comfortable and safe.

Avoid the temptation to let your Italian Greyhound sit in the front seat or roam freely about the vehicle while it's moving. If you have a car accident due to being distracted by your dog, you could be held accountable. Even worse, you, your pooch, or other parties could be seriously injured.

 DO

- Secure your Italian Greyhound inside a hard-cover crate that has been anchored to the vehicle by using a seat belt or other secure means or placed on the floor.

- Bring along plenty of clean drinking water to keep your pooch hydrated, even more so during the warmer summer months.
- Give your dog plenty of rest stops, not only for your Iggy to relieve himself but also so he can stretch his legs and drink some water.
- If you have the air conditioner on or a window open, make sure it is not directly blowing on your Italian Greyhound. If the window is open, make sure your dog cannot stick his head out or accidentally jump out.
- If your pooch suffers from motion sickness, ask your vet to prescribe a mild medication and follow the vet's instructions.
- Make your Iggy feel at home in his crate by bringing along some familiar items such as his blanket, chew toys, etc.
- Bring along a human buddy. Whenever possible, share the driving and dog caretaking duties with a friend or family member. You will be able to use the facilities or grab a quick bite to eat, knowing someone you trust is keeping a watchful eye on your Iggy.

 DON'T

- Never transport your Italian Greyhound in the back of an open pickup truck.
- Do not allow your dog to sit in the front seat and hang his head out of the vehicle while it's moving. He could be injured by particles of debris or get sick from breathing cold air forced into his lungs.
- Never leave your Italian Greyhound alone inside a hot car. It only takes a few minutes for your dog to become overheated. This may cause irreversible organ damage or even death.
- Do not feed your Iggy at least two hours prior to traveling in order to prevent motion sickness.

A year-round hazard is leaving your Italian Greyhound unattended in your car. Any time you leave him alone inside the car, you are sending an unspoken invitation to pet thieves.

If your Iggy is wary about getting into the car, let him explore the vehicle on his own terms with the doors open and the car turned off. Then turn the car on so your dog can get accustomed to the sound of the motor running. Do not forget to praise your Italian Greyhound for his good behavior.

Once your Iggy seems comfortable inside the car with the motor running, place him inside his crate and take him for a short spin around the neighborhood. Be sure someone is sitting beside his crate in the back seat. Make sure the final destination is somewhere fun and memorable for your dog, such as the park, beach, or even your backyard for a game of fetch.

Choosing the Right Crate for Long-Distance Car Travel

Whether your Iggy loves long road trips or quivers at the very thought of getting into the car, you will want to make the journey as comfortable and pleasant for him as possible. Dog travel crates are designed to provide a safe, enclosed place for your pooch to travel in comfort. These crates differ from your Italian Greyhound's home crate, as they come with extra security features such as fasteners to keep the crate secure while traveling.

Here are the factors to consider when choosing a travel crate for your Iggy.

Size – The crate should be big enough for your Italian Greyhound to sit, stand, lie down, and turn around in but small enough to keep him secure. A general rule of thumb is that travel crates should be no more than six inches longer than your pooch. A bigger crate may give your dog more space to move about, but this also means he may involuntarily slide around inside the crate while the vehicle is in motion.

Soft vs. hard cover – As mentioned earlier, a soft carrier may be more comfortable for your Italian Greyhound. However, for car travel, a hard crate provides your dog with more protection if you get into an accident. Another advantage to hard-cover crates is that they are easier to clean up if your dog has an accident or gets carsick.

*Photo Courtesy of
Mark Brennan*

Harness – Due to new state laws, many car crates come with a built-in harness that allows the crate to be securely fastened to the seat belt for extra stability. By fastening the crate to the seat, you are creating a more secure ride for your Iggy, as the crate will not slide around on sharp corners or fly forward if you come to a sudden stop.

Visibility – Iggies are very curious by nature and love to observe their surroundings. Choose a crate that will give your dog an unhindered view and lots of fresh air. If your dog is nervous about car travel, then the more visibility, the better.

Traveling by Plane

Airlines are not only cramming people onto flights nowadays; they are also accommodating a growing number of dogs who are frequent flyers. For first-timers, bringing your Iggy along is definitely more expensive and complicated than flying solo, but it is possible with a little extra research ahead of time.

Generally, veterinarians and breeders do not recommend flying with your pet unless absolutely necessary. Ideally, dogs should not fly unless their owner is permanently moving to a new location or taking a long trip of two to three weeks minimum. This is because flying can be extremely stressful for your Italian Greyhound. Air travel removes your pooch from his comfortable home and familiar surroundings, forcing him into a strange environment with loud noises, bright lights, changes in air pressures and cabin temperature, and, to make matters worse, few opportunities to use the bathroom.

Cargo or carry-on?

Where your Italian Greyhound will be allowed to spend his time during the flight will depend on his size. Rules vary from airline to airline. Typically, your dog will be allowed to fly in the cabin as a carry-on if he is small enough to fit in a carrier under the seat in front of you. Most airlines have a weight limit of 20 pounds for dogs flying in the cabin, though there are some exceptions. Anything larger than that, and your dog will usually have to travel in the cargo hold, along with the luggage and freight.

Every year, hundreds of thousands of dogs fly in the cargo without incident; however, there are many unknown variables that you have no control over once you hand your Iggy off to the airline personnel.

Airlines do their best to make your dog comfortable in the cargo hold. However, baggage handlers are often just trying to get the plane loaded or unloaded on time. They are

HELPFUL TIP
Window Seat

Because of the breed's small stature, your Italian Greyhound may not be tall enough to look out the window. Mental stimulation is important for every dog, and some dogs love to take in the view. Many dog window perches are available for purchase, as well as some DIY plans. Because of their small size, Italian Greyhounds may be able to use cat window perches so long as they can safely reach and exit the perch.

not paid to give your dog extra attention inside the kennel. Unfortunately, many pet owners have horror stories of their pets being injured, becoming seriously ill, getting lost, or even dying after flying in the cargo hold. So, if your Iggy is too big to fit under your seat in the cabin, seriously consider if the risks are worth it.

How much does it cost?

Typically, it will cost approximately $125 each way to fly with your Italian Greyhound in the cabin, but it can vary by airline. The cost of shipping your dog in the cargo hold is relatively cheaper. It depends on the traveling distance, as well as the combined weight of your dog and his crate. The majority of airlines will provide you access to an online calculator to estimate the cost.

Research, research, and research some more.

Airlines have a long list of rules and guidelines for traveling with your dog, and they are constantly changing. It is important to read through them thoroughly before traveling so your Iggy is not turned away before boarding the plane. If you can, a few days before flying, call the airline company to double-check that you have all the required documents for traveling with your Italian Greyhound.

When planning your flight, look for a nonstop flight with no transfers. Avoid traveling with your Iggy during holiday seasons when airports are busy, and flights are packed. This is wise to minimize the risk of any unexpected changes or cancellations.

If your Italian Greyhound has no option but to travel in the cargo hold, be mindful of the weather at your final destination. If you are traveling somewhere cooler, choose flights in the middle of the day when the temperature is not as cold. If you are traveling somewhere warmer, opt for flights later in the evening or in the early morning before the temperatures rise. Keep in mind most airlines will not let your pet travel in the cargo hold if the temperatures are too extreme at the final destination.

The majority of airlines allow only a certain number of dogs on each flight, so always call the airline and make sure they have space for both you and your Iggy. Always make reservations for you and your dog at the same time to avoid unwanted last-minute surprises at the airport.

Consider your destination.

If you are planning on traveling internationally or even to some US states, such as Hawaii or Puerto Rico, be sure to check local animal transportation regulations before purchasing your ticket. Many destinations have a complicated process and lengthy quarantine periods, which may mean you will be separated from your Italian Greyhound for part or most of your trip.

Before traveling, research the departing and destination airports so you know exactly where any pet-relief areas are located inside the airport. If you have flight transfers, your Iggy will thank you for letting him relieve himself and stretch his legs. Consult the terminal so that once your flight lands, you will know where to head with your dog.

Consult with your vet.

Before any flight, be sure to consult with your veterinarian about food, water, and medication. The American Veterinary Medical Association does not recommend sedating your pet prior to flying. There are health risks associated with sedating your dog, and certain airlines prohibit sedating pets without a note from your dog's veterinarian. However, you can ask your vet for his opinion, as he is familiar with your Italian Greyhound.

Photo Courtesy of Katherine Costello

If your Iggy is slightly overweight, your vet can formulate a weight loss plan to help him lose those extra pounds before the big journey. This is important, as obese dogs are at a higher risk of having their airways collapse while traveling.

Many airlines require that your Italian Greyhound have a clean bill of health. Your veterinarian can issue a health certificate stating your dog is healthy enough to fly and is up to date on his vaccinations. If the duration of your trip is longer than the certificate's validity, then you will need to get another certificate from a veterinarian while on vacation to meet the requirements of your Iggy's return flight.

Plan for the airport.

Plan on arriving at the airport with plenty of extra time so you are not stressed and do not feel rushed.

If your Italian Greyhound is traveling in the cargo hold, most airlines require you arrive at least three hours before domestic flights and at least five hours before international flights. You may have to take your Iggy to a separate cargo drop-off section in the terminal, so review your departure and arrival airport maps ahead of time to avoid confusion.

If your Italian Greyhound is traveling with you in the cabin, you can go directly to the passenger check-in desk, where the agent will request to see your dog's health certification and proof of immunizations.

Once you pay the pet carry-on fee, you should head directly to security. Deal with your personal items, such as computers, jackets, shoes, etc., before tending to your dog. Remove your Iggy from his carrier case and carry him through security while his carrier goes through the X-ray machine. To

FUN FACT

Italian Greyhounds in Pompeii

Small Greyhounds are depicted in several famous mosaics in Pompeii. One such mosaic is located in what was once an entrance hall and is accompanied by the inscription "cave canem," which translates roughly to "beware of the dog." Historians believe that this warning may have been meant to caution guests against stepping on the small, delicate dogs on the floor, which were likely early Italian Greyhounds. Similar mosaics and inscriptions can be found throughout ancient Rome.

speed things up, do not forget to remove your dog's harness or collar so it does not set off the metal detector.

If you checked your Italian Greyhound into the cargo hold, be sure to paste a current picture of your dog on the crate along with his name. Also, you can tape a bag of food to the outside of the crate in case of a long delay. Be sure to have a current picture of your Iggy on your phone and a picture of his crate in case the airline accidentally misplaces your dog, which is not likely to happen, but it is better to be prepared than sorry.

Prepare for time in the cabin.

Once inside the aircraft, your Italian Greyhound has to stay in his carrier for the entire duration of the flight. You are not permitted to take him out of his carrier to cuddle him or place his carrier on the seat beside you.

Hydrate, Hydrate, Hydrate – Keeping your Iggy well-hydrated during the fight is vital for his well-being. Many carriers come with an attachable water dispenser, which will keep your Italian Greyhound hydrated during the flight. However, before traveling, you will need to get your Iggy used to drinking water inside of the carrier case or crate.

If your dog is hesitant to drink from the water bottle, then entice him by filling it with lukewarm chicken broth. Water dispensers have a ball inside the cap that rolls around when touched, releasing water. You might have to encourage your Italian Greyhound by rolling the ball around and releasing the irresistible scent of chicken broth. Reward him when he drinks from the bottle, and slowly wean him off the chicken broth by replacing it with water.

Treats – Just as babies cannot pop their ears during the change of pressurization upon take-off and landing, your Iggy can't either. To avoid this, give your pup a few pieces of a jerky treat to chew on to avoid any ear issues during the flight. Be careful not to give him too much, as he could get airsick.

Prepare for potty accidents – To prevent spillage from an unavoidable accident in-flight, place a disposable potty pad on the bottom of the crate. Plus, be sure to bring along a few gallon Ziplock bags in case your Italian Greyhound goes potty mid-flight so you can easily clean up and dispose of the soiled pads.

Upon arrival

If your Iggy traveled in the cargo hold, pick up your checked luggage upon arrival and go straight to your airline's specified location for cargo. Airlines often state that dogs will be available 30 minutes after the flight's

*Photo Courtesy of
Caroline Blackwood*

arrival. If your dog is not picked up four hours from arrival, the airline will hand the dog over to a veterinarian or boarding facility at your expense.

Whether your Italian Greyhound flew in the cabin or the cargo hold, take him immediately for a walk, so he can stretch his legs and relieve himself in a designated relief area for pets either inside or outside of the terminal. Even though the journey may seem complicated, you both will breathe a sigh of relief when you arrive at your final destination together.

Choosing the Right Crate for Air Travel

Yes, we are back to talking about crates and carriers, and with good reason. Whereas a hard-sided crate is recommended for the cargo hold, the best type of crate for traveling in the cabin is a soft-sided carrier, as it can easily fit under the seat in front of you. Hard-cover crates may be quite cumbersome to fit under the seat. Plus, hard-cover crates are heavier to carry around.

The specified carrier dimensions to fit under the seat differ from airline to airline. Just because the crate or carrier you plan to purchase says "airline approved" does not necessarily mean it is suitable to be used on all aircraft.

When choosing a carrier for air travel, look for one that is slightly larger than necessary to give your Iggy a little extra breathing space to stretch out. If you are planning on taking a cross-country or international flight, look for a carrier that expands to give him a little extra space during the long flight.

Familiarize your Italian Greyhound with his carrier or crate well in advance of the actual flight. If possible, take your dog to the airport's departure area several times so he becomes more comfortable with this noisy, strange place.

 A WORD OF CAUTION – *Your Iggy's carrier will count as one of your allotted carry-ons, so be sure to pack accordingly.*

Lodging Away from Home

Hotel Stays

Talk directly with the hotel. Book directly with the hotel over the phone. This way, you will be able to ask any specific questions regarding the hotel's policies and fees for overnight pet guests. Ask the following questions:

- If there is a pet fee, is the fee per night or a flat rate for the entire stay?
- Do they require a damage deposit?
- Is the entire hotel pet-friendly or only a designated floor? If they say the latter, ask whether the restaurants or lobby area are pet-friendly.
- Can you leave your dog in the hotel room alone, or does he need to be supervised? If so, how long does the hotel's policy allow your dog to be left unattended?
- Do they offer dog sitters or dog walkers? If so, what are the costs and availability for your stay?
- Are there any charges associated with damages from your pet?

The majority of hotels charge a nominal fee for dogs; often, $25 to $50 is a standard price per night. Many major hotel chains or boutique hotels offer discounts for pets during their off-season.

Take into consideration your Italian Greyhound's behavior. You never really know how your Iggy will act when traveling until you try it, but taking his behavior at home into consideration will help you determine how he will act at the hotel. For example, if your pooch tends to bark at people walking past the window, then request a hotel room on a higher floor. Or if your pooch gets nervous on elevator rides, request a room on the lower floor so you can just walk up the stairs.

If you have to leave your pup alone in the room, turn the television on so he will not get nervous or excited by hearing people walking and talking in the hallways. If you are unsure how your pup will act, you can always plan a short one-night stay at a local pet-friendly hotel. Or if your

Iggy loves the sound of his own voice, maybe consider staying at a pet-friendly rental property.

Have a backup plan if you cannot leave your dog alone. If the hotel policy is that you cannot leave your dog alone in the room, make sure you have a backup plan. Most hotels offer additional services, such as a dog sitter or a dog walker for hire. Another option is to take your Iggy to a day spa or the groomer for the day.

If the hotel lets you leave your dog alone in the room, always give the front desk staff a heads-up and give them your cell phone number in case of any noise complaints or other issues. Also, place the DO NOT DISTURB sign on the door to prevent a housekeeper from accidentally frightening your pup.

Choose the right pet-friendly hotel. Just because a hotel lets your dog stay as a guest does not necessarily mean it is pet-friendly. Many boutique hotels provide amenities to cater to their four-pawed guests, such as a dog bed, some yummy treats, and food dishes for an additional fee. A few chain hotels even invite their furry guests to their nightly complimentary wine reception.

Research pet-friendly restaurants and activities. If you cannot leave your pooch alone in the hotel room, you are going to want to find restaurants or activities that are pet-friendly. The majority of hotels will provide you with a list of nearby restaurants that allow pets. Often, if a hotel is pet-friendly, at least a part of the lobby or onsite restaurant will accommodate your pooch.

Look for fun activities to do with your Italian Greyhound that are dog-friendly, such as a walking tour of the city or spending the day exploring a dog beach or park. Many galleries, zoos, wineries, and vineyards are pet-friendly if your dog is leashed at all times and under your supervision.

Tips for a quiet hotel stay

Nobody wants to be that person—the one whose dog barks in the hotel room. It can be heartbreaking to realize that your Iggy was upset at being left alone in a strange place and embarrassing knowing you are responsible for disturbing the other guests' peace. Plus, it may cause you an expensive inconvenience if the hotel asks you to leave.

If you must leave your furry friend alone in a hotel room, even if it is for a short period of time, these steps will help you and your dog avoid any problems:

- Do not leave your Italian Greyhound alone until he has become acclimated to the new space. Take the time to establish in your dog's mind that this room is his "new home."
- Try doing a few practices by leaving the room for a few minutes and then coming back inside. This will help your dog understand that if you leave, you will be returning promptly.
- Keep your time away as short as possible.
- If available, upgrade your room to a suite. By having two separate living spaces, you can place your dog's crate in the furthermost corner from the hallway. This will act as a buffer, giving your pooch some space from those strange noises outside his door.
- Tired dogs make less ruckus. Be sure to take your Iggy for a long walk with plenty of opportunities to relieve himself outside.
- Pack something extra special to keep him distracted while you are out and about, such as a toy stuffed with a delicious treat. If your pup's mouth is busy, he will be less likely to bark.
- Help your Italian Greyhound relax by playing classical music and leave it playing when you go out to cover any hallway noises that may trigger barking.

When staying with friends or family

Visiting family and friends is already a challenge, and adding your Iggy into the mix simply makes the whole situation a little more interesting. No matter where you are planning on staying, your pup needs to learn to be a gracious house guest. The sooner you can start teaching your dog proper pet etiquette, the better.

The preliminary step, of course, is to ask permission to bring along your furry friend. Not everyone wants a dog as a house guest. Even dog lovers appreciate an advance warning, as it allows them to puppy-proof their home, such as by putting away those collectible porcelain figurines on display. The strain of an unwelcome dog can permanently damage relationships. So, even if your Italian Greyhound was welcome in the past, never assume he is welcome again—ask first!

Another factor to take into consideration is if the host or other house guests may be allergic to dogs, or maybe there are small children present who are uncomfortable around rambunctious pups, such as your Iggy.

Training is a critical aspect of whether your Italian Greyhound will make a gracious house guest. The better trained your pooch is, the more welcome both of you will be as guests. Ask yourself if your Iggy has mastered the basic commands, such as *sit, stay,* and *come.* It may seem like a long list, but they are key elements for your dog to be a charming guest.

If your Italian Greyhound is prone to bad behavior, such as destructive chewing, nonstop barking, or house soiling, it is unfair to expect your cohost to welcome your dog into their house.

Regular exercise, chew toys, and dog puzzles can keep behavioral issues at bay. Bring your Iggy's crate so that he has a place of his own when he needs a little downtime. Be quick in cleaning up, especially if the mess involves your dog's hair on Granny's black jacket or slopping drinking water on the floor from his dish. Ask your hosts where an appropriate spot is in their backyard for your dog to relieve himself, and be quick to clean up his messes.

If things do not work out as planned, have a contingency plan, such as a pet-friendly hotel nearby or a reputable boarding kennel. No matter how things go, send a thank-you card to express your gratitude and, if necessary, to apologize.

Camping with Your Italian Greyhound

Camping with your Iggy will enhance the adventure of being outside in the great outdoors. Your Italian Greyhound's *joie de vie* will remind you to drink in the moment. However, since camping is done on public land, there are a wide variety of rules and regulations that can vary depending on the destination.

The majority of developed campsites welcome dogs, allowing a specified number of pets per site. For instance, while your furry companion is not allowed on trails in Rocky Mountain National Park, Acadia National Park offers hundreds of miles for dog-friendly trekking and camping. Be sure to do your research before you grab your sleeping bag and tent.

Many states and counties throughout the United States provide an extensive list of dog-related information to help you pick an ideal camping destination for you and your Iggy. This is handy, as some parks and campsites have definite rules for dogs year-round, while others have seasonal rules. For example, in the Sawtooth Wilderness near Sun Valley, Idaho, dogs are required to be on a leash on trails from July 1 through Labor Day.

Rules for camping at regulated campsites or in the backcountry are quite similar. Here are some of the basics:

Co-sleeping – As there may be wildlife roaming near your campsite at night, the rules often will require your dog to sleep with you either inside your car or inside the tent. The last thing you want is your Iggy running into a skunk or a coyote. The best place for your pooch is right by your side at night. You can keep him safe and out of trouble and prevent barking.

Leave no-trace – Depending on the rules of the campsite you are staying at, you may have to pick up your dog's waste and dispose of it later or bury it with dirt. Some parks require you to carry out your dog's waste to prevent the spread of noxious weeds, bacteria, and parasites.

Keep your pooch on a leash while at the camp – If you are staying at a public campsite, there are endless temptations for your pooch to explore, such as your neighbors' sizzling steaks or scurrying squirrels. Most campsites, whether regulated or in the backcountry, require all dogs to be on a leash no longer than six feet long.

Constant supervision – Never assume you can leave your dog alone at the campsite while you run down to the marina and buy a bag of potato chips. Leaving your Italian Greyhound alone, whether tied up or kept inside the car or tent, can be a disruptive disturbance to other campers. It can also put your furry companion in danger, as weather can change quickly, wildlife may wander into your campsite, or there could be other unforeseen circumstances.

Kenneling vs. Dog Sitters

Unfortunately, there will be occasions when you cannot take your Iggy with you, meaning you will have to choose between boarding your dog in a kennel or hiring a dog sitter to watch over him while you are out of town. There is no ideal solution, but taking into consideration your dog's age, temperament, and needs will make the decision a little less worrisome.

Boarding Kennels

Boarding kennels are basically pet hotels for your Italian Greyhound. Your Italian Greyhound's stay at the boarding kennel includes grooming, attention, and daily exercise. Depending on the kennel you choose, they will offer a variety of packages and prices to cater to your pup's individual requirements. If you are considering this option, here are a few advantages and disadvantages:

Advantages to boarding kennels

ADVANTAGES

- Boarding kennels provide a secure environment with experienced, dog-loving employees who will constantly monitor your Iggy to prevent any incidents.
- Often kennels host other friendly dogs, giving your Italian Greyhound plenty of fun opportunities to socialize.
- Your pup will follow a strict schedule during his stay, which will reduce his stress levels. From your Iggy's first day there, he will be fed and exercised according to a schedule.
- Often there is a veterinarian on-site or on-call if there are any emergencies. This option is especially helpful if your pooch has chronic health problems, as he will receive constant monitoring.

Disadvantages to boarding kennels

- With all the different dogs staying at the kennel, things can get quite chaotic and noisy at times, which can be stressful for sensitive dogs. If your Italian Greyhound tends to get nervous in a new environment or around other dogs, maybe boarding your dog might not be the best option.
- Although the kennel staff do their best to keep everything in check, certain situations can get out of control. There is a small risk factor if your Iggy accidentally gets into a scuffle with another dog.
- Depending on the size of the boarding facility, staff could mix up food, toys, or blankets between different dogs. Often, this does not cause too many problems, except perhaps, an upset tummy.
- Keep in mind, if you leave your Italian Greyhound at a boarding kennel, he will spend the majority of his time inside his kennel.

All boarding kennels require that their doggy guests' vaccinations and immunizations be up to date. No matter the age of your dog, he is required to have received his rabies and Bordetella (kennel cough) vaccine at least seven days prior to your dog's planned arrival date.

Bordetella is an airborne upper respiratory infection. There are almost 60 different strains, and the current vaccine only protects against 14. There is no way to fully protect your Italian Greyhound from kennel cough, as it is highly contagious. For this very reason, it is of utmost importance to search for a boarding kennel that prides itself on regularly sanitizing everything your pup might come into contact with, such as playground areas, daycare areas, toys, food and water dishes, etc.

Boarding kennels have the right to refuse admittance to any dog if the pet owner lacks adequate proof of a dog's vaccinations or if the dog has serious health conditions or displays aggressive behavior.

Dog Sitters

A dog sitter is someone who cares for your dog in your home while you are temporarily absent. Typically, the dog sitter will stay in your house or drop by several times a day while you are away, allowing your Italian Greyhound to feel safe and secure in his own territory. Having a dog sitter stay overnight is the ideal solution if your pooch suffers from separation anxiety or you prefer not to leave him alone at night.

Advantages of a dog sitter

ADVANTAGES

- While you are away, your Italian Greyhound is in the comfort of his own home. There is no need to worry about your pooch being exposed to a new environment, people, or other animals.
- The risk of accidents or injury is reduced because a single person is devoted to caring for your Iggy.
- Your dog sitter will carefully follow all your care instructions for your dog and perhaps even water your plants if you ask them to. If you have a younger pup, you can teach the dog sitter how to work on your dog's obedience training and basic commands.
- A dog sitter will directly communicate with you if there are any problems, etc. The direct line of communication will give you peace of mind, so you can focus on your holiday.

Disadvantages to a dog sitter

DISADVANTAGES

- A dog sitter needs to come into your house, and it is imperative you and your Italian Greyhound trust her or him. If your pooch is protective of his home or does not react well to new people, perhaps a dog sitter is not the best option.
- Having a dog sitter stay in your home requires extra preparation, such as readying the guest bedroom where they will stay.

- During holiday season, it can be almost impossible to find a reliable dog sitter. Be sure to book ahead of time.
- If you hire a dog sitter to drop by a few times a day and there's bad weather, they might not be able to get to your house regularly.

Pick the right sitter – Try to choose someone whose energy level and personality match that of your dog. For example, leaving your rambunctious puppy with an elderly relative is a recipe for disaster. Make sure you feel comfortable with the dog sitter and that they understand your Iggy's individual needs.

Finding a professional and responsible dog sitter should not be taken lightly; after all, they will be responsible for your pup's welfare, and you are entrusting them with the keys to your house. Here are a few suggestions to help you find a reputable dog sitter.

Ask your veterinarian – If your Italian Greyhound is elderly or has health issues, finding a dog sitter with a good rapport with your vet will give you peace of mind, especially if there is a medical emergency.

Word of mouth – Anyone can look good on paper, but a qualified, reputable dog sitter will be recommended by a close friend or a relative.

Ask for references – Any reputable dog sitter will be able to provide you with a list of regular clients who would be more than willing to verify their professionalism.

Look for a certified dog sitter – There are two nationwide agencies that train and certify dog sitters—Pet Sitters International (PSI) and The National Association of Professional Pet Sitters (NAPPS). Be sure to check out their web pages to locate a certified dog sitter in your locality, plus you can check out their reviews from previous clients.

Location – Ideally, you want someone who can stay at your house to maintain your Italian Greyhound's regular routine and schedule. This involves keeping your dog on the same walking, feeding, and sleeping routine as when you are at home. If you must change your dog's routine, get him used to the changes a few weeks ahead of time to prevent separation anxiety or other issues.

If you plan on leaving your dog at a friend's house while you are away, you might want to get him familiar with the new location a few times before actually leaving your dog there for an extended stay.

Details – Just as parents leave a checklist for a babysitter, you can make a checklist for your dog sitter. Include important information such as the vet's phone number and address, any medications your dog needs to take while you are away, allergies, feeding schedule, the closest 24-hour emergency veterinary clinic, and any behavioral problems.

Share with the dog sitter any house rules for your Iggy. For example, whether he is allowed on the furniture and how often he gets a treat—basically, any information you feel will keep your pup feeling happy, satisfied, and secure while you are away.

Relax – Now take a deep breath and relax! You have taken all the necessary steps to ensure that your Italian Greyhound has a pleasant experience while you're away, so enjoy your mini vacation.

You will have to take into consideration your Iggy's personality and needs to make the best choice while you are out of town. Carefully consider the advantages and disadvantages of each option and weigh them against your dog's requirements in order to make the ideal decision. If you cannot decide which is the best choice for your canine friend, you can always try a short stay at a boarding kennel and another with a dog sitter before your planned trip to see how your dog reacts.

CHAPTER 10

Living with Your Italian Greyhound

" The journey of life is sweeter when traveled with a dog." – Unknown

Sharing your life with your Iggy involves happy moments, funny moments, sad moments, and everything in between.

Your Italian Greyhound will not only fill your heart with love, but he will make it stronger. Recent studies have shown that having a canine companion can lower your blood pressure, cholesterol, and triglyceride levels. Also, your pup can have a positive effect on your mental health and well-being.

Your dog will be an essential part of your life and family, so you will want to give him the best life possible in every aspect. In this chapter, we will discuss some fundamental day-to-day activities you can do with your Iggy.

Understanding Doggy Language

Since your Italian Greyhound does not speak your language, the only way to truly understand what he is trying to tell you is through body language. For example, determining what your dog's wagging tail or exposed tummy really means can sometimes be the difference between a belly rub or a bite.

Canine communication consists of whining, barking, and growling, but more often, dogs rely on nonverbal body language to express what they are thinking or feeling. Deciphering your pup's body language is no easy feat, as none of his signals act alone and work more as a package. So, be sure to look for every signal, from your Iggy's soft brown eyes to his tail's height. Your dog is trying to communicate with you constantly.

Understanding what your dog is trying to tell you will help you develop a deeper bond of trust and respect. Plus, it will help you predict your pup's behavior and prevent issues before they even occur. To communicate better with your Italian Greyhound, here are some tips on reading dog body language.

Photo Courtesy of Katherine Hagmeier

Tail wagging – Tail wagging is frequently misinterpreted. Pet owners believe a wagging tail means their dog is happy, which is often true, but it can also mean a dog is in pain, aroused, nervous, or overstimulated. To decipher your Iggy's emotions, look at the tail's wag speed and direction as well as the position.

A fast, twitch-like wag generally means your Italian Greyhound is aroused, alert, and possibly irritated. A long, slow, side-to-side tail wag shows your pooch is relaxed and happy to see you.

Tail position – Even though your Iggy's tail may be stubbed, it still holds clues about his emotional state. If you get to know your dog's neutral tail position, it will be easier to recognize when his emotions have shifted.

EXAMPLE *If your dog's tail is pointing to the ground or tucked between his legs, he may be stressed or scared. If your dog's tail is pointed up, it means he is assertive, confident, and perhaps even aggressive. If your Italian Greyhound is relaxed, he will hold his tail in a neutral position.*

Posture – Your dog's posture can tell you a lot about his mood and intentions. A common behavior in Iggies and other gundogs is a raised paw, which is a pointing behavior that indicates nearby prey. But it can also indicate your dog is uncertain about a situation.

EXAMPLE *If your dog shifts all his weight forward as if he is going to lurch, it is a clear indication something has captivated his interest. Or if he is in the same position but growling, it could mean he is being protective or aggressive. If your dog is cowering and hunched toward the ground, he is trying to look smaller and submissive.*

Facial expressions – Your Italian Greyhound has some very expressive facial expressions, but they can be easy to misinterpret. For example, humans tend to yawn when tired or bored, but dogs yawn when they are stressed out.

EXAMPLE *Lip-licking may be an indication your dog thoroughly enjoyed his meal, but it can also be an indication he is anxious. Ever notice your Iggy smiling? If your pup's smile is accompanied by a loose and wiggly posture, then he is trying to tell you he is happy. On the other hand, if his smile is more of a snarl with teeth and growling, then your pooch is not a happy camper.*

Photo Courtesy of
Katherine Costello

Why Exercise Is Important

Being a good puppy parent means providing your pup with daily physical activity. The benefits of regularly exercising your Italian Greyhound are endless. Regular physical activity helps your Iggy to sleep better at night. Just a slight case of sleep deprivation for your dog can cause all sorts of behavioral issues. You will notice your pup's overall mood will improve with daily exercise.

Running Partner

Running with your Italian Greyhound can bring enormous benefits for both you and your dog's physical and mental health. It will help to keep your dog's weight in check. Plus, running can do wonders for your Iggy's mental health. The sights, smells, and sounds your dog will encounter on a run and the change of scenery will provide him with more than enough mental stimulation to reduce anxiety and boredom.

Running is a positive outlet for dogs who exhibit destructive behaviors. Instead of tearing through your favorite pillow, he can burn off his excess energy tearing through the countryside. But before hitting the running trail with your Italian Greyhound, there are a few things you need to consider.

Consider your Iggy's age.

Take into consideration your Italian Greyhound's age and health condition. Similarly, this would apply to running with a dog who suffers from joint problems or has weight issues. If you want to help your dog lose weight, talk first to your vet for some suggestions for an activity that is less painful on his joints.

Remember, it is not a race.

There is no denying the truth: Iggies love to run and run. But if you are trying to break a new sprinting record, it probably is best not to take your dog with you. Remember that you will still need to stop and clean up after your dog, and all dogs can easily get distracted by sniffing their

*Photo Courtesy of
Sarah Evans
Divine Kennels*

surroundings. Running with your dog needs to be a fun occasion for both of you, and your pooch should feel free to stop if he needs to. Instead of breaking records, try to see running as a healthy activity you can do leisurely with your pooch.

Start off slowly.

If you want to start running with your Iggy, take things slowly. Can you imagine how you would feel if someone took you on a five-mile run, and you had not been running in some time? Your Italian Greyhound may be full of energy, but he still needs to build up a tolerance. Start with a mile and slowly work up to a longer distance. Find a running area that both of you enjoy. Remember, never let your pooch off the lead unless he has mastered basic commands and you can trust him to stay close to you at all times.

Do not push your Italian Greyhound too hard.

Do not be fooled by your pup's energy. Dogs do not sweat through their skin; instead, they cool their body temperature down by panting. Pushing your dog too hard for too long can lead to hyperventilation and breathing difficulties. Stop frequently to give your pooch a break; trust me, he will appreciate it. Remember, you and your Iggy are a team, and you need to be aware of his body language, as he cannot tell you when he has had enough.

Hiking Partner

Your Italian Greyhound is an instant companion for adventures in the great outdoors, as he is always ready, willing, and eager to hit the trail. Hiking is one of the best activities you can do with your Iggy, as it will deepen your bond of friendship through shared experiences.

Before you hit the trails with your Iggy, consider the following guidelines.

Make sure dogs are allowed on the hiking trails you will be hiking and obey any restrictions concerning off-limit areas.

Keep your Iggy on a leash at all times. Most national parks allow dogs on the hiking trails if they are always on their leash. Keeping your dog on the leash will prevent him from chasing after wildlife or tearing up the delicate forest undergrowth. Many parks have hefty fines if they find you hiking with your dog off his leash.

Another factor to consider is that your dog can leave behind his predator scent, which may disrupt the local wildlife and hinder feeding and nesting activities. Unleashed dogs can also quickly catch the scent of something and may disappear from your view instantly.

Photo Courtesy of Howard Franks

Never assume that other hikers will love your Iggy as much as you. Always keep your dog on a leash so other hikers do not feel frightened or threatened. This is especially important if you are hiking through bear country. Many unleashed dogs have been mistaken for wild animals and accidentally sprayed with bear spray. Also, never assume other dogs you encounter on a hiking trail will be happy to meet your Italian Greyhound.

Always clean up after your dog. Carry along a small spade and bury his waste in the ground or carry it out with you in a plastic bag. Dog waste contains fecal coliform bacteria, salmonella, and giardia, which can cause other animals to become sick.

Make sure your dog has mastered all the basic commands and is completely vaccinated before hitting the trails. The following is a list of gear for hiking with your Italian Greyhound.

FUN FACT

Zemira the Great

Catherine the Great of Russia had an affinity for Italian Greyhounds. Her favorite of these dogs was named Zemira, who is believed to have slept in a pink, silk-lined cradle in Catherine's room. The royal pair also enjoyed daily walks together in the park. Zemira was immortalized in a painting by Vladimir Lukich Borovikovsky in 1794, nearly 10 years after the dog's death. Zemira was buried in the queen's pet cemetery, in the largest tomb of all the pets interred there.

Collar or a harness – Never use a choke collar, as it could get caught on a twig or branch and strangle your dog. Make sure you can slip two fingers under the collar or harness to prevent your dog from hyperventilating on the trail.

Leash – Make sure you use a heavy-duty leash that can withstand the rigors of hiking. If you plan to use an extendable leash, keep the leash short enough to maintain control over your dog.

Water – Carry at least eight ounces of water per hour of hiking. If you are hiking in hot weather, freeze your dog's water bottles the night before; the ice will melt as you hike, providing your dog with a refreshing cool drink. Water found in ponds, streams, and creeks may contain harmful bacteria and parasites that could cause your Iggy to become sick.

Food – Be sure to bring along enough food for your Italian Greyhound for the duration of the trip. I recommend feeding your pooch in smaller quantities but more frequently to prevent the discomfort of exercising on a full tummy.

Collapsible bowl – A collapsible bowl does not weigh much and will make it easy to give your Iggy water or food during the hike. Most collapsible bowls for dogs can be attached to the outside of your bag for convenience.

Plastic bags or a small spade – Bring a small spade if you decide to bury your dog's fecal matter in the ground, or bring plastic bags if you plan to carry out his waste.

Canine first aid kit – Just as you would bring along a first aid kit for yourself, be sure to bring along extra items for your dog. Be sure your first aid kits have hydrogen peroxide to disinfect cuts, scissors with a rounded tip to cut back any fur around a wound, bandages and gauze, and a small sock to protect a sore or wounded foot.

Reflective lights – Reflective lights can be attached to your Italian Greyhound's harness, leash, or collar to protect him when crossing the road at nighttime.

Specialized clothing – For adverse weather conditions or special activities, have on hand booties, bandanas, canine flotation devices, or insulating jackets. Before heading out into the great outdoors, check the weather conditions and determine what type of clothing your Iggy may require.

Performance Sports

Canine sports are becoming more popular with pet owners around the world. Maybe you have heard of agility, fly ball, or nose work but are unsure what they are. Or maybe you are interested in trying them out but do not know which sport is best suited for your Iggy.

Even though Italian Greyhounds would rather cuddle than play sports, they can still find them enjoyable. In fact, there are some Italian Greyhounds that love to participate in certain performance sports. Here is a list of some you can try with your dog.

Lure Coursing

This can be appealing to Italian Greyhounds since they have a strong desire to run and chase things. Lure coursing is different from other performance sports because it is designed specifically for sighthounds.

The goal is to recreate the experience of going after prey, but instead of using a small animal, a white plastic bag is attached to a pulley system that moves the bag around the course.

You can find lure coursing clubs to join or research the sport online and find ways to recreate it in your backyard.

Canine Parkour

Parkour is a sport that resembles an obstacle course for dogs. It involves objects like logs, park benches, and fire hydrants. The goal is to encourage dogs to use fitness skills, such as balancing, climbing, crawling, and jumping, to make their way through.

You can help your dog prepare by setting up obstacles in your backyard or inside your home, then guiding your dog through them. Make sure to give him treats each time he completes an obstacle to give him the motivation to continue.

This activity can be fun for IGs that are in good shape, but it's not recommended for senior dogs.

Flyball

This sport is like playing fetch but in a competitive form. It includes teams of dogs that race in relay teams to retrieve a tennis ball. The teams usually consist of four dogs and require speed and agility. Since IGs love to run and catch things, they do quite well with this sport.

There are clubs you can join to help your dog practice before competitions, and you can play fetch with your dog at home. If you can't find local clubs, try to reach out to friends with other dogs to set up a team to play in a yard to see if your dog enjoys the sport.

Freestyle Dance

Italian Greyhounds are known for their agility, and this makes them great candidates for dancing. They can learn to perform dance moves either by themselves or with their owners. There are freestyle dance competitions you can enter, or it can be a fun sport to enjoy at home.

Start off small; teach your IG one simple dance move to help build his confidence. Then you can teach him another. Using the reward system (treats and praise) will help your IG want to do the trick. You can make it even more fun by dressing up your IG and bringing out the ribbon wand!

Agility

Agility requires your Italian Greyhound to go through an obstacle course, such as jumping through hoops or over poles, crawling through tunnels, and more as quickly as possible. Your dog will be faulted if he misses an obstacle in the course or disobeys the instructions. Agility is a fantastic way to challenge your pup's mind and body.

Nose or scent work

Nose or scent work involves your Iggy's exceptional sniffer. A course will be set up with hidden scent markers, and your dog's task is to find all the different scent markers in order to get a reward. The course is quite similar to how dogs are trained for search and rescue work or police work. This option is great for a shy dog, as the course is performed by one dog at a time. Nose work may not provide as much physical exercise as the above two options, but it is great mental stimulation for your Italian Greyhound.

Which sport is the best choice for your Iggy? It will depend on your preferences and your dog's personality. For example, if your dog thrives on being active, then give agility a try. If your dog is very social and enjoys being around other dogs, then maybe try flyball. If your pooch is less social and enjoys seeking out objects, then nose work may be best suited for him. No matter what you choose, agility, flyball, and nose work are all mentally stimulating sports.

Show Life

A show dog is not born a show dog. Preparing your dog to become a show dog requires a lot of time, energy, money, care, and determination. Here are some things you should know about show dogs:

Show dogs are not easy to find. Show dogs are not easy to come by, so do not expect to phone a breeder and request a show dog, especially if they have never met you. Show dogs are the cream of the crop, and not every litter produces a show-dog-quality pup. Often, you will have to wait one year or more for a show dog. Some people wait years for a dog out of a specific litter.

Show dogs have to remain intact. Show dogs cannot be neutered or spayed. Often you do not have a say in the gender of your show dog. Show dogs were originally designed to show off the breeding stock of the dog's bloodline. The dog's appearance and structure are judged according to the dog's ability to produce quality pedigree puppies.

Be prepared for co-ownership. The majority of breeders who agree to sell you a show dog will retain partial ownership of the dog. Perhaps the breeder will want to maintain the breeding rights to the dog to protect

the bloodline and prevent the dog from being bred irresponsibly. Be sure to read the fine print on the contract before you sign.

Be determined to work. Show dogs do not get in the ring and automatically strut their stuff. Your Italian Greyhound will need conformation classes to learn how to have a proper gait, be properly socialized, and travel well.

Do not expect to get rich. Dog shows are not money-makers; instead, they are quite expensive. However, if your dog takes first place, you will get bragging rights.

How dog shows work

Each dog registered at the dog show will be presented to a judge by its owner or breeder. However, some pet owners prefer to hire a professional handler or exhibitor.

The sole purpose of a dog show is to evaluate the dog's breeding stock. Your Italian Greyhound will start off in classes competing for points toward his AKC championship. Your dog will win points according to the number of dogs he defeats in the dog show. The more dogs of the same breed who enter a competition, the more points a dog will win. Your dog will need 15 points that have been awarded by three different judges to become an AKC champion.

Dog shows are a process of elimination, and only the Best of Breed winners will be able to compete. Italian Greyhounds compete in the canine Toy Group section. The judges will select the Best in Show winner.

The judges will judge each dog against a written standard describing the ideal dog of the specified breed. The standards for Italian Greyhounds are established by the Italian Greyhound Club. Each judge will give his or her own opinion as to which dog represents the breed's standard appropriately.

CHAPTER 11

Nutrition

> *Select a high-quality dog food that is appropriate for your Iggy's age, size, and specific needs. Look for a formula that contains high-quality protein sources. Italian Greyhounds have a tendency to gain weight, so avoid overfeeding or excessive treats and monitor their weight and body condition regularly.*
>
> EVAN CONAWAY
>
> *azgreyhounds.com*

A balanced and nutritious diet is essential to keep your Italian Greyhound healthy, but providing him with the right amount of nourishment can be tricky.

Obesity is one of the most common dog problems observed by veterinarians and often is due to an unbalanced diet of too many treats and not enough wholesome ingredients. In this chapter, you will learn everything you need to know about feeding your dog at every stage of his life.

Importance of a Wholesome Diet

Every Italian Greyhound is different. Some Iggies love to eat, while others are picky eaters or have sensitive stomachs, and there are also dogs with dietary sensitivities. Deciding on what to feed your dog is a very personal choice; however, his diet will have a direct impact on his health and happiness.

Just like humans, dogs require essential nutrients to develop properly and stay healthy. The wrong diet can lead to a life of health issues and obesity; on the other hand, the right diet can keep your dog slim, healthy, and in tip-top shape.

The old saying "you are what you eat" applies to your Italian Greyhound as much as yourself. Dog food made with high-quality ingredients equals a better quality of life, resulting in fewer infections, digestive issues, skin conditions, and so on. The impact of a wholesome diet does not end there, as it can also directly impact your dog's personality and behavior.

Your dog's behavior is a direct result of activity in his central nervous center. If he is not receiving the necessary nutrients, he will be lethargic, moody, and inactive. Here are a few examples of how the food you give and the frequency by which you feed your Italian Greyhound will impact his mood and behavior.

Unbalanced diet – Many health and behavioral issues in dogs are caused by a poorly balanced diet. For example, a diet deficient in nutrients may cause your Iggy to suffer from frequent urinary tract infections that cause him to become irritable due to discomfort and pain. Make sure your Italian Greyhound only eats a well-balanced, high-quality dog food to maintain good mental and physical health.

Inadequate food – If your Iggy is not consuming enough calories throughout the day, he will be hungry and may engage in disruptive behaviors such as scavenging through your neighbor's garbage or eating feces. Dogs who are not receiving sufficient nutrients in their diet may develop a condition called pica, which causes them to eat non-food items such as soil and plants.

Pet food ingredients – The ingredients in your pup's pet food may also affect his behavior. For instance, research has found that senior dogs who receive a diet rich in antioxidants are able to learn complicated tasks faster than dogs who do not. Studies have shown that senior dogs who have always received a high-quality dog food suffer from fewer behavioral changes common to cognitive decline.

A well-balanced diet will promote stable blood sugar levels throughout the day, which will directly affect your Italian Greyhound's serotonin levels. Serotonin improves not only your dog's mood but also his concentration, behavior, and training response. Another advantage to a wholesome diet is your Iggy's immune system will be in excellent condition.

Talk to your veterinarian before changing your Italian Greyhound's diet. Your vet will recommend a brand of food that is suitable for your dog's age, size, weight, medical history, and lifestyle. Nutrition has an extensive impact on your dog's overall health, so make sure you feed him a wholesome diet.

Here are some common health issues related to your Iggy's diet.

- Heart disease – Dogs often have issues with heart disease, especially if their diet is not well-balanced. Increased levels of sodium are one of the main factors of heart disease in dogs. Since high-quality commercial dog foods are low in sodium, the main source of sodium is probably coming from those table scraps you are slipping your dog under the table.

- Diabetes – Overweight dogs tend to develop diabetes as they age. There is no known cure for diabetes. A dog with diabetes will require daily insulin shots, a special diet, and extra medical attention. The best and only prevention is to keep your Italian Greyhound on a healthy diet and give him an active lifestyle. Avoid dog food that contains starchy fillers and sugar, which offer little to no nutritional value and will spike your dog's blood sugar level.

- **Obesity** – Obese dogs are prone to arthritis, diabetes, breathing issues, high blood pressure, and cancer. Decreased life expectancy is linked to obesity in dogs. Your Iggy does not need excessive calories each day. Be sure to follow the instructions on the food bag for his weight, size, and age.

- **Pancreatitis** – Pancreatitis is caused by a diet high in fats. Consult with your vet to see if your dog's current dietary fat intake may be increasing his risk of pancreatitis.

Food allergies and sensitivities

Food allergies and sensitivities are not the same thing. It is important to take into consideration how a particular food affects your Iggy. If your dog's energy level is normal for his age, if his coat and skin are healthy, if his stools are brown and well-formed, and if he appears to be healthy, then his food is doing its job.

However, if your Iggy has diarrhea, skin issues, or an extremely itchy coat, your dog may have a food sensitivity. In this case, discuss the issue with your veterinarian. He will be able to help you create a feeding plan that works best for your dog's health. Often, your veterinarian will place your dog on an elimination diet and slowly reintroduce foods to determine what foods are causing the allergic reaction.

A food allergy involves the immune system and is often caused by a protein molecule. Food allergies present an immediate immunological response, such as anaphylactic shock, which may mean your dog is having difficulty breathing. In this case, you should take your pooch to the nearest veterinarian clinic immediately. A less severe reaction may present with facial swelling, hives, or itchiness. If you suspect your Italian Greyhound has a food allergy, it is vital that you talk to your vet to identify the cause.

A food sensitivity is an abnormal response to a certain ingredient. Food sensitivities can easily be managed and often will disappear over time. If you suspect your dog has a food intolerance, talk to your vet, look for a hypoallergenic food that avoids common allergens, such as beef or wheat, and choose a dog food with a single protein source.

Human Foods to Avoid

Slipping your Iggy a morsel or two under the table may be tempting, but it can cause your dog some serious health issues or even be fatal. You might be surprised at some of the foods your furry friend needs to avoid at all costs!

Alcohol – Even the tiniest amount of any type of alcohol can be fatal for your Iggy. Alcohol causes dogs to have coordination problems, vomiting, diarrhea, breathing issues, and even death.

Avocado – All dogs are allergic to persin, which is found in high quantities in avocados. Persin is not only found in the flesh of the avocado but also in the leaves, peel, bark of the tree, seed, etc. If you have an avocado tree in your backyard, be sure to keep your dog away from it at all times.

Bones or fat trimmings – It might seem like second nature to give your pooch a bone to chew on, but dogs can easily choke on them, or the bone may splinter and become lodged in his throat or cut up his digestive system. Furthermore, pieces of grease or fat can cause your Italian Greyhound to develop pancreatitis.

Caffeine – All types of caffeine are fatal for your dog, including cocoa, energy drinks, guarana, tea, caffeinated, carbonated beverages, and soda. If your dog accidentally consumes a product with caffeine, go immediately to the nearest veterinarian's office.

Chocolate – Dark, white, and milk chocolate are deadly for dogs. Even the smallest morsel can cause diarrhea, vomiting, cardiac failure, seizures, and even death.

Dairy products – Dairy products such as milk, whipped cream, and ice cream can cause your dog to experience digestive discomfort and diarrhea. Many dogs who are lactose intolerant have extremely itchy

skin. That said, the majority of dogs can tolerate cheese and yogurt due to the natural digestive enzymes and probiotics.

Garlic and onions – Keep all types of garlic and onions far away from your pooch, including fresh, dry, powdered, dehydrated, or cooked. Even the smallest pinch can cause your Iggy's blood count to drop, causing him to become anemic.

Grapes or raisins – Grapes and raisins seem the perfect bite-sized treat for your dog, but just a few can cause kidney failure. If you think your Italian Greyhound may have consumed some grapes or raisins, call your veterinarian if you notice any sluggish behavior or severe vomiting.

Macadamia nuts – Eating just three macadamia nuts can cause your Iggy to become seriously ill. Eating chocolate-covered macadamia nuts will intensify the symptoms, which will eventually lead to death. Macadamia nuts cause vomiting, muscle tremors, fever, and loss of muscle control.

Pitted fruits – Fruits such as peaches, persimmons, cherries, and plums have pits or seeds that can get lodged in your dog's intestines, causing a blockage. Some pits, such as from a plum or a peach, contain cyanide, which is fatal if consumed.

Raw eggs – Raw eggs are a source of bacteria, such as salmonella or E. coli. Avoid feeding your Iggy raw or undercooked eggs or any type of raw animal products, such as fish, beef, pork, or chicken.

Raw yeast dough – Before baking, yeast dough needs to rise. If your Italian Greyhound eats some raw dough, it will continue to rise inside his stomach, stretching your dog's abdomen, causing extreme pain. The yeast can also cause alcohol poisoning.

Salt – A word of caution: do not share your salted popcorn or pretzels with your furry friend.

Too much salt can cause sodium poisoning, vomiting, diarrhea, fever, or seizures and may be fatal if left untreated.

Xylitol – Xylitol is a common sweetener used in baked goods, toothpaste, and diet products. It causes your dog's blood sugar levels to drop, which leads to liver failure.

If your Iggy got into the pantry and ate something he shouldn't have, call your local vet immediately or call the ASPCA Animal Poison Control Center at (888) 426-4435.

It is not advisable to make a practice out of giving your Italian Greyhound leftovers, bits of meat, or other scraps, as he may begin to refuse to eat his normal food. Also, it can unbalance your dog's regular diet, causing him to gain weight. Human foods can cause gas, which may not be a problem for your dog, but it could be for you!

After all that talk about harmful human foods for your pooch, you are probably wondering: "Is all human food bad for my dog?" Although you may use great self-control to keep your Italian Greyhound on his canine diet, sometimes you may not be able to resist the urge to slip him a piece of cheese.

Before giving your dog any foods that are not on this list, do some research to make sure they are safe. If your pup experiences any sort of reaction or allergy, immediately consult a veterinarian. Here are some of the best human food choices for your four-pawed furry friend:

Peanut butter – Peanut butter is a favorite treat for Iggies around the world. Also, it is an excellent source of protein, healthy fats, vitamin B, and niacin. Be sure to only use unsalted peanut butter. Make sure you are not using sugar-free or lite peanut butter, as it may contain artificial sweeteners such as xylitol.

Cooked chicken or turkey – Cooked chicken is a healthy source of protein and makes a great alternative to high-calorie treats used in obedience training. Plus, if you accidentally run out of dog food, it makes a healthy meal replacement.

Cheese – Cheese is an excellent snack for your pooch if he is not lactose intolerant. Choose low-fat varieties and do not overfeed, as most cheeses are high in fat and may cause constipation. Cottage cheese is typically a good option for Italian Greyhounds.

Carrots – Carrots are a yummy, low-calorie snack for your dog and are great for your dog's teeth. They are also high in fiber, beta-carotene, and vitamins. You can feed your dog raw or cooked carrots; just be sure to cut them into small pieces to prevent him from accidentally choking on them.

Yogurt – Yogurt is high in calcium and protein. Also, its active probiotics can aid your dog's digestive system and improve his breath.

Salmon – Salmon is an excellent source of omega-3 fatty acids, which will help keep your Iggy's coat healthy and shiny and support his immune system. Try adding cooked salmon to your dog's kibble, or slip him some unwanted fish skins.

Pumpkin – Pumpkins are part of the squash family, all of which are excellent sources of fiber, beta-carotene, and vitamin A. Plus, pumpkin can keep your dog's GI tract moving and aid digestive issues.

Eggs – A scrambled egg will give your Italian Greyhound's diet a protein boost. Eggs are remarkably high in protein and a source of digestible riboflavin and selenium. Always thoroughly cook the eggs to avoid any risk of salmonella.

Green beans – Green beans are another healthy snack for your Iggy as they are a source of protein, calcium, vitamin K, and iron. Raw and cooked green beans are filling and low in calories. Just remember to only serve them without salt or other seasonings.

Apple slices – Sliced apples are high in fiber and vitamins and are a healthy treat for your pooch. Additionally, apple slices are known for cleaning dogs' teeth and freshening their breath. Before giving your dog a few apple slices, make sure to remove the seeds and the core, as they can be a choking hazard.

Oatmeal – Cooked oatmeal is an excellent source of soluble fiber, which is especially beneficial to senior dogs with bowel irregularity issues. It is a fantastic grain option for dogs allergic to wheat. Always cook oatmeal before serving it to your pup, and only use oatmeal that has no added sugar or additives.

Photo Courtesy of Leslie Teed

If you decide to give your pooch a treat or two from your table, make sure it is not seasoned, fatty, salty, or raw. Certain fruits, such as thin slices of apples, bananas, or watermelon, make yummy treats for your Italian Greyhound. Be sure to remove any seeds, peels, or stems that could get stuck in your dog's digestive tract.

Cooked, plain white rice or noodles with a piece of boiled chicken might be the best solution if your pooch has an upset tummy.

Commercial Dog Food

In the last few years, commercial dog food has improved enormously. A few decades ago, there were only a few generic brands of dog food on the shelves, whereas today, you can find countless brands that cater to different breeds, ages, and dietary restrictions. However, with so many choices out there, it can be overwhelming to narrow down what type of dog food is best suited for your Iggy.

Learning about how commercial dog food is made will help you understand the nutritional value of the food you are feeding your Italian Greyhound. There are two main types of commercially prepared dog food: canned food and dry kibble. Commercially produced fresh dog food is a newcomer to the dog food aisle and is quickly gaining popularity but is not yet widely available.

Wet dog food

Wet dog food may be sold in cans, boxes, or single-serving pouches, often consisting of 35 to 75 percent water, depending on the quality. Be sure to look for the moisture content on the label. Wet foods contain a variety of meats, such as beef, chicken, lamb, salmon, or venison.

Once the can or package is opened, it must be refrigerated to maintain its freshness, and most dogs will not eat cold food. To solve this problem, you can warm up the meal portion before serving. Note that wet foods have the highest cost per serving, and cheaper brands of wet food are high in fillers, sugar, and fat.

Wet dog food is made using fresh and frozen meat. Many commercial brands use animal parts such as organs or fatty tissue. One of the advantages of these parts is they have a higher nutritional value than meats typically consumed by humans. The meat is then ground and mixed in large machines to ensure even distribution of calories and nutrients.

The packaging method used for wet food uses a high-heat sterilization method to kill off any bacteria, but an unwanted side effect is that it also destroys nutrients and vitamins. The sterilization and vacuum-sealing process ensure a longer shelf life without the need to use harmful chemicals.

However, due to the processing method, wet foods are notorious for being void of nutrients. If you want your dog to get his daily nutritional requirements, you will need to give him a huge portion at each meal, which will eventually result in weight gain.

Dry food

The vast majority of dogs throughout the United States are fed dry kibble.

Dry dog food contains similar ingredients to wet dog food, but instead of adding gravy and canning the product, the meat mixture is pulverized and mixed together to create a consistent mass of dough that can then be cooked. The dough can be manufactured by one of the following methods:

Baked – The dough is extruded through specially shaped holes and then baked at a low temperature. Once baked, the kibble is left out to dry and then sprayed with fats, oils, minerals, and vitamins. Often, baked kibble contains wheat gluten to aid in binding the ingredients together.

Cold-pressed – This is a newbie in the dog food aisle that is quickly gaining popularity with both pet owners and dogs alike. Cold-pressed dog food often prides itself on only using the freshest of ingredients. The manufacturer will grind the ingredients together, forming a thick, coarse paste, which is then left to dry before being pressed out to remove the excess moisture. It is then baked at a very low temperature to prevent any nutrient loss.

Extrusion – This method is similar to baking, except before extruding the dough through specially shaped holes, the mixture is first cooked in huge steam and pressure cookers to kill off any bacteria. Then, when the mixture cools, it is pressed through an extruding machine, shaping the kibble. After this, the kibble is placed into a high-heat convection oven to remove any excess moisture.

It is worth mentioning that this type of kibble's double exposure to extreme heat removes the majority of the nutrients and vitamins.

Freeze-dried – The fresh food is mixed together, then ground into a coarse paste, formed into small pieces of kibble, and placed inside a type of vacuum oven that removes all excess moisture. The process preserves the majority of the nutrients, making it one of the healthiest food choices for your Iggy.

Freeze-dried foods have a long shelf life without the need for harmful preservatives. Some freeze-dried foods may need to be rehydrated with water before serving. This is one of the most expensive dry dog food options.

Fresh food

Fresh dog food is quickly gaining popularity in the dog food aisle, as it is a convenient option for homemade dog food. Fresh dog food manufacturers pride themselves on using only fresh, organic ingredients and human-grade proteins. Many companies provide the option of using recyclable, reusable serving trays.

One of the main advantages of fresh dog food is its high nutritional value due to the low level of processing required. On the other hand, since it does contain preservatives, fresh food has a maximum life span of seven to 14 days and will need to be stored in the refrigerator. It is not recommended to freeze fresh dog food, as many of the nutrients will be lost.

Wet dog food vs. dry dog food

As you can see above, both wet dog food and dry can be good choices, depending on the quality of ingredients and the process used to manufacture the dog food. However, they each offer different benefits and drawbacks depending on your Italian Greyhound's nutritional needs.

As you can see, there are quite a few factors to take into consideration when choosing the best dog food for your Iggy. Ultimately, choosing the right dog food is a very personal decision and depends on your budget and personal preferences. The right dog food for your Italian Greyhound will meet his nutritional requirements and keep him happy and healthy.

BENEFITS OF WET DOG FOOD COMPARED TO DRY DOG FOOD

Wet Dog Food	Dry Dog Food
Higher moisture content – Your veterinarian may recommend a wet dog food diet if your dog frequently suffers from urinary tract infections or dislikes drinking water.	**Dental health** – One of the main advantages to dry food is it acts like a toothbrush, helping to remove and prevent the buildup of plaque and tartar on your dog's teeth.
Palatability – Wet dog food is preferred by dogs who are finicky eaters. Also, wet dog food is ideal for concealing medications. It is ideal for elderly or sick dogs whose appetite has decreased.	**Convenience and cost-effectiveness** – Kibble's popularity is due to the convenience of feeding and cost (as with most things, the larger the bag, the better the savings). In addition, it stays fresh longer than wet foods once the package has been opened.
Easier to chew – Dogs who have dental issues or other oral abnormalities may find eating wet food easier than dry food.	**Food enrichment** – Kibble is easy to use with food puzzles that help to keep your dog mentally stimulated and improve the quality of his life.
Satiety – Wet dog food tends to cause a longer-lasting feeling of being full. Increased satiety is especially useful in managing your dog's weight.	

How to Read Dog Food Labels

The dog food nutrition label is similar to the nutrition facts on packaged food for humans. The label is designed to help you compare products and learn more about what you are considering purchasing and feeding your dog.

 Quick tip: *Look past the attractive packaging and marketing; instead, learn to read the ingredients.*

 General rule of thumb: *If humans are not allowed to eat it, then you should not feed it to your dog either.*

Just as with packaged food for humans, dog food must list the ingredients according to weight, starting with the heaviest. But a word of caution: if the first ingredient is a protein, keep in mind that proteins are typically about 75 percent water.

Dog food labels are required to contain:

- Product brand name
- Quantity displayed in terms of weight, liquid measure, or count, depending on the formulation of the dog food
- Ingredients listed in descending order by weight
- Feeding instructions for your dog's age, activity level, and weight
- Nutritional statement backed up by research and testing to prove the food provides the required daily nutritional requirements
- Manufacturer's name and address
- Calorie statement and the life stages the food is appropriate for

Continue reading to learn which ingredients to avoid and why they can harm your Italian Greyhound's health.

Artificial preservatives – Avoid dog foods that contain ethoxyquin, BHA, and BHT on the ingredient list. The National Institute of Health has deemed BHA and BHT to be carcinogenic and unfit for human

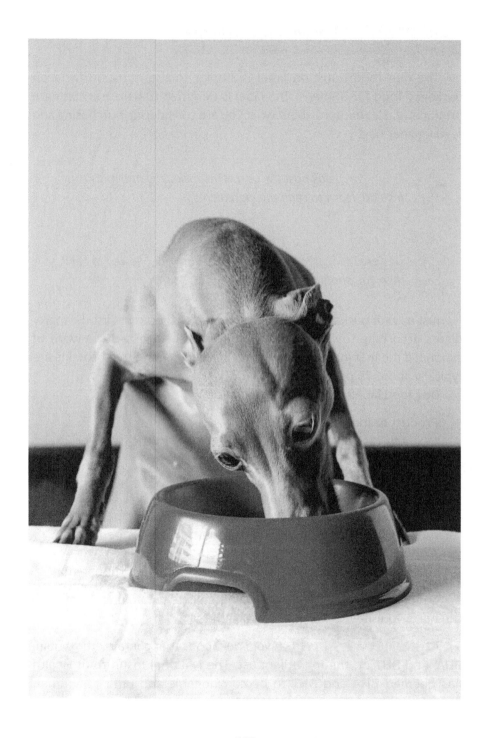

consumption. Ethoxyquin is linked to cancer, chronic immune diseases, and kidney failure in both humans and animals.

Corn and rice fillers – Corn and rice fillers are commonly used for fattening up animals, and the last thing your Iggy needs is a carbohydrate-rich diet. A low-protein diet is one of the main causes of obesity in smaller breeds, such as your Iggy. A diet high in corn and rice can cause chronic digestive issues, such as bloating, gas, and diarrhea.

Food coloring – Many dog food manufacturers add food coloring to their kibble and/or treats to make them look more appealing and appetizing. But your Italian Greyhound is not concerned about the appearance or color of his food; he just cares whether it is tasty. Avoid dog foods that contain food dyes such as Blue 2, Red 40, or Yellow 5 because they are linked to allergies, hyperactivity, and cancer.

MSG – Monosodium glutamate (MSG) is a well-known flavor enhancer for Chinese food and dog food. MSG overstimulates your dog's brain, causing him to produce a hormone called dopamine, making him become addicted to his food. Recent studies have shown when dogs regularly consume foods with MSG over time, they can develop brain damage, obesity, and behavioral issues.

Nondescript fats – Fat is essential for your Iggy's overall health. Many dog food manufacturers list generic animal fat as one of the ingredients, which often is fat derived from sick or rancid animals. Choose a dog food that specifies the type of fat used, such as salmon fat instead of fish fat or coconut oil instead of vegetable oil, etc.

Propylene glycol – Propylene glycol is a common ingredient for antifreeze and is extremely toxic for dogs. However, many dog food manufacturers add it to their products to reduce moisture from building up inside of the packaging, prevent bacterial growth, and lengthen the product's life span.

Rendered foods – Rendered meat is often listed on the ingredient list as animal by-product meal, which is a mix of animal parts such as blood, brains, spleens, entrails, and internal organs. Often, it includes discarded animal parts that were considered unfit for human consumption.

The nutritional value of rendered meat is extremely low, and it can be a source of salmonella and toxins.

Sugar – Many dog foods contain sugar to mask a bitter flavor and to improve texture. Once your Italian Greyhound is addicted to sugar, it is extremely difficult to switch him to a healthier, sugar-free alternative. Sugar additives to watch out for are cane sugar, beet pulp, corn syrup, sucrose, fructose-glucose, xylitol, molasses, and sorbitol.

Some dog owners shy away from buying food that contains synthetic preservatives such as BHA (butylated hydroxyanisole), BHT (butylated hydroxytoluene), or ethoxyquin. These synthetic preservatives prevent fat from turning rancid and can keep dry dog food fresh for at least a year. The FDA has approved these preservatives as safe for animals in small amounts.

Ethoxyquin came under scrutiny after a long list of complaints concerning some dogs who were given food with this preservative, such as skin allergies, reproductive problems, cancer, and organ failure. The FDA requested dog food manufacturers reduce the amount of ethoxyquin to half of the previously approved amount.

Some dog food manufacturers have opted to use natural preservatives such as vitamin E (mixed tocopherols), vitamin C (ascorbic acid), and plant extracts such as rosemary. These natural preservatives help to keep dry food fresh but for a shortened life span. Be sure to check your dog food bag for the "best by" date on the label before buying or feeding it to your Iggy.

Deciphering terms

Recently there have been so many new trends in the dog food market that it can be challenging to decipher the terms. Here are some terms that can be difficult to understand:

Organic – As of the moment this book went to print, the US Department of Agriculture (USDA) was still developing official regulations regarding the labeling of organic foods for pets. In the meantime, dog foods that claim to be organic must meet the requirements established by the USDA's National Organic Program, which means organic dog food has to meet the same standards as organic human food.

Organic dog food must contain no artificial sweeteners, preservatives, flavorings, or food colorings. Plus, meat and meat by-products must be sourced from animals with no antibiotics or growth hormones. Generally speaking, dogs with sensitive tummies do better on an organic diet. Note: "Natural" dog food is not the same as "organic." The term "natural dog food" refers to the lack of artificial ingredients used in the product.

Grain-free – Recent studies by the FDA have discovered grain-free dog foods are linked to canine dilated cardiomyopathy (CDC), which causes a dog's heart to enlarge and prevents the blood from circulating freely throughout the body. The FDA recommends pet owners avoid feeding their dogs grain-free foods. Dogs need a diet based on high-quality proteins, natural fats, vegetables, and whole grains to meet their dietary needs.

New proteins – The term new proteins refers to new meats in the dog food market, such as bison, kangaroo, rabbit, lamb, and other exotic animals. At the moment, it is difficult to rate the benefits of this food due to a lack of research on the different nutrient profiles when compared with common proteins, such as beef, chicken, or fish.

Human-grade dog food – This is defined as legally edible and safe for human consumption. Human-grade dog food is tightly regulated by the FDA and the USDA. Also, the Association of American Feed Control Officials (AAFCO) requires that human-grade dog food be manufactured, packaged, and held in accordance with federal regulations for manufacturing, packaging, and holding human food.

Light, low-calorie, and low-fat – If labeled with one of these terms, dog food must have a significant reduction in fat or calories when compared to the brand's standard dog food. The AAFCO requires that any dog food label claiming to be light, low-calorie, or low-fat must show the reduction on the label and name the product in comparison.

Good foods to watch out for

Finding a wholesome, healthy, and delicious food for your Italian Greyhound may seem like a challenge, but it is not impossible. When

Photo Courtesy of
Jackie Keeney

choosing a dog food for your pooch, look for a variety of ingredients such as meat, veggies, grains, and fruits. Look for some of the following ingredients on the nutrition label:

Meat – Your Iggy is a high-energy dog who needs plenty of healthy proteins to maintain his body, muscle, and immune system. Look for commercial dog foods made from human-grade proteins, such as beef, chicken, salmon, rabbit, etc.

Whole-meat meal – Often, meat meal is from by-products such as rendered meats, whereas whole-meat meal is a high source of protein and is simply a fancier way of saying ground beef. However, the ingredient list should specify the type of whole-meat meal used, such as chicken, beef, etc. Meat meal contains more protein, as it is ground up, then dried to a 10 percent moisture level, making the protein level at least 65 percent and the fat level at least 12 percent.

Carbohydrates and grains – Whole grains are an exceptional source of energy for your Italian Greyhound, and they improve his digestion. Avoid dog foods made from corn, soy, or white rice; instead, look for higher-quality ingredients, such as brown rice, whole oats, barley, and peas. Carbohydrates and grains should never be one of the first ingredients on the list.

Vegetables and fruits – Both provide essential nutrients, minerals, vitamins, fiber, and antioxidants. For example, sweet potatoes are an excellent source of potassium, vitamin B, and antioxidants. Unsweetened cranberries provide vitamin C, prevent urinary tract infections, and protect your pup's teeth from harmful bacteria.

Fats – Fats are necessary for your Iggy's overall health, proper cell function, and digestion. Fats help your Italian Greyhound absorb minerals and vitamins and keep his coat and teeth in tip-top shape. Look for dog foods that contain wholesome fats like omega-3 and omega-6 fatty acids, canola oil, salmon fat, olive and coconut oils.

Word of caution

Pay attention to the product name, as it will give you a clue about the ingredients in the dog food you are considering. Most dog owners base their decision on a specific ingredient. Many brands will highlight that ingredient on the product's label.

Stay away from commercial dog foods that use the term "with," such as "with chicken" or "with beef." Manufacturers are only required to use 3 percent of protein in dog food. Avoid dog food whose labels include the wording "flavor," such as beef or chicken flavor, as this indicates it was made with an exceedingly small percentage of the actual product and mostly contains artificial flavoring.

Just because a dog food manufacturer claims to provide everything your Italian Greyhound needs for his optimum health does not necessarily mean the food is really healthy. Take the time to carefully read the ingredient list and make a decision based on the ingredients, not based on the attractive packaging.

B.A.R.F. Diet

The B.A.R.F. diet stands for two common phrases: Biologically Appropriate Raw Food and Bones and Raw Food. B.A.R.F. was developed by nutritionist and veterinarian Dr. Ian Billinghurst, and the main principle behind the diet is feeding canines a diet similar to what they would eat in the wild. The raw diet is composed of proteins, vegetables, and fruits that are all uncooked.

The B.A.R.F. diet basically consists of a hearty portion of protein, such as muscle meat, raw meaty bones, organ meat, and a moderate quantity of vegetables and fruits. Some pet owners also add supplements to their dog's diet under the guidance of their veterinarian.

According to recent studies, there are quite a few health benefits to feeding your Iggy a raw food diet:

● **Healthy weight** – Your Iggy will have a leaner, more muscular build and will maintain a healthy weight.

● **Improved appearance** – Most pet owners who feed their dogs a raw food diet notice an overall improvement in the appearance of their skin and hair. Plus, their dogs have cleaner teeth and fresher breath.

● **Increased energy** – Many pet owners who feed a raw diet to their canines state their dogs have increased energy levels.

● **Improved bowel movements** – Dogs who suffer from diarrhea with a regular diet often have firmer and smaller stools on a raw food diet.

However, there are many disadvantages to giving your Italian Greyhound a raw diet, such as:

● **An unbalanced diet** – An unbalanced diet can cause nutrient deficiencies and future health problems.

● **Bacteria and other pathogens** – Raw dog food, if not stored correctly or consumed immediately, becomes an ideal breeding ground for potentially dangerous bacteria or pathogens that can make your dog very sick.

● **Cross-contamination** – The risk of contamination with raw meat can make humans extremely ill.

● **High cost and time investment** – Providing your dog with human-grade proteins each day can be very expensive, not to mention being time-consuming to prepare.

If you decide to give your Italian Greyhound a raw food diet, be sure to consult with your vet beforehand to decide whether it is suitable for your dog's health and lifestyle. Your veterinarian will need to closely monitor your dog's overall health for the first few months to ensure he has no allergies or other health issues.

If you decide that a raw food diet is something you are interested in but do not feel comfortable preparing your pup's meals every day, ask your veterinarian to recommend a company that makes raw dog food in your locality.

Even though what you decide to feed your dog is a very personal decision, you should be aware that a raw diet is not appropriate for every dog. For example, a raw food diet is not recommended for dogs with health issues such as kidney and liver failure. Dogs with cancer, on chemotherapy, or dogs with other immunosuppressive diseases also should not be on a raw diet. Due to the lack of calcium and the potential for harmful bacteria, raw food is not recommended for puppies.

Making Homemade Dog Food

Is homemade dog food healthier than commercial dog food? Many pet owners assume it must be better because eating a home-cooked meal is better than chowing down on fast food, but does this hold true for your Italian Greyhound?

Many dog food recipes fall short of the nutrients needed to keep your Iggy strong and healthy, such as iron, copper, calcium, and zinc. A recent study by the University of California School of Veterinary Medicine tested more than 200 online recipes written by respected veterinarians. Unfortunately, the researchers discovered more than 90 percent of the recipes lacked essential nutrients for canine health.

One of the main advantages of preparing your own dog food is you know exactly what you are feeding your dog. Commercially made dog food is convenient and is a fantastic way to ensure your Italian Greyhound is receiving all the nutrients he needs. However, making your pup's homemade meals involves more than just throwing a bunch of ingredients into the slow cooker and hoping for the best. It involves careful planning to prepare a well-balanced and complete meal that meets all your dog's nutritional needs.

If you decide to make your dog's meals yourself, be sure to consult with your vet before switching him over to the new diet. A homemade diet is not recommended for puppies or expecting mothers.

As I mentioned before, Italian Greyhounds are high-energy dogs and need a well-balanced diet to maintain lean muscle and support their immune system. Your dog's daily diet requires protein (animal meat, seafood, dairy, eggs, and so on), fat (from animal organs or oil), and carbohydrates (grains and vegetables). Your Italian Greyhound will also need calcium from dairy products or eggshells and essential fatty acids (oils, egg yolks, oatmeal, etc.).

The following guidelines will help you create your own balanced, homemade dog food recipe:

Meat products – Protein should make up 50 to 65 percent of your Iggy's diet. As it is the main component of your dog's meal, choose organic lean meats without skin and fat. Include in your dog's diet boneless chicken, beef, and fish. Make sure the meat is cut into small pieces, as it will facilitate chewing and digestion. Incorporating up to 5 percent beef liver is a nutritious and tasty addition.

Eggs – Eggs are an excellent source of protein; however, medium-sized dogs such as your Iggy should only eat one whole egg per day.

Dairy – The majority of dogs can tolerate plain yogurt, cottage cheese, and ricotta. If your pooch suffers from lactose intolerance, try substituting dairy products with goat milk. Avoid using other types of cheese as they tend to be high in cholesterol, fats, and calories.

Starchy vegetables – Beans, peas, potatoes, squash, and sweet potatoes are all great sources of fiber for your Italian Greyhound. If your pooch is overweight, you will need to reduce the percentage of starchy vegetables in his dog food. Cook all grains, beans, and starchy vegetables to make them easier to digest.

Other vegetables – Leafy veggies are high in fiber and low in calories, plus they are full of wholesome nutrients for your pooch. Avoid using raw, cruciferous vegetables, such as broccoli and cauliflower, as they can cause digestive issues for your dog. Chop and blend the vegetables together before adding them to the meat mixture when cooking.

Fruit – Fruit supports your Iggy's digestive health and provides a long list of vitamins, nutrients, and antioxidants. Apples, bananas, berries, and papaya are all excellent options. Avoid grapes and raisins as they cause kidney failure.

Grains – Whole grains such as quinoa, barley, brown rice, oatmeal, and pasta are all excellent sources of fiber. All grains need to be well-cooked so they can be properly digested by your Italian Greyhound. Note: white rice has low nutritional value and should only be used to settle an upset tummy.

Supplements – Even the best homemade dog food recipe, using the highest-quality organic ingredients, will still lack certain nutrients such as calcium. Another reason to add supplements to your dog's homemade food is if you are freezing the food into daily portions; many nutrients are lost when food is frozen and then thawed. Closely follow the instructions on the supplement packaging for your dog's weight, size, and age. If you have doubts, talk to a pet nutritionist.

Make sure the homemade diet is working.

After your Italian Greyhound has been enjoying his homemade meals for one to two months, take him to the vet to make sure he is not gaining or losing too much weight. If your dog's weight has changed slightly, check it again in a few weeks. Your vet will regularly check your dog's coat, skin, teeth, and body condition for any issues that might be related to his homemade diet.

Are meatless diets safe for my Iggy?

Due to climate change and ethical considerations, many people have decided to become vegetarians or vegans, and they often wonder if their dogs can be vegetarian or vegan too. Can dogs be healthy on a meatless diet?

Dogs are not considered to be obligate carnivores. Obligate carnivores, such as cats, have to eat animal proteins, as their body needs the amino acids found in animal proteins. This means, theoretically, dogs can eat a plant-based diet and get amino acids from plants or produce them in their own liver. There have been a few pilot studies that have shown dogs, even high-energy dogs such as Italian Greyhounds, thrive on a meat-free diet.

One of the main side effects of meatless diets is they tend to make the dog's urine more alkaline, causing painful kidney and gallbladder stones that often need to be surgically removed. Veterinarians do not recommend feeding your dog a meatless homemade diet. Getting the right nutrients is difficult in a normal homemade dog food and almost impossible for a meatless diet.

The good news is there are quite a few meatless dog foods on the market, and more are being launched all the time. There are some great meatless diets out there that are complete and balanced. If you do not want to purchase a meatless dog food, ask a veterinary nutritionist to help you plan a balanced recipe for your dog's lifestyle and age.

Remember, if your dog has any medical conditions or is prone to an upset stomach, it is best to discuss your options first with your veterinarian.

A Basic Recipe for Homemade Dog Food

The following recipe is a healthy alternative to canned dog food, as it is loaded with iron from fresh protein and veggies. It can be stored in the fridge for up to a week or be frozen and reheated later. The recipe below is a basic guideline that you can adapt to your Italian Greyhound's personal preferences.

As mentioned before, be sure to cook all animal products thoroughly to kill any harmful bacteria, and cook all grains, starchy vegetables, and beans to make them easier for your Iggy to digest. Before switching your dog to a homemade diet, be sure to discuss your dog's specific nutritional needs with your veterinarian. Remember that switching your dog's food to homemade from kibble is a slow process, so patience is essential.

Doggy Stew

Ingredients

Total: Makes four cups (32 fluid ounces)

- 1 pound chicken or beef, without fat, skin, or bones (cut into small pieces)
- 4 oz. of beef liver, chopped
- 1 medium, steamed sweet potato, chopped
- 1/2 cup steamed green beans, chopped
- 1 cup cooked quinoa or oatmeal
- 1 cup spinach, blended with a cup of water
- 1 tbsp fish oil or coconut oil

Directions

1. Sauté the meat and liver together with the oil in a large pot until thoroughly cooked.
2. Add the rest of the ingredients and leave to simmer on low heat for 10 to 15 minutes.
3. Let cool and serve.
4. Store the leftovers in the fridge for a maximum of five days.

Weight Monitoring

Dogs, like people, have a harder time getting around if they are overweight. Losing weight can be a challenge for dogs at any age, but even more so as they get older. Despite the challenges, weight loss for dogs of any age is worth the effort. Slender pups enjoy longer lives, show fewer visible signs of aging, and have fewer chances of developing canine arthritis.

Health problems that are more common in overweight dogs include pancreatitis, diabetes, heart disease, joint pain, ruptured ligaments, hip dysplasia, compromised immune systems, and different types of cancer. If you cannot feel your Italian Greyhound's ribs and shoulder blades, if his waist is not discernible (a tuck behind his ribs), or if there is a roll of fat at the base of his tail, then it is time to face reality and put your pooch on a diet.

If in doubt, ask your vet for his professional opinion about your dog's weight.

Here are some weight loss tips for your Italian Greyhound.

Feed your dog more protein and fewer carbohydrates.

When it comes to weight loss, the ratio of carbohydrates to fats and proteins matters more than calorie counting. Iggies thrive on a high-protein diet, as it builds lean muscle and improves mood and mental agility. If your Iggy is overweight, look for a dog food that is high in protein, low in carbs, and moderate in healthy fats.

Avoid feeding your Italian Greyhound a high-fiber diet.

Fiber will not satisfy your dog and can interfere with nutrient absorption. Instead, look for dog foods that contain whole grains, such as quinoa, whole oats, and brown rice, as they are an excellent source of fiber and protein yet are low in carbohydrates.

Reduce your Iggy's portion size.

Instead of making drastic changes, start slowly by cutting back your dog's meal portion size by 5 percent. Reduce this by 5 percent every three weeks until you are giving your pooch the amount of food specified for him on the dog food package. This strategy prevents your Iggy from losing weight too fast and then gaining it back. Slow, steady weight loss means long-term success.

Measure everything your Italian Greyhound eats.

One of the reasons your Iggy is overweight is probably because you have been eyeballing his dog food. The only way to accurately measure your dog's food is either by using measuring cups or, even better, by using an electronic scale to weigh every meal. This takes a lot of discipline on your part, but you will be surprised to find that you were often feeding your dog twice as much as required. You can find a small scale at an office or kitchen supply store or online.

Make your dog's weight loss a family project.

Feeding your furry friend a smaller portion will not help him lose weight if he is getting breakfast leftovers, an afternoon snack, and/or a treat or two throughout the day. Discuss your dog's diet plan with the entire family, and be sure they cooperate. Allot each family member a certain number of training treats to give your Italian Greyhound each day, and encourage everyone to focus on calorie-free treats and rewards such as playing fetch, games, or praise.

HELPFUL TIP
Weight Management

Because of their small stature, it's easy for Italian Greyhounds to become overweight. This can be caused by lack of exercise or poor diet. Excessive use of treats is another leading cause of obesity in dogs. You can easily determine whether your dog is overweight by checking that his ribs are not visible but can be easily felt under a thin layer of flesh and that the hip bones are barely visible. Italian Greyhounds are also prone to hypothyroidism, which can be made worse by weight gain. If you're concerned that your dog is overweight, talk to your vet about an effective strategy for weight management.

Rethink the treats you give your dog.

Treats and rewards often have three to five calories, and they can quickly add up in a training session. Instead of store-bought treats, try using pieces of cut-up skinless chicken breast. Most dogs are more concerned about the number of treats they are receiving and do not notice the size of the actual treat, so cut up chewy treats into smaller pieces. Use raw baby carrots, zucchini slices, or small slices of apple, banana, or melon for a healthier treat.

CHAPTER 12

Grooming Your Italian Greyhound

Good grooming helps your Iggy feel and look his best. Routine grooming sessions give you an opportunity to examine your pup's coat, eyes, teeth, ears, and nails for any health problems.

Brushing

Adult Italian Greyhounds have beautiful, long, feathered ears and silky hair under their chest, legs, and underbelly. This must be regularly brushed to keep it clean and free of knots. Regularly brushing your dog for a few minutes at a time can accomplish a lot in terms of keeping him clean, as it removes dirt, burrs, and grass.

Get your dog accustomed to being brushed while he is standing, as a groomer would, instead of lying down. If you have a hard time remembering to brush your Iggy daily, place his brushes in a place where you will see them, such as beside the television remote.

All dogs shed, and your Italian Greyhound is no exception. By nature, Iggies do not shed too much, but excessive shedding can easily be prevented by providing your dog with a healthy diet, plenty of exercise, and fresh air. If you notice, while brushing your dog, that he is losing more hair than normal, the cause may be one of the following factors:

- Hot spots
- Sarcoptic mange
- Food-related allergies
- Parasites, such as fleas, lice, or mites

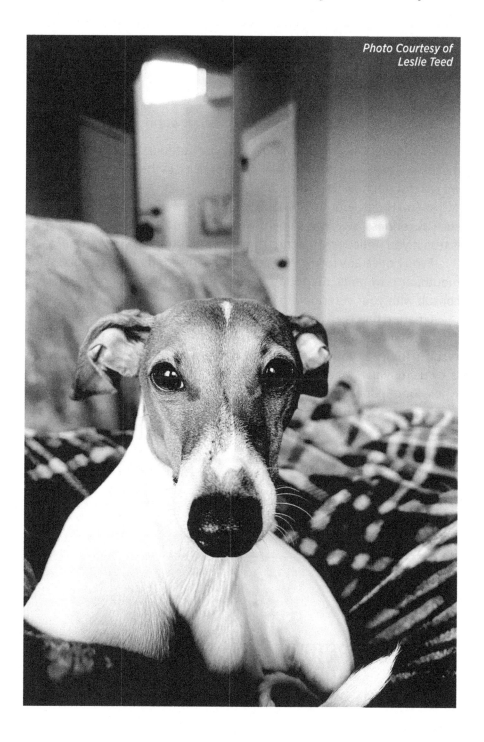

Photo Courtesy of
Leslie Teed

- An immune disorder, such as adrenal or thyroid diseases
- Cancer
- Anxiety or stress
- Pregnancy or lactation
- A bacterial or fungal infection, such as ringworm

Your Italian Greyhound will love running outdoors year-round, which means you will need to check him daily for ticks. In the following chapter, we will discuss how to remove a tick.

As you brush your pooch, look for sores, rashes, or signs of infection, such as redness, swelling, skin inflammation, and tenderness. The same is true if you notice any patches of dry, brittle skin.

If you notice any foreign objects lodged in your dog's eyes, ears, skin, mouth, or paw pads, do not attempt to remove them yourself—always consult with your veterinarian beforehand.

If matted hair is an issue, leave your household scissors in the drawer where they belong. One wrong movement by a nervous pooch could result in injury to you or your dog. The best way to remove a knot or mat is by using your fingers, some pet-friendly conditioner, a comb, and a whole lot of patience.

Bathing

> Wash your Iggy in warm, soapy water, rinse him in warm, clear water, and dry him off with a clean towel. Keep his nails trimmed and get experienced help if you have any troubles. And of course, be careful that you don't drop him or hurt him at any time, in any way.
>
> CAROL A. HARRIS
> *Bo-Bett Farm*

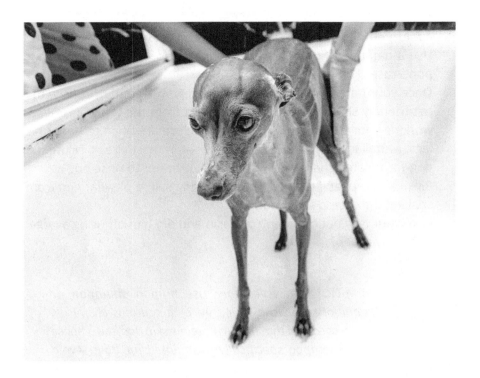

Your Iggy is an active dog and will need to be bathed at least every six weeks, sometimes more often. Regularly bathing your dog will help to keep his coat clean, short, and tangle-free.

Never spray your pooch with scents or perfumes. Dogs are very sensitive to fragrances, and most fragrances contain harmful ingredients that can make your dog very sick if he ingests them while cleaning himself. Fragrances can result in respiratory problems. The best way to keep your Italian Greyhound smelling his best is by regularly bathing him.

How to give your Iggy a bath

1. Before your Italian Greyhound's bath, take extra time to brush out any extra hair, debris, or heavy dirt. Place your pup in a large basin or tub filled with approximately four to six inches of lukewarm water.
2. Thoroughly wet your dog using a large pitcher or spray hose. If using a spray nozzle, make sure the water is neither too hot nor too cold.

3. Avoid getting water or soap in your Iggy's eyes, nose, and ears. Use a damp washcloth to remove any dirt or debris around your pup's face.

4. Once your Italian Greyhound is completely wet, gently massage the pet-friendly shampoo into his coat. Start from the top of his head, working your way down to his tail. Pay close attention to under his legs, as Italian Greyhounds tend to sweat in these areas. Dilute the dog-formulated shampoo in water so it is easier to rinse out.

5. Rinse and repeat if needed. Hold your dog still to prevent him from shaking the excess water out.

6. Take your Iggy out of the tub or basin and dry him off using a large, fluffy towel.

 REMINDER – *Never ever use human shampoo or conditioner to wash your Iggy, as it contains chemicals and fragrances that may irritate his skin. Instead, choose a high-quality shampoo specifically formulated for dogs. Avoid using inexpensive dog shampoos as they often are made with harsh ingredients.*

Since your Italian Greyhound is a water dog, he can easily confuse bath time with playtime. If your dog has a hard time standing still, ask a family member to help you.

Nail Clipping

Most Iggies are squeamish about having their nails trimmed, so do not expect it to be your favorite shared activity, no matter how many treats your pooch gets afterward.

Chances are your Italian Greyhound's nails will need to be trimmed every four to six weeks or so unless he is running around on hard surfaces such as cement that keep his nails short. A general rule of thumb: if you can hear your pup's nails clicking against the floor or his nails snag on the carpet, then it is time for a trim.

If possible, get your Iggy used to having his nails clipped at a young age by rubbing your hands up and down his legs and gently pressing down between his toes each time. Never forget to give your pooch a yummy treat, followed by a big, boisterous "Good boy!" After about two weeks of massaging your Italian Greyhound's feet, you can attempt clipping his nails. This method works especially well if your older dog is ticklish or wary about having his feet touched.

If you are unsure about how to cut your Iggy's nails, ask your veterinarian or groomer; they will gladly give you a short demonstration on how to trim his nails to the right length.

There are two different types of nail clippers—scissor-type or guillotine. Both styles come highly recommended, so choose the style you feel the most comfortable with. Another option is a nail grinder, which sands the nails down; however, it makes a loud grinding noise, and the vibration can frighten you and your dog.

Be sure to give your Italian Greyhound a vigorous workout to burn off excess energy before clipping his nails. If your dog is skittish, ask a family member to help you. There is no need to clip all your dog's nails at once; you can clip one paw at a time, with breaks in between.

How to clip your Iggy's nails

1. Hold your Iggy's foot steadily but gently as you spread out each toe. Hold the nail clipper at a slight angle, snipping from the top to the bottom. Cut off the tip of the nail. Avoid giving the nail a blunt edge; instead, follow the natural curvature of the nail.
2. Snip off the tip of the nail, avoiding the quick. The quick is the darker-colored circle inside the nail, which is the blood vein. If you accidentally cut the quick, you will have one very unhappy dog.
3. If you accidentally cut your Iggy's nail quick, use a nail cauterizer, such as cornstarch or styptic powder, which you can apply with a Q-Tip. Be sure to have a moist washcloth on hand to clean up the mess. Cutting your dog's nail quick hurts, and trust me—he will remember this unpleasant experience for a long time.
4. Once you have finished clipping your pup's nails, do not forget to generously praise your Italian Greyhound with yummy treats and a healthy scratch behind his ears.

If you are using a nail grinder to trim your Italian Greyhound's nails, follow the method above; simply hold your pup's foot and grind a little off each nail. Do not forget to trim your Iggy's dewclaws. Since they do not touch the ground, they tend to grow longer and will eventually grow back into your dog's paw, which can be very painful and may cause health complications.

If your Italian Greyhound has darker nails, you will need to be extra careful because it is almost impossible to notice the nail quick. If you have a hard time keeping your hands steady or your pooch shows aggressive behavior while getting his nails clipped, feel free to ask the groomer to clip his nails for you.

Importance of Good Dental Care

You have probably heard the expression a dog's mouth is cleaner than a human's mouth. The truth is a dog's mouth is no cleaner than a human's mouth; it just is home to an entirely different group of bacteria.

Your Italian Greyhound can develop dental issues such as tartar, plaque, and gingivitis. As if bad breath was not enough, these canine

dental problems can lead to life-threatening infections, not to mention dental extractions, which can be very costly to treat. The only way to prevent this is by practicing good oral care.

Since your Iggy cannot brush his teeth on his own, you will need to brush his teeth regularly. Older dogs can learn to be comfortable with getting their teeth brushed, but you can make things easier for yourself by starting early with your dog when he is still a puppy.

Get your pooch used to having his teeth cleaned by gently massaging his gums for about 20 to 30 seconds daily for about two weeks. Once he is comfortable with you touching his gumline, do the same procedure daily but including his teeth for another two weeks.

How to brush your Italian Greyhound's teeth

1. Place a pea-sized amount of canine toothpaste on the tip of your finger, then let your dog smell it and taste it.
2. Gently massage the toothpaste onto his gums. This will allow him to get used to the texture and the flavor.
3. Use a double-headed canine toothbrush held at a 45-degree angle to clean below the gumline.
4. Work on one spot at a time until your Iggy gets used to the feel of the toothbrush inside of his mouth.

Your pup may not be keen on getting his teeth brushed at first, but over time he will get used to it. Choose a time when he is more likely to sit still for the entire procedure, such as after a vigorous walk or a game of fetch outside.

Make sure you speak softly and soothingly throughout the entire process, and do not forget to reward your dog with a yummy treat afterward. Be cautious not to overdo it the first few times or if your pooch becomes agitated. Take your time and increase the length of each session slowly.

If brushing your pup's teeth ends with tears, hurt feelings, or blood, there are still a few other choices you can make to improve his oral health. Dry kibble is better for your Iggy's teeth than soft or wet food, as soft food can become stuck between his teeth, causing tooth decay. There are also synthetic bones and chew toys that have been specifically designed to strengthen your dog's gums and teeth.

Never use human toothpaste or mouthwash for your Italian Greyhound, as it contains fluoride, which is toxic for dogs. Look for a specially formulated toothpaste at your local pet store; often, they come in a variety of flavors such as beef, chicken, or salmon. There is also dog mouthwash that is diluted in water to kill bacteria and prevent plaque buildup.

Routine dental cleanings

No matter how disciplined you are about cleaning your Italian Greyhound's teeth, you will never really be able to give him a deep, thorough cleaning with just a toothbrush. Even if your dog has healthy teeth, it is wise to have your veterinarian give him an annual cleaning to remove any plaque and tartar buildup, clean the gum line, and polish his teeth.

Common Dental Issues in Italian Greyhounds

No matter how often you brush your pup's teeth, you should inspect the inside of his mouth at least once a week. If you notice any of the following signs, take your dog to the vet as soon as possible:

- Bad breath
- Constantly pawing at his face or mouth
- A change of eating or chewing habits
- Depression
- Excessive drooling
- Red, swollen, painful, or bleeding gums
- Bumps or growths inside the gumline
- Yellowish tartar buildup along the gumline
- Discolored, missing, or misaligned teeth

Doggy dental care may be a hassle, but regular maintenance is a money saver in the long run and may even be a lifesaver. Letting your dog's teeth deteriorate leads to expensive and painful vet visits down the road. Many dogs will need to be given anesthesia to have their teeth and gums cleaned.

Gingivitis – Gingivitis is caused by an accumulation of plaque, bacteria, and tartar around the gum. Signs are swollen, bleeding gums, and extremely bad breath. Fortunately, it can easily be cleared up with regular brushing.

Mouth tumors – Mouth tumors look like small bumps or lumps on your dog's gums. They can be extremely painful and irritating for your dog while eating or drinking water. Mouth tumors will need to be surgically removed by a vet.

Periodontal disease – This gum infection results in tooth loss and a high risk of the infection spreading throughout the body, causing all sorts of maladies. Watch out for bad breath, nasal discharge, mouth pain, lack of appetite, and loose teeth.

Proliferating gum disease – This occurs when your dog's gumline is over his teeth, causing a gum infection. It can easily be treated with antibiotics.

Salivary cysts – These are fluid-filled blisters located under your dog's tongue or along the corners of his mouth. They will need to be professionally drained and cauterized. Often the salivary gland will need to be surgically removed.

Moral of the story: keep your Italian Greyhound's teeth sparkling white, and you will both be smiling.

Paws

Your Iggy's paws are made for stomping. Your pooch uses his paws for just about everything. You need to keep your dog's paws in tip-top shape by regularly checking them for pebbles, splinters, or any other type of debris that may get stuck in there. If you find a splinter, use a pair of tweezers to gently pull it out. Regularly trim the fur between your Iggy's toes as it could become matted, making it painful for your dog to walk.

Paw pads can crack and bleed if they get too dry. Never use lotions or moisturizers designed for humans on your Italian Greyhound, as they will soften the pads, leading to further injury. Instead, use a high-quality, dog-formulated paw moisturizer on his feet. Give your pooch a paw massage by rubbing the moisturizer between the pads on his feet.

Winter paws – Winter is not only harsh on you but also on your Iggy's paws. You need to worry about frostbite or hidden debris in the snow that could cut your dog's paws.

The salt used to melt the ice can burn your pup's paw pads, causing them to become chapped or cracked. Rock salt or other ice-melting chemicals is made from toxic chemicals that could be ingested by your pooch if he licks his paws. After coming in the house from a walk, wash your dog's paws in warm water to remove excess chemicals. Using doggy booties and limiting outdoor exposure are the best options.

Summer paws – Asphalt and pavement can get hot enough to scorch your pup's paw pads. Check the ground temperature with the palm of your hand; if you cannot rest it there comfortably for 30 seconds, then the ground is definitely too hot for your dog. Paw pads can easily become burned and blistered. If the ground is too hot, stick to grass or shady places when walking your pooch.

Ears

Your Italian Greyhound's long, drooping ears allow him to catch a scent while hunting. But those adorable floppy ears can also trap water and bacteria, leading to painful ear infections. Routine preventative care will reduce your pup's chances of infection and improve the overall health of his ears.

Plucking the ear hair is the best method as it removes both the strand and the root. However, since you have not removed the hair follicle, be aware that the hair strand will grow back. It is not recommended to trim the hair strands as the shortened hairs create a trap for bacteria, yeast, and debris.

Dog ear powder – This powder is designed for plucking hairs out of your pup's ears. The powder lets you grip the strands and makes for easier removal.

Hemostat – A hemostat is an essential tool designed to grip your Iggy's ear hairs; it is similar to a pair of tweezers but sturdier. It is not recommended to extract the hair strand using your fingers, as it will not extract the hair root. Plus, pulling the hair out with your fingers will be more painful for your dog.

How to pluck hairs from your Italian Greyhound's ears

1. Choose a moment when both you and your pup are relaxed, such as when your dog has burned off some of his access energy with a vigorous walk or a game of fetch.
2. Position your dog so you have a clear view inside of his ear. Gently bend back the ear leather, sprinkle a light dusting of dog ear powder in the ear, and using a disinfected hemostat tool, grip a few hairs, lock, and quickly pull up.

*Photo Courtesy of
Patti Bryan*

3. Only pluck hairs you can see, as digging around in your dog's ear can cause more damage than good. Therefore, only pull out what you can easily see and grab.
4. Throughout the entire process, use a soft, calming voice, and be sure to reward your Iggy afterward with a nice, yummy treat.

Never insert a Q-Tip in your Italian Greyhound's ears, as it could easily slip deeper in the canal, causing injury. Another word of caution: do not clean your pup's ears too often, as they could become irritated or infected.

How to clean your Iggy's ears

1. If your Italian Greyhound's ears appear to be dirty or waxy, use a small piece of gauze or a cotton ball dampened in mineral oil or a liquid ear cleaner formulated for dogs.
2. Gently fold back your pup's ear and carefully wipe away any ear wax or debris you can see.
3. Instead of rubbing the ear to remove the debris or ear wax, gently wipe it away.

Most Italian Greyhounds need to have this type of ear cleaning every two to three weeks to keep bacteria and ear infections at bay.

Regularly check your Italian Greyhound's ears if you notice any of the following symptoms.

- Brownish or yellowish discharge
- Red and swollen inner ear canal
- Hearing loss
- Excessive shaking of the head or tilting to the side
- Scabby skin around the ear flap
- Strong odor emanating from the ear
- Loss of balance
- Ear scratching or wiping ears on the floor or rubbing ears against the furniture

Photo Courtesy of
Tara Hannum

If you notice a brownish or black buildup of earwax (that looks like coffee grounds) in your Italian Greyhound's ear, he could have microscopic ear mites. Be sure to make an appointment with your vet as soon as possible.

Eyes

Regularly check your Iggy's eyes. Have your dog sit in a well-lit part of the house, preferably with natural light. Your dog's eyes should appear bright and clear, and the area surrounding the pupil should be white and not yellow. There should be no crusty discharge at the corner of his eyes. Using your thumb, gently pull down the lower part of your dog's eyelid to observe the inner lining; it should be a pale pink color and not red or white.

On a daily basis, use a clean, damp cotton ball or dog-formulated eye wipe to wipe any gunk away from your dog's eyes. Be careful not to touch your dog's eyeballs. If recommended by your vet, you can use canine eye drops to get rid of tearstains on your Italian Greyhound's face.

The following symptoms are clear indications your Iggy may have an eye infection.

- Crusty gunk and discharge around the corners of his eyes
- Cloudiness
- Swollen eyelid
- Unequal pupil size
- No desire to open his eyes
- Teary eyes and tearstains

Keep the hair around your Italian Greyhound's eyes trimmed. Use a small pair of scissors, like cuticle scissors, to minimize the risk of injuring your dog. Long hair around the eyes can accidentally poke or scratch the pupils. Air conditioners will dry out your dog's eyes, causing irritation and possibly infection.

Anal Glands

Italian Greyhounds are prone to anal gland problems; unfortunately, this condition can cause painful sores around the anus. Both female and male Iggies have a pair of anal glands found under the skin that surrounds your dog's anal muscles. Often, they are referred to as scent glands, odor glands, or stinky glands.

These glands hold an oily substance that is released in minute amounts when one dog meets another, which explains why dogs sniff each other's rear ends. The anal scent tells the other dog the unfamiliar dog's gender, health, and general mood. Also, the oily substance is released every time your dog has a bowel movement.

Often, when a dog is scooting his rear end on the ground after having a bowel movement, the anal sacs are engorged (swollen). Your Italian Greyhound will need your help to express his anal glands; otherwise, they could become infected or even break open and will need to be treated by your veterinarian.

How to tell if your Italian Greyhound needs his anal glands expressed

- Scooting his rear end on the ground
- Excessively licking or biting his butt
- Red, swollen skin around his anus
- Bleeding or discharge from around the anus

Most Italian Greyhound owners prefer to ask their groomer or vet to express their dog's anal glands. If your dog's anal glands have not been expressed in quite some time, and the oily substance has become solid (impacted), then your veterinarian will need to sedate your dog for the extraction as it is very painful.

Anal glands are expressed in a similar fashion as you would pop a pimple, but due to the location and the discomfort your dog is experiencing, it can be a challenge.

How to express your Italian Greyhound's anal glands at home

To begin, you will need a pair of disposable latex gloves, Vaseline or a similar lubricant, paper towels, a warm, soapy washcloth, and someone to help you restrain your Iggy. The smell is not for the faint of heart.

1. Place your dog on the table with his rear end facing you. Your dog should be standing on all fours. Have your helper gently restrain the dog by placing one arm underneath and around your dog's neck and the other arm hugging your dog's body.
2. Put on latex gloves and lubricate your index finger.
3. Lift your Italian Greyhound's tail and insert your index finger about one inch into his rectum.
4. Place your thumb on the outside of your dog's anus. Using your thumb and index finger, feel for a firm pea-sized object. The anal glands should be located at the four o'clock position and the other at the seven o'clock position.
5. Once you have located the anal glands, using your other hand, place a paper towel in front of your dog's anus, as the glands tend to squirt outward. Using light pressure, gently milk the anal glands. When you can barely feel the gland, it is completely expressed.
6. Follow the same procedure with the other gland.
7. Once you are finished draining both anal sacs, use the warm, soapy washcloth to clean the area.
8. Reward your dog with some treats and lots of praise.

Professional Grooming

Grooming your Italian Greyhound may seem like an easy way to save money and bond with your pooch. But the grooming process is not for everyone, as it takes time, patience, and it is a whole lot trickier than it sounds. Thankfully, there is a stress-free option! Professional groomers have the skills and expertise to make sure your pooch gets a trim and bath. After all, your furry friend deserves to be pampered.

There are pros and cons associated with taking your dog to a professional groomer. Here is the nitty-gritty:

ADVANTAGES

- Professional groomers have years of experience and can groom your dog in less time than you.
- Groomers use professional equipment and tools, ensuring a top-notch job.
- Groomers provide specialized treatments, such as de-shedding.
- Groomers provide a quick medical exam, and upon request, they will pluck and clean your Iggy's ears and express his anal glands.
- Most groomers include nail trimming.

DISADVANTAGES

- The cost can add up, especially if your pooch gets groomed every six to eight weeks.
- Some Italian Greyhounds suffer from anxiety and stress from being left alone at the groomers for two to three hours.
- Finding the perfect groomer for your Italian Greyhound takes time.
- Transporting your dog to and from the groomer may be troublesome if he does not enjoy long car rides.

In the end, the decision to use a professional groomer or not depends on your personal preference and situation. Ask yourself if you have the time and patience to groom your Iggy yourself or if you can afford to send him regularly to the groomer.

Many dog owners prefer combining both methods in order to save money, and in the meantime, they can gain experience grooming their dogs themselves at home. For example, they may get their dog professionally groomed once every four to five months, and in between, they will do minor grooming touch-ups and baths.

Before you choose a groomer, take the time to research your options. Ask friends and colleagues for recommendations. Once you have narrowed down your options, be sure to ask the groomer the following questions to get a better picture of their operation. Feel free to ask any other questions that concern the well-being of your Italian Greyhound.

Can I see your facility?

The grooming facility should be clean, well-ventilated, and modern. The washtubs and tables should be sturdy. As you observe the facility, ask yourself if you feel comfortable leaving your furry companion there. If the groomer is standoffish and refuses to let you into the facility, move on to the next option on your list.

HELPFUL TIP
To Brush or Not to Brush?

Italian Greyhounds' short fur coat is not prone to excessive tangles and knots, but that doesn't mean you don't need to brush them at all. Detangling is just one of the roles of brushing. A good-quality brush will help remove dirt and excess dander as well as dead hair. When choosing a brush for your Italian Greyhound, look for a slicker brush to gently remove excess hair and dirt.

Do they have liability?

Any reputable groomer will have liability insurance, as they will be a registered business. Using a groomer with liability coverage will give you peace of mind if your Iggy has an unfortunate accident while in the groomer's care, as any medical expenses incurred will be covered.

What is the total cost?

Never assume that one groomer will charge the same as another. Always ask what services are included in a basic grooming. Groomers often charge different fees depending on the dog's size, coat, and temperament. Often groomers offer discounts for regular dog clients.

What type of training have they received?

Many groomers are self-trained. Be sure to look for a groomer who has been professionally trained through an apprenticeship, etc. Ask the groomer how long they have been professionally grooming dogs and if they have experience grooming Italian Greyhounds.

CHAPTER 13

Preventative Medical Care

By making your Italian Greyhound's health a priority, you will avoid many medical problems and increase the well-being of your furry friend. Get the facts about preventive care, vaccines, parasites, and alternative medical treatments to enhance your dog's quality of life.

Choosing Your Italian Greyhound's Veterinarian

Choosing a reputable veterinarian for your Iggy should not be taken lightly.

Before you start checking out different veterinary clinics in your locality, make a list of your priorities for your Italian Greyhound. This will help you narrow down your options when choosing a vet and help you ask the right questions. Consider your dog's age, family history (if known), and any health concerns. For example, if your furry friend is getting older, look for a vet who specializes in geriatric care.

Here is a basic checklist of essential requirements for veterinarians (requirements may vary depending on your dog's needs):

- Proximity to your house – If there is an emergency, can you get to the veterinary clinic quickly?
- Pricing – Every veterinary clinic has different prices; make sure the clinic you choose fits your budget.
- Do the clinic's hours work with your work schedule, or will you need to take time off to take your Italian Greyhound there?

- Does it have up-to-date facilities with cutting-edge medical technologies and care?
- Check for generous appointment times, as you do not want to feel rushed during the visit.
- A smaller practice means you will most likely see the same vet every time you visit, plus your Italian Greyhound can develop a rapport with the medical staff.
- Does the staff have knowledge of alternative and holistic treatments?
- Is the staff involved in the local animal welfare community, such as pet rescue organizations?

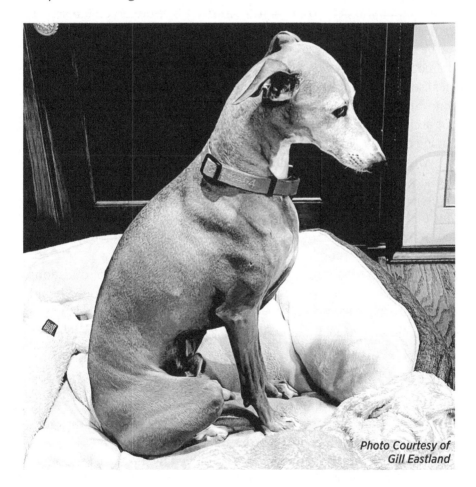

Photo Courtesy of
Gill Eastland

Once you have narrowed down what you want from a veterinarian, it is time to search for a few candidates. The best place to start is by word of mouth. Ask fellow dog owners whose pet care philosophies are in line with your own about their vets. Or ask a friend or family member for recommendations. Many veterinarian clinics offer a referral program, which means discounts for you and your friend who referred you.

If you are new to an area, you can check the American Animal Hospital Association (AAHA) website; you will find a list of accredited veterinarians in your locality, as well as an evaluation of the facility, staff, patient care, and equipment.

Whether you get a referral from a friend or from an online search, you will want to make sure the veterinarian clinic is accredited by the AAHA. The AAHA regularly evaluates veterinary practices throughout the United States on their standard for patient care, pain management, facilities, surgery, medical records, cleanliness, anesthesiology, and more. Unfortunately, veterinary clinics are not required to be accredited by law, but accreditation shows you their philosophies are committed to maintaining only the highest standard of care or service.

When you finally narrow the list down to one or two veterinary practices, you should ask to take a tour of the facility. Any reputable vet will be more than happy to show you around and make you feel comfortable. One of the main aspects to observe is if the staff is caring, calm and courteous. Another important aspect is the cleanliness of the lobby, waiting rooms, and exam rooms.

In addition to getting a feel for the facility, ask plenty of questions. Vets appreciate when pet owners are interested in their pet's health and well-being.

Here are some questions you should ask when interviewing the vet.

- How are overnight patients monitored?
- Are all diagnostic tests, like blood work, ultrasounds, X-rays, etc., done on-site or in another referred location?
- Are all the veterinary technicians employed by the clinic licensed by the state to practice on animals?

- Does the facility refer patients to specialists if needed? (Their answer should be affirmative.)
- What types of payment plans does the practice accept? Are there special payment plans for major surgeries or treatments?

The questions above are simply a guideline. Feel free to ask any other questions that concern you and your Italian Greyhound.

The in-person visit should leave you with a positive feeling about the practice and the staff. Communication is a vital part of quality health care for your Iggy, as he cannot explain to the doctor where it hurts; it is up to you to do the talking. So, you need to feel comfortable asking the vet questions.

Once you have chosen a vet, be a good client. Show up early for appointments to allot time to fill out any necessary paperwork, etc. Be your Italian Greyhound's advocate, but know when to step back and let the vet take over. Be patient; emergencies may take precedence over routine appointments.

If you have problems with your vet, do not hesitate to switch facilities. Veterinary clinics expect clients to come and go. However, before you depart, be sure to request a complete copy of your Iggy's medical file. You can ask that your dog's health records be faxed or mailed to either you or the new vet.

Microchipping

Each year, more than eight million pets end up in a shelter across the country, and fewer than 20 percent are reclaimed.

A microchip is about the size of a grain of rice. It is implanted in your Iggy's neck and your dog will not even notice it is there. The average cost to get your dog microchipped is around $30 to $50, depending on your vet.

Generally, the entire process takes only a few seconds or about the time it takes to give your dog an injection. It will take more time for you to fill out all the paperwork involved than it will to insert the microchip! Microchipping does not necessarily have to be completed by a vet, but it is highly recommended you use a vet's service.

If your dog is squeamish around injections and needles, you might want to consider getting him chipped at the same time he is being neutered. Most pet owners opt to have their pooches chipped when they are spayed or neutered for this very reason. The pain is similar to using a needle to draw blood; some dogs flinch, while others do not.

If your Italian Greyhound happens to get lost, he may have on his collar and ID tags, but if your dog is a victim of theft, the thief will most likely remove the collar and ID tags and toss them in the trash. Whereas, with a microchip, the people who find your dog can take him in to be scanned either at a local shelter or vet's office, so you can be reunited with your Iggy. Or if someone else says your dog is their dog because they purchased it from the thief, you can prove the dog is yours.

Pet doors can be programmed to recognize your dog's microchip, letting him come into the house but keeping other animals outside. However, a microchip will not prevent your Italian Greyhound from being accidentally hit by a car, so never let him run loose.

One of the biggest misconceptions about microchips is that your dog can be tracked. In order to know your Iggy's whereabouts, the chip will need to be scanned. Trust me, you will never regret getting your dog chipped, but if your pooch gets lost, you will always regret that you did not.

Neutering and Spaying

There are numerous caring and health-conscious reasons to spay or neuter your furry canine friend.

Spaying is a simple surgical procedure performed by your veterinarian that involves removing your female dog's ovaries and uterus. Here are some reasons why you should consider spaying your Italian Greyhound:

- Spaying reduces the risk of urinary infections and breast cancer. It is highly recommended to spay your Iggy before her first heat to prevent health complications in the future.
- If your unspayed Italian Greyhound accidentally mates with a larger dog, her uterus may be too small to accommodate the litter and could rupture, causing serious injury. Spaying limits this risk.

- Spaying prevents unwanted pregnancies, which saves you from unplanned expenses.
- A spayed dog will not go into heat. A female dog in heat will urinate all over the house and yowl loudly while trying to attract a mate.

*Photo Courtesy of
Caroline Blackwood*

Neutering is a simple surgical procedure performed by your veterinarian that involves removing your male dog's testicles. Here are some reasons why you should consider neutering your Italian Greyhound:

- Neutering prevents testicular cancer.
- Your Iggy will not roam about the neighborhood in search of a mate. An unneutered male dog will do everything in his power to find a mate, including digging a hole under the fence or running across a busy highway.
- A neutered dog will be less aggressive and better behaved than an unneutered dog. Also, he will not have the desire to mark his territory by spraying urine everywhere.

Neutered and spayed Italian Greyhounds are both much better behaved as they will focus their undivided attention on their human family instead of finding a mate. Many aggression issues are eliminated when your pet is neutered or spayed.

Many concerns you may have about getting your dog spayed or neutered are just misinformation. Consider the following:

Will your dog feel remorse or loss? No. Dogs do not suffer from emotional insecurities or experience societal pressures to have a family like humans do. They do not need to procreate to feel emotionally fulfilled.

Does spaying or neutering cause obesity? Contrary to popular opinion, spaying and neutering will not make your Iggy fat. However, a lack of exercise and over-feeding will.

Are there negative side effects? As with all surgical procedures, there are certain risks, but these are minor and rare, and often occur when the procedure is not performed by a reputable veterinarian.

Many states have established low-cost programs for spaying or neutering, which makes these types of surgeries an affordable option for all pet owners. The webpage for the Humane Society will provide you with a list of local, affordable clinics and funding options to help you cover the cost of the procedure. If you are not planning on professionally breeding your pooch, then you should definitely consider getting your Iggy neutered or spayed.

Vaccinations

Vaccinating your Italian Greyhound is a necessity if you want to give him a long and healthy life. Your veterinarian will help you determine a vaccine regimen for your Iggy by taking into consideration his health, lifestyle, and the area where you live.

Vaccinations are designed to help your dog fight off organisms that cause diseases. Vaccines are made up of antigens, which the immune system identifies as the same disease-ridden organism, but without actually causing your dog to become sick. When the vaccine is introduced into the body, it instructs the immune system how to fight off the real virus in its entirety, hence building antibodies.

The AAHA recommends all dogs receive core vaccines throughout their lives. Your veterinarian may recommend other noncore vaccines depending on geography, lifestyle, and current prevalence of the disease. For example, a noncore vaccine for kennel cough is required for dogs who frequent doggie daycare, a kennel, grooming facilities, and so on.

Puppies – A puppy's mother will pass on antibodies while nursing her pups. When puppies are six to eight weeks of age, they will receive a series of three core vaccines administered by a veterinarian at three-to-four-week intervals. The final dose should be administered when your Italian Greyhound is 16 weeks of age.

Adult dogs – Depending on your Iggy's lifestyle, he will require annual vaccines or booster shots every two to three years.

Rabies – It is mandatory throughout the United States

FUN FACT

Italian Greyhound Health Foundation (IGHF)

The Italian Greyhound Health Foundation (IGHF) is a 501(c)(3) nonprofit whose mission is to fund research and educate the public about genetic diseases to which Italian Greyhounds are predisposed. Some of the diseases of interest to the IGHF include progressive retinal atrophy (PRA), glaucoma, and enamel hypoplasia. For more information about this organization, visit the Italian Greyhound Club of America website at www.italiangrey-hound.org.

for all dogs to be vaccinated against rabies. However, each state and county have different laws regarding the administration of rabies vaccines. For example, some states require an annual vaccine, while others mandate doses once every three years.

The majority of dogs experience no side effects from being vaccinated. However, there are exceedingly rare cases of severe side effects. Reactions are often short-lived and rarely require veterinary care. Here is a list of common reactions:

- Lack of appetite
- Sluggishness
- Vomiting
- Swelling, pain, redness, or hair loss around the injection site
- Fever
- Diarrhea

Schedule your Italian Greyhound's vaccinations when you will be around to monitor him for a few days. If your dog experiences any severe symptoms, like seizures, difficulty breathing, or lameness, call your vet as soon as possible.

Internal Parasites

Internal parasites may be parasites or worms. The idea of your dog having creepy crawlies moving about inside his internal organs is always unpleasant. But understanding the symptoms, risks, and treatment options is part of being a responsible puppy parent.

If internal parasites or worms in dogs are left untreated, they can cause serious, long-term health problems for your pooch. These types of parasites can be passed to your dog from contaminated soil or other dogs' stool, and certain types of worms may even infect humans.

There are five main types of worms that commonly affect Italian Greyhounds: hookworms, whipworms, heartworms, roundworms, and tapeworms. By familiarizing yourself with these common parasites you will learn how to keep your dog safe. While each parasite affects dogs differently, there are some general warning signs that your Iggy may have parasites:

- Abdominal pain
- Vomiting
- Diarrhea that lasts longer than twenty-four hours
- Unexplained weight loss
- Pot-bellied appearance
- Extreme lethargy
- Dehydration
- Poor coat appearance, hair loss, or hot spots
- Coughing

Here are some common internal parasites that may affect your dog.

Roundworms – Roundworms are one of the most common types of internal parasites in dogs and can be transmitted to humans. Many puppies are born with roundworms as they are passed on from their mother. Roundworms can be diagnosed by your vet with a small fecal sample and treated with deworming medications. If left untreated, roundworms can cause your puppy to become anemic, retard his growth, and may be fatal in some cases.

Whipworms – Whipworms live in the large intestine and colon. Dogs can become infected by whipworms by consuming an infested substance, such as fecal matter, soil, food, water, or animal flesh. Eggs can survive in soil for up to five years, which is another reason to clean up after your pooch when he relieves himself. Severe cases of whipworms can cause weight loss, inflammation, diarrhea, and anemia. Often, three-monthly treatments will be required to eliminate whipworms.

Tapeworms – Tapeworms are intestinal parasites that are often transmitted through a flea bite or when a dog consumes dead animals or fleas infested with tapeworms. When a dog consumes a flea infested with tapeworm eggs, the egg will attach itself to the dog's intestines and hatch. Infected dogs may scoot their rear end on the ground.

Photo Courtesy of
Tara Hannum

Often, pieces of the tapeworm may break off and resemble small pieces of rice in a dog's stool. If you suspect your Italian Greyhound has tapeworms, take a stool sample to your vet for diagnosis. Treatment involves an oral medicine, an injection, and fumigating your house for fleas. Infected fleas may infect humans.

Hookworms – Hookworms can be fatal in puppies if left untreated. There are several types of hookworms that attach themselves to the dog's intestinal wall to gorge themselves on blood, causing anemia. Your dog can get hookworms from ingesting contaminated fecal matter, or they can be passed on to puppies through their mother's milk. Humans can become infected with hookworms. Treatment involves a deworming medication, which will need to be administered twice.

Heartworms – Heartworms are transmitted through a mosquito bite but can be easily prevented by giving your dog regular heartworm medication. Heartworms grow and multiply at an extraordinary rate inside your dog's heart, causing heart disease, heart failure, organ damage, and ultimately a painful death. Mosquitos carrying the heartworm parasite can be found in all 50 states.

The best approach to heartworms is prevention, as treating heartworms is extremely expensive and can have serious side effects. Also, treating heartworms requires keeping your dog confined without exercise for long periods of time in order to prevent heart damage. Even if your dog is regularly taking heartworm preventives, he will need to be tested regularly for worms.

How to diagnose worms

Some internal parasites, such as tapeworms, may be observed in your dog's fecal matter. However, most parasites will need to be diagnosed by your vet via a microscopic examination of the stool sample. If your dog exhibits any of the symptoms listed above, your vet will ask you to bring in a stool sample. Even if there are no symptoms, it is wise to take a stool sample with you to your dog's annual check-up.

Your vet will set up a regular deworming schedule for your Iggy to treat different types of intestinal parasites, as well as preventive heartworm medication. The bottom line—prevention, flea control, and regular testing are the best actions to prevent consequences caused by internal parasites.

Fleas and Ticks

Your Italian Greyhound's soft, warm coat provides the ideal environment to harbor ticks and fleas. These insects feed on your dog's blood and may cause health problems ranging from allergic reactions to serious, life-threatening illnesses caused by a tick bite. Despite the fact that fleas and ticks are more common during the warmer months, you will need to ward them off year-round.

Fleas – One of the most common external parasites, fleas not only affect your dog but can also invade your house. These blood-sucking insects have the ability to jump almost three feet and can survive in even the harshest environments. An average life span for a flea may be anywhere from 12 days to an entire year. During that time, they can produce millions of baby fleas, which will produce even more offspring.

Symptoms your Iggy has fleas

- Hair loss
- Allergic dermatitis
- Flea droppings can be found throughout your Italian Greyhound's coat. Use a fine-toothed comb, especially around his abdomen, ears, mouth, and tail. Flea droppings look like tiny dirt particles or sand.
- Flea eggs look like white grains of sand.
- Excessive biting, licking or scratching
- Hot spots or scabs

Fleas are expert stowaways. They quickly attach themselves to animals while outside or can jump from one dog to another. If not controlled, fleas can invade your house within a day or two.

If not controlled, fleas can cause serious health complications for their host. For example, a flea consumes approximately 15 times its body weight in blood each day, causing your Iggy to become anemic. Some dogs have an allergic reaction to flea bites, which is called allergic dermatitis.

If your Italian Greyhound has fleas, all your resident pets will need to be treated. Also, your indoor environment will need to be fumigated to kill any pesky fleas and their eggs. Your veterinarian will be able to confirm your suspicions of a flea infestation and most likely will suggest one or two of the following treatments:

- Oral or topical treatment or dog-formulated shampoo for your Iggy.
- Thoroughly cleaning your house, including bedding, rugs and upholstery. A severe infestation will require professional help, which means you and all your pets will have to temporarily evacuate your home.
- If your puppy gets re-infested every time he goes into the backyard, you may need to fumigate your lawn.

Flea prevention

- Wash your Italian Greyhound's bedding at least once a week in hot, soapy water and brush him using a flea brush.
- Rake up any grass clippings or leaves in your backyard, as fleas tend to conceal themselves in dark, moist areas.
- There are preventive flea-control measures available either by prescription or over the counter. Be aware some flea collars can be carcinogenic for animals and humans. Always consult with your vet beforehand.

Ticks

Ticks are considered parasites as they feed on the host's blood. Ticks are experts at concealing themselves by burrowing into their hosts and then gorging on their blood. Ticks can transmit a long list of serious diseases. Transmission varies by certain areas and climates. Ask your vet what types of ticks are in your locality.

Ticks are most active during late spring and early summer. Ticks prefer to burrow into their host's head, neck, ears, and feet but can be found in other places. Ticks jump from one animal to another.

How to check your Iggy for ticks

Ticks are about the size of a pinhead and are often not noticed until they bite your dog and begin to swell up with blood. If you live in an area where ticks are prevalent, be sure to regularly check your dog. Carefully run your fingers through his coat, paying extra attention to warm spots, such as inside his ears, on his feet, and on his head. Repeat this every time he comes inside from playing outside.

Health complications caused by ticks:

- Blood loss and anemia
- Tick paralysis
- Allergic dermatitis
- Lyme disease – Deer ticks are the primary carrier of Lyme disease, which causes depression, fever, loss of appetite, painful joints, and kidney failure; it needs to be treated with antibiotics.

If you find a tick attached to your Italian Greyhound, it is important to be careful when removing it, as the tick's blood could infect your dog or you if you accidentally come into contact with it.

Follow these instructions to safely remove the tick.

1. Prepare a glass jar with rubbing alcohol inside; this is where you will place the tick. This allows you to take the tick in for testing at your veterinary clinic. Put on latex gloves and ask a family member to distract your Iggy while you extract the tick.
2. Using a pair of disinfected tweezers, gently grasp the tick as close as you can to the dog's skin. Pull straight up using even pressure, then place the tick into the jar with rubbing alcohol. Do not twist the tick out, as this could leave the head attached inside the dog or cause the tick to regurgitate infected fluids.
3. Disinfect the bitten area and the tweezers; wash your hands with warm, soapy water afterward. Monitor the area for the next few weeks for any signs of an infection. If there is a sign of infection, take your Italian Greyhound and the tick to the veterinarian for a check-up.

Photo Courtesy of Lisa Sholes

Many products used to treat or prevent fleas are also useful in killing ticks.

Keep your yard tick-free by keeping the grass cut and by removing any large weeds that could be hiding places.

Holistic Alternatives to Conventional Veterinary Medicine

Holistic veterinary care is a new term that can easily be misunderstood. Often holistic care is combined with conventional medicine to treat injury or disease and to aid the dog's healing process. For example, if your Italian Greyhound had surgery for a hip replacement, he will need to take medications to fight off infection. But some veterinarians recommend using a holistic treatment such as acupuncture or massage to naturally ease the pain and hasten the healing process.

Below you can find a list of some of the most popular holistic treatments used by concerned pet parents. Some of these treatments have been scientifically proven. If you have doubts or questions as to what type of treatment is best suited for your Iggy, be sure to discuss the options with your veterinarian to find the best treatment for your dog.

Canine acupuncture

Acupuncture uses needles to stimulate pressure points to release the buildup of certain chemicals in the muscles, spinal cord, and brain, thus promoting better health. There is plenty of anecdotal proof that acupuncture can relieve dogs of joint and muscle pain, encourage healing post-surgery, and even treat cancer or trauma.

Hydrotherapy

Hydrotherapy, in layman's terms, means physical therapy in water. This type of therapy is highly recommended for dogs in need of low-impact exercise due to joint pain caused by arthritis or recovery from an injury or surgery. Hydrotherapy is proven to build muscle, improve mobility, decrease stress, and increase circulation.

Chinese herbal medicine

Chinese herbal medicine has mastered the art of combining certain herbs to relieve pain, improve and restore organ function, and strengthen the immune system. Many pet owners rave about Chinese herbal medicine as they have seen their pups' physical and emotional states improve with the use of the herbs. As with all herbs, make sure they are safe to use alongside your dog's conventional medications, such as blood thinners or diuretics.

Magnetic field therapy

According to the Veterinary Clinics of America, magnetic therapy is gaining popularity in the United States to treat illness and injury; however, there is not much evidence that the application of magnets can heal your Italian Greyhound. Magnet field therapy is affordable, non-invasive, and has virtually no side effects.

Canine massage

Canine massage encourages healing, improves circulation, stimulates nerves, relieves stress, and relaxes your dog's muscles. One of the biggest advantages of a doggy massage is that it makes your pooch feel good and strengthens the bond between a person and the dog. Massages will not cure your Iggy's cancer or injury; they will, however, make him feel relaxed and loved.

Nutritional supplements

Nutritional supplements are required if you are feeding your dog a homemade or raw diet. Look for nutritional supplements that include calcium, omega fatty acids, vitamins, and amino acids.

When choosing a holistic treatment or supplement for your dog, be sure to use good judgment and always consult with your veterinarian to see if the treatment will help your dog. Note: just because herbal supplements state they are healthy and beneficial does not mean that they are harmless. Always thoroughly research a product before giving it to your dog.

Dog Depression

Dogs, like humans, experience depression. However, they cannot simply tell us that they are feeling sad or depressed. Currently, there is not as much research about dog depression as there is for humans, but there is plenty of unofficial data pointing to the fact that dog depression does exist.

Often doggy depression is obvious, such as when your Iggy sleeps all day in the dark corner of the laundry room when another furry friend dies. Other symptoms may not be so straightforward, as your dog may be moping around the house after a move to a new area.

How can you tell if your Italian Greyhound has canine depression? You will be surprised to discover many of the symptoms are quite similar to humans.

Changes in appetite – Some pups lose interest in food when they become extremely sad, and they may start losing weight. Alternatively, other dogs may use food as a type of solace when they are feeling blue, which leads to weight gain.

Sleeping all day long – Iggies love to sleep, especially when they are snuggled up beside you on the couch. However, if you notice your pooch continues to sleep long after you get home, barely reacting to your presence, then it is a warning sign something is wrong. If you cannot find any physical problems, then your dog may be depressed.

Lack of interest – If your Italian Greyhound begins to lose interest in activities that he used to love, such as playing fetch or going for walks, then take note. Dogs who begin to slow down or lose interest in everyday activities may be experiencing canine depression.

Excessive licking – Excessive paw licking may be a sign of deep-rooted psychological issues. Research has proven that dogs will lick or chew their paws to comfort themselves.

Avoidance and hiding – When your dog hides, it can be one of two things—illness or injury (with depression being included under the illness category). If your dog is avoiding his human family and hiding, it could mean that something is upsetting him. If there is no physical reason, then it is emotional.

Never assume your Iggy is depressed. First, get your veterinarian to rule out any physical or medical reasons causing his change in behavior. Then, if medical issues are ruled out, your vet will give you suggestions to help your furry friend beat the blues.

Pet Insurance

No matter how cautious you are with your Italian Greyhound, unwanted accidents happen—and often they are expensive.

Veterinary costs are higher than ever. According to the American Pet Product Association, dog owners spend an average of $248 for annual check-ups. What happens when the unexpected occurs? Costs can add up even more! For example, a typical corrective surgical procedure, such as removing cataracts in a senior dog, can cost $1,200 and up. Foreign body removal can cost a whopping $3,600 without insurance.

Pet insurance can help to defray these costs. Currently, more than 15 different insurance companies in the United States offer pet insurance, but less than 1 percent of dog owners purchase this type of insurance.

Here are a few benefits and drawbacks of pet insurance.

> **PROS**

- Gives you peace of mind knowing you have the resources for any unforeseen medical costs if your Iggy becomes injured or ill.
- Pet insurance gives vets the opportunity to give your pooch top-notch care without having to worry about incurring too many medical costs for you.
- Pet insurance helps your dog live a longer and healthier life, as you will not hesitate to take your dog in for medical treatment before his condition worsens.

◄ **CONS** ◄

- Some insurance companies look at factors such as the dog's age, whether he is a purebred or a designer breed dog, and the dog's living environment. Depending on these factors, the monthly insurance could increase.
- Many insurance companies have a waiting period, such as a 48-hour period before approving accident insurance and a 14-day waiting period before approval for treating illnesses.
- Depending on the fine print of the insurance plan, it may exclude pre-existing illnesses, pregnancy and/or birth, routine vaccines, and dental maintenance.
- The majority of pet insurance plans require you pay for the entire veterinary cost up front and, afterward, submit a claim for reimbursement.

The final price of pet insurance depends on the age of your Italian Greyhound and the type of coverage you choose. Pet insurance works similarly to human health insurance. Once you choose a plan that works for you and your Iggy, you can expect to pay a monthly premium of about $20 to $50. The deductible depends on the insurance plan you choose.

NOTE: *Your pet insurance will be void if your Iggy is not up to date on his vaccinations and deworming. Also, if your dog gets sick from something that is preventable by being vaccinated, most insurance companies will not cover the expenses.*

Unfortunately, there is no right or wrong answer regarding whether or not you should buy pet insurance for your Italian Greyhound. If you do opt to purchase the coverage, as with all insurance plans, be sure to read the fine print very carefully.

Consider Self-Insuring

If you feel pet insurance is too costly for your monthly budget, then another practical option is to set up a personal savings account for your

Italian Greyhound. You can always deposit an established amount into the account on a monthly basis and only withdraw from it for medical care for your dog. This is only a good option if you are disciplined with money.

The bottom line—veterinary care can add up quickly, especially if your pooch needs costly diagnostics, care, and treatment. If you decide to purchase pet insurance, be sure to read the fine print to understand exactly what you are getting yourself into.

CHAPTER 14

Breed-Specific Diseases

All dogs, purebred and mixed breeds, are prone to diseases and abnormalities which may be genetic. Your purebred Italian Greyhound is no exception.

Many of these health issues can be unapparent to the average person for years and can only be detected by a medical screening performed by a veterinarian.

Understanding some of the health problems that may affect your Italian Greyhound can help you take precautions to avoid future troubles. For example, if a certain dog breed has an inherent risk for intervertebral disc problems, then precautions can be taken to avoid having him running up and down the stairs or jumping off the furniture.

Common Hereditary Diseases and Illnesses for Italian Greyhounds

By purchasing your Iggy from a reputable breeder, you will be able to verify the health of at least up to three generations of your puppy's family health. However, if your pooch was adopted from a shelter, he most likely will not come with a pedigree ensuring a clean health background, so it will be even more useful to be aware of which breed-related health problems to watch out for.

Photo Courtesy of
Amaya Asante

Acral Mutilation Syndrome

Acral mutilation syndrome (AMS) is a serious but very rare hereditary disease. AMS causes progressive degeneration of the sensory neurons of the dog's spinal cord, resulting in a loss of pain sensation in the outer extremities, such as the hind legs. Dogs with AMS will often chew, bite, and self-mutilate their outer extremities, resulting in bacterial infections and ulcers.

Puppies with AMS are often much smaller when compared to their littermates. Often, by the age of three months, the puppy will begin excessively licking, biting, and chewing on his hind feet. The puppy will have no pain or temperature sensation in his feet.

Unfortunately, there is no known treatment for AMS, but there are ways to prevent the dog from mutilating himself, such as Elizabethan collars or cones, bandages, doggie booties, and muzzles. Topical application of specially formulated ointments that taste bad may deter the dog from licking a certain area. Talk to your vet for additional alternatives. If all attempts to prevent the canine from self-mutilating are unsuccessful, then your vet may suggest euthanasia.

AMS is an autosomal-recessive condition, which means the affected dogs must inherit two copies of an abnormal gene (one from each of the parents). If a dog inherits only one abnormal gene from one of his parents, he will have no symptoms of the disease, but the dog will be a carrier and will pass the abnormal gene on to any future offspring. Reputable breeders will test both parents prior to breeding for AMS. The Kennel Club Breed Register also has a record of DNA results tests carried out by different breeders.

Even though this condition is extremely rare, make sure the breeder tests the parent dogs prior to breeding. Also, make sure there is a clause in the breeder's contract that you will be refunded your money if the dog has a genetic disease such as AMS.

Eye Problems

Nothing is as traumatic to the quality of your dog's life as losing his vision. Unfortunately, Italian Greyhounds can inherit or develop a number of different eye conditions, and some may cause blindness if not treated in time.

Ectropion is a genetic defect that causes the eyelids to droop, exposing the eyeball to environmental contaminants that cause irritation, drying, and infections. The good news is this condition can easily be surgically corrected.

Progressive retinal atrophy refers to a group of different degenerative diseases that affect a dog's vision. This disease causes the light-sensitive layer of cells inside the eye, the retina, to slowly deteriorate over time, eventually leading to blindness. Retinal dysplasia is diagnosed in puppies around two to three months of age, and a later-onset form is diagnosed in dogs between the ages of four to nine years.

Progressive retinal atrophy is an inherited disease that occurs in a long list of breeds and mixed-breed dogs. Affected dogs should not be used in breeding. If a dog develops progressive retinal atrophy, its parents and all its siblings from previous litters should be prevented

Photo Courtesy of Marcy Ringer

from breeding. Unfortunately, there is no known cure for progressive retinal atrophy.

Cone degeneration is often referred to as day blindness, as affected dogs experience temporary blindness when exposed to daylight. Cone cells are responsible for helping a dog see in high light, and rod photoreceptors are responsible for helping canines see in low light. Affected dogs have normal vision in low light, and light sensitivity begins eight to 12 weeks after birth. By the time an affected dog is an adult, it will have completely lost all cone cells; however, it will be able to see normally in a low-light situation.

As this is a genetic condition, and some dogs may be carriers without showing symptoms, many reputable breeders will test the parent dogs for this mutation. It is recommended dogs with this genetic defect be eliminated from breeding lines. There is no known cure.

Keratoconjunctivitis, also known as dry eye, is common in Italian Greyhounds. The tear ducts no longer produce enough tears to keep the eyes moist, which results in sore, itchy eyes and infections. Often, symptoms include discharge, squinting, pawing at the eyes, and a dull, dry appearance of the eye. If you notice any of these conditions, please call your vet immediately. There is no cure for this disease, but you will need to apply ointment or prescription eye drops for the rest of your dog's life.

Bone and Joint Problems

> 66
>
> *Italian Greyhound puppies think they can fly, and many think nothing of launching off the back of a sofa onto a hard floor, so leg breaks can be an issue up to 18 months; you'll want to keep accident insurance up to age 24 months, just in case. Do NOT allow puppies under 18 months on furniture or up stairs or steps until you are sure they know how to get down safely.*
>
> LYNNE EZELL
> *Uwharrie*
> 99

Joint dysplasia and musculoskeletal problems have been reported in Iggies.

Joint dysplasia is a deformity of the joint that occurs during growth. Joint dysplasia often occurs in the hip joint. The thigh bone and socket for the pelvis need to grow at the same speed. However, in joint dysplasia, this growth does not occur, resulting in a loose joint, which is followed by osteoarthritis or degenerative joint disease as the body tries to stabilize the loose joint.

FUN FACT
Long Live the Greyhound

Italian Greyhounds are a long-lived breed that lives from 12 to 14 years on average. It's not uncommon for a healthy Italian Greyhound to live beyond this estimate and up to 18 or 19 years! Good preventative health care and regular exercise are two of the keys to your dog's longevity, but genetics may also play a role.

Joint dysplasia is a genetic disease, but the extent of damage can be affected by diet, environment, exercise, growth rate, and hormones. Medium-sized and larger dogs are most prone to joint dysplasia. Care should be taken to keep your dog at a healthy weight, especially during his growth cycle, by feeding him a healthy, balanced diet. Avoid overfeeding your puppy, and do not give him calcium supplements until he is at least two years old.

An Italian Greyhound's kneecap (patella) may slip out of place; this is called patellar luxation. When this happens, you may notice your Iggy picking up his back leg and hopping for a few strides. Your dog will kick his leg out sideways to pop the kneecap back into place, and after that, the dog will walk normally again. Most likely, your pooch will only require arthritis medication, but when symptoms are more severe, surgery may be required to realign the kneecap to prevent it from popping out of place.

Italian Greyhound pups can suffer from another condition called eosinophilic panosteitis, which is a painful inflammation of the long, slender leg bones. This condition usually begins when the pup is six to 10 months old, and it shifts from leg to leg. Your vet will squeeze or palpate your dog's legs, and if he exhibits pain, the vet will take an X-ray to diagnose the condition. Panosteitis is normally treated with pain medication.

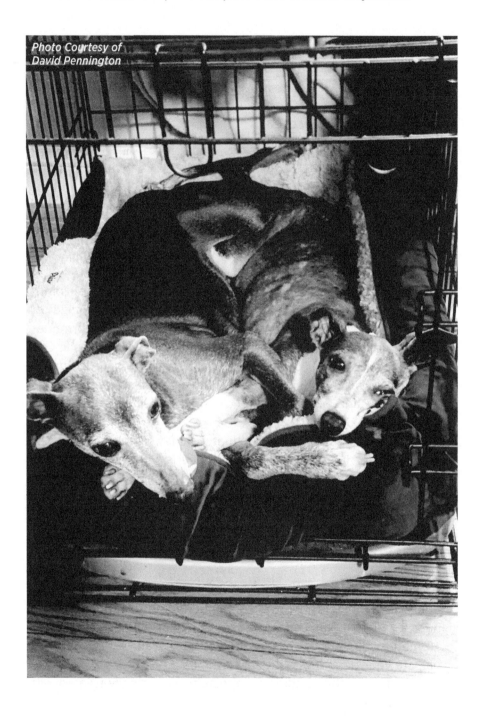

Photo Courtesy of
David Pennington

Nerve Diseases

Neuronal ceroid lipofuscinosis is a progressive neurological disease found in Greyhounds. Clinical symptoms often appear in younger dogs between one to three years of age. In the early stages, the dog exhibits rear-leg weakness and imbalance, which generally progresses rapidly to all four legs; some dogs also lose their vision. There currently is no cure for this disease, but there is a genetic test available. Dogs carrying this genetic mutation should not be used for breeding, as it will be passed on to future generations.

Skin Infections

Italian Greyhounds are susceptible to many different types of skin infections and diseases. The most common is Malassezia dermatitis. When it affects the skin, it leaves greasy, hairless areas around the face, neck, and throat, with a distinctive unpleasant odor. In the ears, it causes itchy red and brown discharge. This condition can easily be treated, but your dog may have flare-ups for the rest of his life.

Dental Abnormalities

Teeth abnormalities are common in purebred dogs like your Iggy. The most common abnormality is an overbite or an underbite called a malocclusion or a bad bite. Another condition is oligodontia, which is a condition where only a few teeth are present. Misaligned teeth may also occur and can cause numerous dental issues but can easily be corrected with braces or extractions.

Other Common Diseases or Health Conditions

Not all diseases and health conditions are hereditary. Diet, life-style, and just plain bad luck are all factors that can affect your dog's long-term health.

Arthritis

As your Iggy ages, you may notice that he begins to show lameness in his legs or struggles to stand up after lying down on his bed. The sooner your vet can diagnose this condition, the better to minimize discomfort and pain. Most likely, your vet will take an X-ray to see how much damage has been caused to your dog's bones and joints; surgery is a good option in severe and life-limiting cases. Keep in mind that obese or overweight dogs will develop arthritis sooner than dogs with a normal weight.

Aortic Stenosis

Aortic stenosis is a hereditary cardiovascular condition. Affected dogs are born with a narrow aorta, which prevents newly oxygenated blood from being pumped out of the heart into the body. Consequently, the narrowed aorta causes the entire heart to work twice as hard to provide the body with oxygen-rich blood needed to perform bodily functions.

Symptoms of aortic stenosis often are identified early, including fainting, poor growth, sluggishness, and exercise intolerance. Since the dog's heart is constantly overworking, it grows bigger and bigger over time. Affected dogs tend to develop a constant cough as the heart takes up more space and pushes against the lungs, causing breathing difficulties and heart rhythm abnormalities. Sadly, sudden death is a likely outcome for affected dogs with aortic stenosis.

Vets often identify this condition in the first year of a dog's life via a simple medical exam. The vet will hear a characteristic murmur known to be caused by aortic stenosis. If your Italian Greyhound has aortic stenosis, your vet will recommend reducing the impact of the heart's work by reducing exercise to a bare minimum, along with beta-blockers to reduce a dog's blood pressure.

Discoid Lupus Erythematosus

Discoid lupus erythematosus is an autoimmune disease that causes the immune system to attack its own skin, causing painful inflammation and tissue damage. Discoid lupus erythematosus is the most common type of lupus in dogs but is still extremely rare. Dogs with this autoimmune disorder develop a crusty scab around the nose, as well as skin pigmentation loss.

The underlying cause of discoid lupus erythematosus is unknown. Veterinarians have observed that prolonged exposure to ultraviolet light appears to worsen the condition. Affected dogs respond well to a topical steroid medication or ointment. Apply the cream when your dog is distracted, such as during mealtime, to prevent him from licking it off.

Von Willebrand's Disease

This is one of the most common hereditary canine disorders, as it has been reported in more than 50 different dog breeds, including the Italian Greyhound. This disease is a blood disorder that prevents the canine's blood from clotting properly. Most dogs with Von Willebrand's disease show no signs or symptoms and may go years before the condition is discovered when a dog has surgery or gets injured.

In very rare and severe cases, symptoms may begin to occur in dogs younger than 12 months of age. Some common symptoms may be spontaneous nosebleeds or bleeding from the gums, excessive bleeding from the vagina during the heat cycle, bloody stools, or visible blood in the urine.

If your veterinarian diagnoses your Iggy with von Willebrand's disease, he will know to use medications while operating on your dog to stabilize bleeding and promote blood clotting. Your vet most likely will tell you to avoid giving your dog certain medications that have anti-platelet or anticoagulant properties, such as aspirin, NSAIDs, ibuprofen, and more.

Gastric Dilation Volvulus

Gastric dilation volvulus is a life-threatening condition in dogs, as it causes the dog's stomach to expand to the point that neither food nor gas can be expelled. This condition is believed to be caused when a dog eats a large meal; however, the actual cause is not completely understood. An expanded stomach can rotate inside the abdomen, which is called volvulus. When a rotation occurs, it can lead to a blockage in the blood supply to the dog's spleen and stomach.

When this condition occurs, your vet will need to quickly stabilize your dog by decompressing the stomach, followed by surgery to return the stomach to its original place. During the surgery, the vet will evaluate any damage to the surrounding organs. If this painful condition is left untreated, it can result in a ruptured stomach wall, put excess pressure on the lungs, causing decreased breathing, and finally, it can be fatal.

Hepatitis

There are two types of hepatitis in dogs: infectious canine hepatitis and canine chronic hepatitis. Infectious canine hepatitis is a contagious disease caused by a canine adenovirus, and symptoms can vary from fever to lethargy, thirst, or death. If infectious hepatitis is left untreated, it causes chronic hepatitis, affecting the liver to the point of causing inflammation and cell death (necrosis).

If your dog has a fever for more than one day, take him to see the vet immediately. The sooner your dog starts treatment, the better the outcome. This condition can be prevented by routine vaccinations. However, dog owners must stay vigilant and keep their dogs' vaccines up to date, as the disease can develop quickly.

Myasthenia Gravis

Myasthenia gravis is a condition that causes a miscommunication between the nerve and muscle signals. Affected dogs will exhibit extreme lethargy and muscle weakness. Dogs with congenital myasthenia gravis are usually diagnosed between six to eight weeks of age. Acquired myasthenia gravis is more like an autoimmune disease and is not hereditary. It tends to be diagnosed in dogs between two to four years of age.

Most affected dogs can be treated with medication they will need to take for the rest of their lives. If left untreated, the affected dog will eventually have difficulty swallowing food, and it may accidentally inhale food, liquid, or vomit, which will result in aspiration pneumonia. Aspiration pneumonia is extremely serious and requires costly veterinarian care until the dog's condition can be stabilized.

Cruciate Ligament Disease

Cranial cruciate ligament disease occurs when the tough fibrous tissue attached to the hip and knee bone prevents the knee from

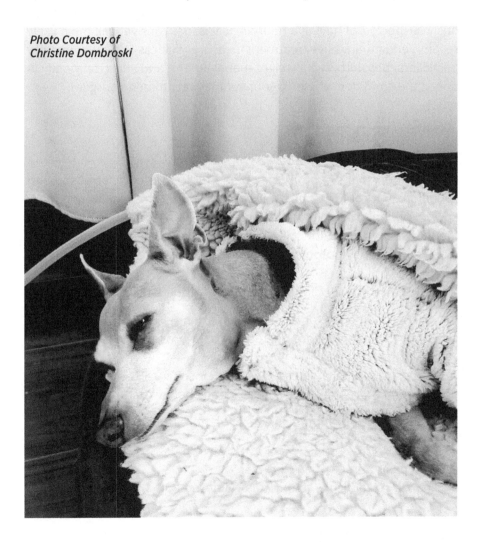

Photo Courtesy of
Christine Dombroski

moving forward, and at the same time, it does not prevent the knee joint from over-extending or rotating. The precise cause of this condition is unknown, as the ligament degenerates slowly over time, similar to a fraying rope. Factors such as obesity, hormonal imbalance, and inflammatory conditions of the joint may play a role in this condition.

One of the most common signs of cruciate ligament disease is a dog limping after exercise or standing up after sitting for a long period of time. In severe cases, affected dogs cannot stand up and may be erroneously suspected of having a neurological issue. Your vet will most likely recommend noninvasive treatment measures such as anti-inflammatory painkillers, physiotherapy, weight management, and exercise modification. If the condition worsens, your vet may recommend surgery.

What to Watch for

Any abnormal symptom may be an indication of a serious health condition, or it could just be a minor health issue. The important thing is knowing when to seek veterinary help and how urgently help is required. Many diseases that affect Italian Greyhounds have a characteristic combination of symptoms that will be a clear indication to take your dog to the vet.

Call the veterinary clinic if you notice any of the following symptoms:

- Change in appetite or water consumption
- Tartar buildup, foul breath, red gums, or broken teeth
- Itchy skin, hair loss
- Lethargy, mental dullness, or excess sleeping
- Unusual aggression, fearfulness, or any behavioral changes

Seek emergency medical care immediately if you notice any of these signs:

- Lumps or bumps of any size
- Inability or difficulty to urinate or defecate; discolored urine

- Scratching or shaking the head, tender ears, or ear discharge
- Reluctance to run or play
- Leg stiffness, reluctance to rise, sit, use stairs, run, or jump
- Redness, itching, or any other abnormalities involving the eyes

Your Italian Greyhound counts on you to take good care of him and give him a long and healthy life. Your goal should be to provide your Greyhound with the best health care possible: health care based on his breed, lifestyle, and age. Please contact your vet whenever you have a doubt about your dog's health.

CHAPTER 15

Caring for a Senior Italian Greyhound

> *You'll want to make sure to keep your older dog's teeth clean and use a good-quality food made for senior dogs. Exercise is still important for an aging Italian Greyhound, though, of course, his exercise needs will be different from that of a younger, more active dog.*
>
> DEBORAH FUXA
> *Azygous Italian Greyhounds*

Your Iggy has become more than a four-legged companion. He is part of your immediate family. Just as your pooch has cared about you over the years, you want to care for him throughout his life, even more so as he ages. Dogs age quite similarly to humans. They, too, lose control of their physical and mental abilities.

As your Italian Greyhound ages, you are going to notice some changes, such as slowing down, decreased agility and mobility, and personality changes. Perhaps your pooch will become less enthusiastic about his favorite activities, such as going for walks, eating, or even playing a game of fetch. But with love and care, you can help your Iggy age gracefully.

Physical and Mental Signs of Aging

It is a well-known fact that dogs age faster than their pet owners. Generally, a smaller breed like your Italian Greyhound enters the senior years at around seven or eight of our years. The more aware you are of the typical signs of aging, the sooner you can make your pup's later years more comfortable.

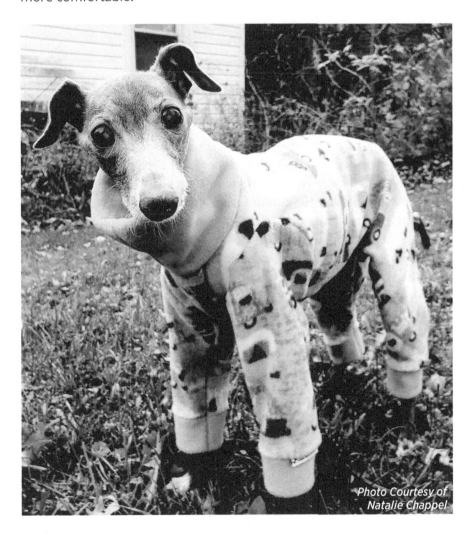

Photo Courtesy of
Natalie Chappel

Here are some common physical and mental signs of aging your Iggy may experience.

- Bathroom issues
- Hearing loss
- Mobility issues
- New lumps and bumps
- Aches and pains
- Poor vision
- Stinky breath
- Weight change

As your Italian Greyhound ages, you will also notice behavioral changes. Changes in your dog's temperament and behavior may be an indication of physical issues. For example, your normally mellow friend could suddenly turn into an old grouch. He may be in pain from arthritis. Or maybe your hyperactive Iggy suddenly wants to sleep all day long. Senior dogs need more rest, so let them sleep.

Your senior Italian Greyhound may also begin to display cognitive symptoms, such as forgetting where his water dish is or simply barking at nothing. Your dog may seem to be going senile, which is entirely possible as dogs can develop cognitive problems just like humans. Many behavioral changes are caused by canine cognitive dysfunction syndrome (CCDS). CCDS is similar to Alzheimer's disease and affects around half of all dogs over 11 years of age.

At around 15 years of age, almost 70 percent of all dogs begin to experience symptoms associated with CCDS. Some behavioral changes your Iggy might display are:

- House soiling
- Increased anxiety
- Fear of familiar people and objects
- Compulsive behaviors
- Excessive barking and vocalization
- Change in activity level
- Insomnia, sleepwalking, or restlessness

If you observe your Italian Greyhound displaying any of these symptoms, consult with your vet. Your vet will make a diagnosis by asking you a few questions during the visit. There is no cure for CCDS; however, there are medications and therapeutic options.

Illness and Injury Prevention

> **"**
>
> *The average life span of an Italian Greyhound is 12 to 15 years, but many dogs live as long as 18 years. Like many dogs, and even people, they can develop arthritis, digestion problems, or vision and hearing problems as they get older. But because they can't tell you what they're feeling, you have to use observation to monitor for any potential issues. Older dogs should be seen by a vet more frequently, so that the vet can find problems that we can't necessarily see.*
>
> KAREN HAREN
> *Bethany Italian Greyhounds*
>
> **"**

Strained muscles, sprains, and pulled ligaments are all common senior canine injuries. As your Italian Greyhound ages, he will become more susceptible to injury due to brittle bones and arthritis. Research shows dogs experience a similar pain threshold as humans. You can easily reduce injuries by incorporating these strategies into your dog's daily life.

Avoid extreme temperatures – Elderly Italian Greyhounds are more sensitive to extreme temperature changes. They can suffer more easily from heatstroke, frostbite, and hypothermia than younger dogs. If the weather outside is too hot or too cold, keep your pooch inside.

Daily exercise schedule – Even though your senior Iggy has gotten slower in the last few years, that does not mean he does not need regular exercise. Switch up your dog's exercise routine by taking him for shorter walks. Instead of walking on cement, take your canine for a walk on a dirt or grass path, as it will be softer on his sore joints.

Ramp up – Climbing stairs, jumping up on the couch, or getting into the car may become a challenge for your senior dog. At your local pet supply store, you can find a variety of ramps to help your pooch with these movements.

Slip-proof your home – Your Italian Greyhound may lack the agility he once had during his younger years. Your hardwood or tile floors may cause him to slip and slide, causing injury. Place rugs in areas your dog tends to spend the majority of his time, as this will help him feel more secure and sure-footed.

Photo Courtesy of Michael Delizia

Soft, fluffy bed – Your Iggy will thank you for a soft, fluffy bed that supports his old bones and joints. Invest in a doggy bed with soft sides, so your senior pooch can rest his head on a soft surface while he observes his surroundings.

Take it slow – Your elderly Italian Greyhound will need extra time for eating, walking, going to the bathroom, etc. Be patient with him and give him the time he needs. Your furry friend also will appreciate any extra attention, love, and affection from you, like cuddling on the couch.

Weight control – Since your senior Iggy is less active, he is burning fewer calories, meaning unwanted weight gain. Extra weight puts pressure on your old dog's bones, joints, and heart, which could cause additional health problems. Consult with your vet for recommendations to improve your dog's diet.

Signs of illness or pain

Each dog will display pain and suffering differently. Any change in your Italian Greyhound's behavior may be an early indication that he is ill or in pain.

When your dog is in pain or is ill, his eating or drinking habits will often change. He might lose interest in food or drink excessive amounts of water. He may become withdrawn, be aggressive when petted, or seem unwilling to go for a walk. Your dog may display one or more of these signs of ill health:

- Runny nose, runny eyes, or discharge coming from the ears
- Excessive drooling
- Vomiting
- Diarrhea
- Constipation
- Difficulty urinating
- Coughing
- Hot spots, excessive scratching, or skin sores under his coat
- Limping, swelling, and lack of mobility

If you notice that your Italian Greyhound is displaying any of these symptoms for more than 48 hours, consult with your veterinarian.

Age-Related Diseases and Conditions in Italian Greyhounds

During your Iggy's golden years, he may begin to experience age-associated illnesses and diseases. Many of these conditions can be treated if identified early, so be sure to consult with your vet immediately. The following health issues are commonly associated with geriatric Italian Greyhounds.

Arthritis – Just like people, dogs develop arthritis as they age. The most common type of arthritis in aging Italian Greyhounds is osteoarthritis, also called degenerative joint disease. This condition affects the hips, knees, shoulders, and elbows. The changes in joints result in pain, stiffness, and lack of mobility. Osteoarthritis is progressive, meaning there is no cure, but there are many treatments, such as chiropractic, hydrotherapy, and acupuncture, which are known to slow the progression and ease the joint pain.

Cancer – Unfortunately, cancer is common in older dogs. Different types of cancer can cause a variety of symptoms. Often, symptoms may be dismissed as signs of aging, such as lethargy or a lack of appetite. As your Iggy ages, it is vital he receives routine wellness screenings with your vet. Lab work, additional diagnostic imaging, and exams can pick up on anything that is unseen to the naked eye. The sooner the cancer is caught, the better the chances of your dog's survival.

Cataracts – Cataracts cause your Iggy's eyes to lose transparency, causing them to appear cloudy. The cataract prevents light from passing through your dog's lens, blocking his vision. Most elderly dogs who develop cataracts will not completely go blind, and they adjust to their loss of vision. Your vet will need to diagnose the cause of the cataract before coming up with a treatment plan.

Glaucoma – Your dog's eye is made up of a jelly-like substance called aqueous humor. This liquid is constantly being produced by the eye. Normally, the eye drains itself of the old fluid, but if this does not occur, then glaucoma happens. Glaucoma in dogs can have one of many causes, so be sure to consult with your vet to find the correct treatment for your dog.

Hypothyroidism – Hypothyroidism is common in older Italian Greyhounds as their thyroid gland becomes weaker and underactive. One of the main indications of hypothyroidism is unexplained weight gain, lack of interest in playing or going for walks, and separation anxiety. Additional symptoms are brittle hair and itchy skin. The good news is that this condition can be easily treated with prescription medications.

Diabetes – Italian Greyhounds are prone to developing canine diabetes. Diabetes occurs when the pancreas stops producing normal amounts of insulin and may be caused by an inherited predisposition, diet, obesity, and certain medications, such as steroids used for treating allergies. Diabetes can easily be regulated with insulin shots and a change in diet.

Incontinence – Age takes a toll on your dog's organs, muscles, and nerves, making it more challenging to hold his bladder and bowels the way he used to. Incontinence may be an indication of other health complications, so you will need your vet to rule out some issues first. If the vet does not find any health problems, you may need to let your Iggy out more often for potty breaks or have him wear a doggy diaper.

Kidney Disease – Kidney disease often develops slowly, starting off as renal insufficiency and progressing to full renal failure. Once this disease starts to progress, there is no cure, but if caught in time, it can be successfully treated to slow the progression. Signs of kidney disease include increased thirst, frequent urination, lack of appetite, vomiting, and lethargy.

Lenticular Sclerosis – This condition is often confused with cataracts as it also causes the dog's eyes to form a white, cloudy sclera. Lenticular sclerosis, however, does not affect your Italian Greyhound's vision. But to be on the safe side, get your dog's eyes checked out by your vet.

Muscle Atrophy – Muscle atrophy is common in older Italian Greyhounds as they become less active with age. This condition causes rear leg weakness, limping, ataxia, paw dragging, flabby muscles, and weight loss. Muscle atrophy can be caused by a number of conditions, such as arthritis, injury, and sore muscles from lack of exercise. Your vet will need to give your dog a check-up to diagnose the cause of your Iggy's muscle atrophy before treating it.

Photo Courtesy of Katherine Hagmeier

Nutrition Needs

Every Italian Greyhound has different nutritional needs, and senior dogs are no exception. Once your pooch reaches his golden years, it can become a challenge to understand his new dietary requirements. However, switching your dog's regular dog food for a bag of senior dog food may not be enough.

Watch those calories – Younger senior dogs tend to gain weight, while older senior dogs tend to lose weight. As your pooch ages, he begins to slow down, which means he burns off fewer calories and those unneeded calories are stored as fat. Research shows senior dogs require 20 percent fewer calories than adult dogs in order to maintain a healthy weight. If your Iggy starts losing weight, you may need to give him extra calories to help him stay healthy.

Nutrient-rich dog food – Even though your Italian Greyhound may require fewer calories, he will need a premium diet that provides all the required nutrients to stay healthy. Recent studies have discovered that food rich in L-carnitine helps elderly dogs to burn off stored fat for energy. So, make sure your Iggy receives a diet rich in lean red meats, chicken, fish, healthy fats, and dairy products.

Protein – Protein is vital for your Italian Greyhound's overall health. As your dog ages, he begins to lose muscle mass, even if he is still leading an active lifestyle. As his muscle mass depletes, so does his protein reserve, causing his immune system to weaken. As your dog's immune system weakens, so does his ability to fight off infections and illnesses. Your senior Iggy's diet should be made up of 40 percent protein. Avoid dog foods that contain fillers. Instead, opt for foods rich in lean red meats, fish, chicken, and dairy products.

Fiber – Fiber is essential in helping your Iggy lose weight, alleviating constipation, and controlling blood sugar levels. However, certain cellulose-based fibers are difficult for your dog to digest and prevent other nutrients from being absorbed. Avoid giving your dog foods that contain bran flakes, psyllium husks, and dried peas. Research shows soluble fibers help senior dogs regulate glucose levels and absorb nutrients better. Some beneficial soluble fibers for your dog are sweet potatoes, carrots, brown rice, milled flaxseed, wheatgerm, kale, and kelp.

Sodium – Your senior Italian Greyhound will need a low-sodium diet if he has hypertension, cardiac, or kidney problems. Most commercial dog food is extremely high in sodium, so look for brands that are low in sodium or make your own homemade dog food.

If your senior Iggy will not eat

It is common for senior dogs to lose interest in food. Try adding one to two tablespoons of bone broth or a small amount of canned food to entice your dog. If your elderly pooch refuses to eat for more than 48 hours, consult with your vet to rule out any underlying health problems.

Bone broth is a delicious, nutrient-dense superfood that will improve your Italian Greyhound's health and get him to gobble up his dinner. Bone broth is a stock made from simmering raw bones for several hours, either in your slow cooker or on low heat on your stovetop. Bone broth is jam-packed with nutrients that will improve your dog's overall health; plus, he will devour his food.

How to choose a premium senior dog food

Unfortunately, the FDA has not established any official regulations for senior dog foods, which is why you need to educate yourself on how to find a premium-quality dog food for your Italian Greyhound.

Beyond the caloric intake and protein content, there are several ingredients that can benefit your Iggy's overall health. Here are a few key ingredients to look for when choosing a premium senior dog food.

Glucosamine and chondroitin – These supplements help your senior dog's cartilage and joints so that he can move around with less pain.

Antioxidants – Antioxidants provide much-needed support for your elderly pup's immune system, helping him to fight off diseases and illnesses.

How to make bone broth for your Iggy:

Ingredients

- 4 pounds of raw bones with marrow (you can use chicken, turkey, rabbit, beef, or oxtail bones)
- 1/3 cup fresh parsley, chopped
- 3 stalks of celery, chopped
- 1/4 cup organic apple cider vinegar (helps to pull the marrow and minerals out of the bones)
- 6 to 7 quarts of water

Directions

1. Place all the ingredients in a large pot or the slow cooker.

2. Cook on low heat for 8 to 12 hours on a low simmer or for 24 hours in the slow cooker on the lowest setting. Stir occasionally and add extra water if necessary.

3. Allow to cool. Remove the bones, celery, parsley, and discard. Note: you should never feed cooked bones to your Italian Greyhound.

4. Once the broth is completely cool, place in the refrigerator overnight. It will form a layer of fat on top, which can easily be skimmed off and discarded.

5. Freeze in small portions in Ziploc baggies, then thaw before serving to your Iggy. Give him one to two tablespoons with each meal.

Decreased levels of sodium and phosphorus – Lower phosphorus helps to maintain healthy kidney function, and lower sodium levels keep your Iggy's blood pressure normal.

Omega-3 fatty acids – Healthy fats found in fish oil and nut and plant oils help to decrease inflammation caused by arthritis and improve kidney and liver health.

Extra fiber – Many senior Italian Greyhounds suffer from constipation, so extra fiber may help. However, too much fiber can cause other problems, so the best way to control constipation is to make sure your dog gets enough exercise and add a soluble source of fiber occasionally to his food, such as canned, unsweetened sweet potatoes.

When choosing a senior dog food, it is important to consider your Italian Greyhound's individual needs and recognize that these needs can change over time. So, just because one type of senior dog food is suitable for your dog now does not mean it will always be. The right dog food will have a direct impact on your dog's health, so take your time to research and talk to your vet to find the best diet for your faithful companion.

Look for a senior dog food made from premium-quality ingredients such as human-grade organic lean red meats, free of artificial preservatives. No matter how healthy your Iggy is, there is no need to put a strain on his immune system by feeding him poor-quality, generic dog food with little to no nutritional value.

Transition your pooch slowly to a new senior dog food. It is best to start gradually by adding a small amount of the new food to his current food. Each day you can add a little more of the new food. Ideally, this process should take seven to 10 days to completely switch your dog to the new food.

Listen to your vet's recommendations, especially if your dog has been diagnosed with a condition such as diabetes, kidney, liver, heart disease, arthritis, etc. Your vet will most likely recommend a prescription diet. While these diets often do not include the word "senior" in the title, they are formulated to manage disease conditions commonly seen in elderly dogs.

Exercise

As your Italian Greyhound ages, his mobility is going to decline. However, this does not mean he should not be getting any exercise. Actually, by helping your senior dog maintain an active lifestyle, you are decreasing his risks of geriatric ailments, such as arthritis and muscle loss. Although your old pup may not be chasing the ball as fast as he used to, there are still plenty of safe physical activities.

Here are a few suggestions to keep your senior Iggy active.

 DO

- Establish a regular exercise regime. The more active your Italian Greyhound is, the more agile he will feel, even if it is several short walks a day instead of one or two long walks.
- Consider the climate before going for a trot around the block. Elderly dogs are more sensitive to extreme weather conditions. During the warmer months, take your Iggy for a walk in the cooler times of the day, and during the colder winter months, buy your dog a little jacket and booties.
- As your pooch ages, he may lose his hearing and eyesight, so stick with the familiar walking routes. New surroundings may cause your furry friend to become anxious and confused.
- Be sure to consult with your vet to learn if your Iggy is receiving enough exercise, especially if he has a medical condition.

 DON'T

- Never stop taking your Iggy for daily walks! Maybe your pooch will not be able to endure longer strolls, but he will still be grateful to go for shorter walks. Walking gives your dog the opportunity to stretch his legs, sniff out his surroundings, and enjoy the fresh air.
- Do not set the pace; instead, let your Italian Greyhound set the pace. If your dog needs to sit or lie down for a minute or two, then let him rest.
- Do not forget that indoor playtime is exercise. If the weather outside is too extreme, then keep your pooch active by playing hide-and-seek inside.

Exercise helps keep your Italian Greyhound's mind stimulated, his weight healthy, and his body agile. Regardless of your furry friend's physical limitations, there are plenty of appropriate exercises for your senior dog:

Walking – All dogs love going for walks, despite their age or health issues. Walking is one of the best low-impact exercises for your elderly dog, as it improves his mental and physical health. Footing will impact your dog's walking ability, so grass and dirt are recommended surfaces. Avoid asphalt or rough gravel surfaces that may damage your dog's paws.

Swimming – Swimming is easy on your elderly dog's body, especially on the joints, while providing a total body workout. An added bonus is your Italian Greyhound loves water and will be the happiest dog while he swims around a dog-friendly pool or lake. Swimming is often used as a form of physical therapy for dogs that have undergone major surgery for injuries.

There are plenty of other ideas to keep your senior dog active, such as playing fetch in the backyard or sniffing games that lead him to a treat. Give your Iggy time to follow his surroundings by sniffing out every shred of grass. However, whatever type of physical activity you choose for your dog—do not overdo it!

How much exercise is too much?

Each dog's physical tolerance levels vary depending on weight, lifestyle, exercise history, and overall health. Your Italian Greyhound may be pushing himself past his comfort zone just to please you. Here are a few tell-tale signs your dog has pushed himself past his physical limitations:

Excessive drooling or panting – It is perfectly normal for your Iggy to pant a little after playing a game of fetch; however, excessive panting and drooling are a clear indication that he is dehydrated or overheated.

Reluctant to play – If your Iggy stops playing and wants to sit down, then he is telling you he is tired and needs to rest.

Limping or muscle atrophy – If your Italian Greyhound starts to favor his hind legs by limping while exercising—stop immediately!

Observe your dog for the next 24 hours and if the limp does not go away, take him to see your vet as soon as possible.

Coughing or hacking – If your Italian Greyhound begins to cough or hack while exercising, it may be a sign of his trachea collapsing or other health conditions. Repeated hacking can sound like your dog is honking. If your senior buddy begins to make coughing or hacking sounds while exercising—stop immediately! If you notice the coughing noise returns every time that he exerts himself, consult with your vet.

It helps to keep an exercise journal of your Italian Greyhound's daily exercise regimen and adjust his routine as needed. Whenever you notice your dog is experiencing pain or discomfort, slow down his workout. Do not hesitate to check in with your vet if you have any questions or concerns.

Photo Courtesy of Cynthia Chavez

Old dog, new tricks

You have most likely heard the saying, "If you don't use it, you lose it!" Elderly people play sudoku, do crosswords, or complete brain teasers to keep their minds sharp and alert. Your faithful old companion needs to keep learning new activities to keep his mind stimulated. When your dog is forced to focus on something, it tends to slow down cognitive degeneration.

Here are some ideas to keep your canine's mind sharp.

- Explore new places, such as parks, beaches, or a ferry boat ride.
- Teach your Iggy new tricks or reinforce old ones.
- Reactivate old instincts with a game of tug-of-war.
- Take your faithful old companion swimming or, even better, to a local natural hot spring.
- Play a short game of fetch or hide-and-seek.
- Introduce new toys or games that involve sniffing out a yummy treat.

Grooming

Grooming is essential throughout your Italian Greyhound's life, but even more so as he gets older. Grooming sessions are an excellent opportunity to observe any changes in your dog's overall health, as many underlying health issues are revealed through the health of his skin and coat. Fur can begin to thin, and skin irritation, new growths, or lumps may start to appear.

One of the best gifts you can give your aging Iggy is daily grooming, as it keeps him looking and feeling his best. Plus, he will drink up the extra attention from you. Your dog is never too old to be pampered!

Typically, elderly dogs who loved getting groomed in their younger years suddenly start to resist the process due to joint pain. Senior dogs may squirm and bark to vocalize their objections to being groomed.

However, at the end of the grooming session, your Italian Greyhound will be prancing around like he was still a puppy!

Your older Iggy will thank you for his grooming session. A warm bath will relieve those itchy sections your dog is no longer able to reach. Plus, your pooch will drink up the extra attention and the treats during the grooming and afterward. Nothing is more satisfying than seeing your freshly groomed old companion swagger away, feeling renewed and refreshed.

If you prefer to take your Italian Greyhound to a professional groomer, avoid using a discount service that may neglect your dog. Not every groomer has the ability or the patience to deal with your faithful old companion's aches and pains, so choose carefully. Look for a groomer who has experience with grooming geriatric dogs.

If you decide to groom your senior Italian Greyhound at home, be sure to review the detailed instructions in Chapter 12 of this book and take into consideration the following suggestions to adapt the process to your old friend. These tips can go a long way in ensuring your elderly dog will receive the level of care and respect he deserves.

Whether you decide to groom your elderly Italian Greyhound at home or use a professional groomer, consider the following suggestions beforehand:

Keep sessions short – Lengthy grooming sessions can expose your older dog to unnecessary discomfort, pain, and stress. Many reputable groomers with experience grooming geriatric dogs will schedule multiple grooming sessions instead of one. For example, the first session may include a bath and, the following week, a haircut and brushing.

Watch for signs of discomfort – Your older dog will communicate his discomfort through body language or by vocalizing. If you notice your Iggy whimpering, squirming, shivering, or even growling, then you need to stop the grooming session. Let your dog take a short rest or find a more comfortable position. If your dog becomes agitated or stressed, then discontinue the session and continue another day.

Understand your dog's limitations – It is more than likely your senior Iggy may not be able to handle the same grooming regimen as when he was younger. Pressure sores and benign fatty tumors mean your dog's coat cannot be trimmed as short as usual. Or if your pooch has poor eyesight, clipping too close to his face may cause him anxiety.

Bathing – If you decide to bathe your elderly pooch at home, there are a few precautions you can take to ensure his well-being and comfort. When bathing your dog, place a nonskid mat in the bottom of the basin or tub to secure his footing. Make sure the water is warm enough that your Iggy is not shivering during the bath. Often, geriatric dogs need a special shampoo to treat dry skin or other conditions.

After thoroughly rinsing out the shampoo, dry your dog with warm, fluffy towels. Before using the blow dryer, let your Italian Greyhound shake himself off. Never use the blow dryer on the hottest setting. Instead, use the cool setting. Be sure to get your old dog as dry as possible, as water trapped close to the skin may cause hot spots.

Brushing – Before you start brushing your Iggy, inspect the brush to make sure it's in good condition. If the brush's teeth are bent or broken, it is best to discard it and get a new one, as the teeth can scratch an older dog's thin, vulnerable skin or damage his coat.

Unfortunately, arthritis and joint pain may make it difficult for him to stand in the same position for long periods of time. Place a blanket on the floor and have your Italian Greyhound lie on his side while being brushed. Despite common belief, matted, tangled hair does not provide your dog with extra insulation as much as clean, tangle-free hair will.

While brushing your Iggy, be on the lookout for bare patches and brittle hair. This may be an indication of health conditions. Also, use your fingers to feel for any new lumps, warts, or sores on your dog's skin. If you notice anything suspicious, consult with your vet.

Nail trimming – Your elderly Iggy will need his nails trimmed more frequently than when he was younger. If your old dog suffers from arthritis or joint problems, it is even more reason to keep his nails trimmed, as the nail length affects your dog's posture and can force him to torque his spine, causing additional discomfort. In the past, his long walks on the sidewalk naturally kept his nails trimmed, but because of his shorter, golden-year strolls, he needs some extra help to keep his nails short.

Sanitary areas – The glands and groin area are normally cleaned by your dog daily, but with old age he may need some help. Regular trimming of the groin area will prevent any fecal matter or urine from getting trapped. Typically, all dogs express their anal glands when they defecate. But smaller breeds, such as the Italian Greyhound, may need help expressing their anal glands as they age.

Saying Goodbye

For every person who loves and shares their life with an Italian Greyhound, the dreaded and inevitable day will come when you have to ask yourself whether or not to intervene in how or when your beloved four-pawed friend's life must come to an end. The very thought of having to say goodbye to your best friend for the last time is definitely heart-wrenching.

More often than not, when we start to observe signs that our dog is dying, we start second-guessing ourselves or go into denial. This often causes our beloved dogs to suffer far longer than they should have to. The question is, how do you know? When is the right time to put your best friend to forever sleep?

Tell-tale signs your dog is dying

Prolonged lethargy or disinterest – One of the most common signs of the dying process is finding your dog lying in the same spot (often not where he would normally rest), barely acknowledging you or other family members. Dogs may become lethargic due to other health conditions, but if the veterinarian has ruled this out and the lethargy lasts for more than a few days, then maybe it is time to consider saying goodbye.

Stops eating or drinking – Another classic sign something is wrong with your Iggy is when you offer him the tastiest treat imaginable and he refuses to even sniff it. Often, at this point, the dog will stop drinking water as his organs are starting to shut down. Try keeping your dog hydrated by giving him water using a dropper or turkey baster, but if he still refuses to swallow, there is not much you can do at this point. Be sure to rule out other health conditions with your vet.

Lack of coordination – The next sign is when your dog begins to lose balance and motor control. When your elderly Italian Greyhound tries to stand up, he may be very wobbly or disoriented. Or he could shake or convulse while lying down. In this case, make your dog as comfortable as possible and remove any objects he could knock over if he tries to stand up. Note: saying goodbye to your dog means protecting him, creating a safe area for him, and providing whatever help he needs.

Incontinence – When a dog is dying, often he will not even move from the spot to relieve himself, even if he has diarrhea. This is an indication that your dog's organs are starting to shut down. During this stage, make sure you keep him and his bed clean and dry.

Labored breathing – As heartbreaking as it sounds, toward the end, many dogs display labored breathing. Your dog's breathing may become difficult, with lengthy gasps between each breath. This is an extremely hard moment, as you know, at this point, your dog is suffering.

Seeking comfort – This is one of the hardest moments, as despite your dog's quickly deteriorating health, he will look for comfort from his people—from you. During these final hours, be with your dog, reassuring him of your love and affection.

Making the decision

The signs above are not always consistent, as some dogs suddenly pass away in their sleep without any indications, and other dogs exhibit even more signs. Part of preparing to say goodbye to your Iggy is realizing you may have to make the difficult decision for your dog by intervening. Be sure to talk over the decision with your significant other and come to a mutual agreement.

Once you come to a decision to intervene due to your dog's suffering, discuss the options with your vet.

Veterinarians are required to follow a set of guidelines called the "Humane Euthanasia Protocol," whether the euthanasia is performed inside the clinic or in the tranquility of your own house. The entire process is painless and stress-free for your Italian Greyhound. The Humane Euthanasia Protocol is considered the most humane way to put your dog to sleep.

The Humane Euthanasia Protocol

1. The veterinarian will inject your Iggy with a pain tranquilizer.
2. Once your dog is relaxed and sedated, your vet will insert an IV to administer the euthanasia solution.
3. The vet will leave you alone with your dog for a few minutes for any final goodbyes, then return to administer the final drug to stop his heart.

In certain parts of the United States, veterinarians are not required by law to adhere to the Humane Euthanasia Protocol. Instead, they practice a quicker and more affordable method to stop the animal's heart with a single injection of barbiturates. Barbiturates cause the animal's central nervous system to slow down, causing a painful death. This type of euthanasia is not humane, as it is not pain-free, causing the animal short-term distress and anxiety.

Ensure your veterinarian applies the Humane Euthanasia Protocol on your dog. If not, look for another veterinarian who will.

Most dogs are euthanized in the veterinary clinic, but many vets will make house calls. If your vet is unable to make house calls, you can find an extensive list of reputable veterinarians throughout the United States and Canada in the In-Home Pet Euthanasia Directory.

Here is a quick overview of the pros and cons of getting your Iggy euthanized at home versus at the clinic.

At-home euthanasia may be the right choice for you if:

● Your Italian Greyhound is too sick to be transported comfortably to the veterinary clinic.
● You personally feel more comfortable grieving at home.

Photo Courtesy of Mark Brennan

- Car trips or visits to the veterinary clinic cause your dog anxiety and stress.
- Money is not an issue, as at-home procedures cost more.

Vet clinic euthanasia may be the right choice for you if:

- You want your usual vet to perform the procedure, but they are unable to perform house calls.
- You prefer a more neutral environment for the procedure.
- Your dog is still mobile enough to be comfortably transported in your car.
- Cost is a concern.

Whether you decide on euthanasia at home or at the veterinary clinic is a very personal decision. There is no right or wrong answer.

The cost of clinical euthanasia can be between $80 to $350, depending on where you live. The cost of at-home euthanasia can cost between $300 to $800. The higher cost may include add-ons, such as cremations, funeral services, or getting the vet to take an impression of your dog's paw to cast into a memento.

It is highly recommended you pay for the euthanasia before the procedure as emotions can be running high when the procedure is final, and the last thing you need is to relive the heartbreak by receiving the bill later. When it is all over, you can request the veterinary clinic dispose of your dog's body for an extra cost. Some clinics offer cremation or a professional burial service at a nearby pet cemetery.

Take your time grieving your Italian Greyhound and come to terms with your loss. Everybody does it in their own way. Saying goodbye to your Iggy does not mean forgetting about him. With time, you may start thinking about opening up your heart to another dog.

Made in the USA
Las Vegas, NV
06 March 2024

86752465R00174